Also by Rivanna Heights Media

Epic Historical Mysteries by Logan Cross

Conspiracy Theories Unveiled by Logan Cross

Pickleball Made Simple by Blake Foster

Cryptocurrency Investing 101 by Jordan Taylor

Artificial Intelligence for Beginners: 2 in 1 Value Collection

The Complete Beginner's Guide To ChatGPT

& AI-Proof Your Career

Ryan Harper

RIVANNA HEIGHTS — MEDIA —

Rivanna Heights Media

Contents

The Complete Beginner's Guide To ChatGPT

Introduction 3

1. Foundations of ChatGPT and AI 6
2. Mastering Prompt Engineering 18
3. Business Productivity with ChatGPT 33
4. ChatGPT for Your Personal Life 48
5. Ethical Use and Social Implications 63
6. Advanced Features and Customization 75
7. Staying Ahead with ChatGPT 88

Conclusion 104

References 106

AI-Proof Your Career

Introduction: The New Rules 111

AI's Impact on Careers

1. Welcome to the AI Career Revolution 114
2. AI 101 for Career Climbers 118
3. The Great Job Shuffle: Who's Safe, Who's Sorry? 128
4. Skilling Up for the AI Age 135
5. The Human Edge: Outsmarting AI in the Workplace 146

Embracing the AI-Driven Workforce

6. Navigating the Ethical Minefield of AI at Work 160

7. The Global AI Race: Opportunities in a Borderless Job Market 168

8. The Entrepreneur's AI Playbook 176

9. Future-Proofing Your Career: The Long Game 185

Thriving in an AI World

10. AI and Remote Work 194

11. AI and Personal Branding 207

12. AI and Work-Life Balance 216

Conclusion: Your Next Chapter 223

Appendix: Tools Featured in This Book 226

Acknowledgments 233

The Complete Beginner's Guide To ChatGPT

Master Practical AI and Effective Prompts to Gain an Edge in Just 7 Days

Ryan Harper

Rivanna Heights Media

Get Your Free Guide: 10 Ways to Make Money with AI!

To thank you for reading this book and to help you get the most out of the tools and exercises you'll find here, I want to offer you something special. I've created a free guide that reveals 10 breakthrough strategies for making money with AI.

Not only will this guide provide you with ideas, but it will also complement the exercises in this book, giving you even more tools to apply what you learn right away. As you work through the activities and explore the opportunities that artificial intelligence can offer you, you can start thinking about how to implement these strategies in your own life or business.

Download your free guide now by clicking or scanning the QR code:

Introduction

Imagine the sense of empowerment and accomplishment you could feel by mastering a powerful AI tool like ChatGPT in just a week. Let me share a quick story: Sarah, a small business owner, struggled to keep up with customer inquiries and manage her marketing efforts effectively. After dedicating one week to fully understanding and integrating ChatGPT into her business, she saw a remarkable transformation. She automated customer service, freeing up valuable time, and created personalized marketing content that significantly boosted her engagement rates. This achievement improved her business and instilled a sense of empowerment and accomplishment. You, too, can experience this by embarking on the same journey.

ChatGPT is a game-changing AI technology that is reshaping industries and can be mastered in just seven days. If you're new to AI, the idea might seem intimidating, but rest assured, it's more within your reach than you think. This guide is tailored to take you from a curious beginner to a confident user, dedicating a small portion of your day for one week to understanding and applying ChatGPT. You'll be pleasantly surprised at how practical and straightforward the learning journey can be.

My vision for this guide is simple: to break down the barriers of AI and make ChatGPT approachable and valuable for you. Whether you're looking to enhance your professional skills, streamline tasks, or satisfy your curiosity about AI, this book promises to equip you with the necessary knowledge and skills to make a tangible difference in your life.

You, the reader, might be someone overwhelmed by technology, a busy professional looking for efficiency, or a lifelong learner eager to explore new tools. No matter your background, this book is crafted for your success. It's structured to provide a practical, engaging, and empowering journey through the world of AI, with each day's learning designed to build on the previous one.

Think of this book as a week-long conversation with a supportive friend who's there to guide you through the complexities of AI. The style of this book is conversational and optimistic, designed to keep things light, engaging, and, most importantly, understandable. There is no jargon, no overwhelming details—just clear, actionable steps that lead to actual results. You'll feel comfortable and at ease, as you embark on this journey with a supportive companion.

We'll start with the basics of AI and ChatGPT and quickly move into practical applications. By the end of the week, we'll explore some advanced features and ethical considerations. Each chapter includes hands-on exercises to reinforce what you've learned and see the technology in action.

On a personal note, my journey into AI started much like yours might today - curious and a bit unsure. Within a week of diving into ChatGPT, I was fascinated and saw significant improvements in managing my tasks and information. This experience ignited my passion to share these benefits with others, especially those who might feel hesitant about stepping into AI.

The 7-Day Structure: Mastery in One Week

The book is structured into seven chapters to make your journey effective and manageable. Each chapter represents one day of focused learning, designed to help you build upon the previous day's knowledge, leading you to master ChatGPT by the end of the week.

On **Day 1**, you will lay the groundwork by understanding the foundational concepts of AI and ChatGPT. This day is all about simplifying the technology and preparing you for the more detailed applications that will follow. By the end of this day, you'll have a solid grasp of ChatGPT and how it works, setting the stage for the rest of the week.

Day 2 focuses on mastering the skill of prompt engineering, which essentially means crafting clear and precise instructions to receive the best responses. This skill is crucial as it helps you frame the right questions to get the most accurate results. By the end of this day, you'll be able to create effective prompts that enhance your interaction with ChatGPT, ensuring you get the most useful output.

On **Day 3**, you'll explore how ChatGPT can enhance business productivity. From managing emails to optimizing customer service and creating content, you'll discover practical ways to integrate ChatGPT into your business workflows, improving creativity, efficiency, and productivity. This day will show you how to leverage AI to streamline your professional tasks.

Day 4 shifts focus to your personal life. You'll learn how to integrate ChatGPT into your daily routines, such as managing schedules, enhancing health and wellness, and budgeting. By the end of this day, you'll see how ChatGPT can simplify and enrich your life, making everyday tasks more manageable.

On **Day 5**, the focus will shift to ethical use and the social implications of AI. You'll gain an understanding of the ethical considerations and societal impact of using technologies like ChatGPT. This day will guide you on using ChatGPT responsibly and thoughtfully, making you aware of the broader implications of AI.

Day 6 is dedicated to exploring ChatGPT's advanced features and customization options. You'll explore its more sophisticated functionalities and learn how to tailor It to meet specific needs. By the end of day 6, you can customize ChatGPT's features to suit specialized tasks, enhancing its value and effectiveness for your unique applications.

Finally, on **Day 7**, you'll learn how to stay ahead with ChatGPT by keeping up with the evolving landscape of AI and continuously improving your skills. You'll be introduced to resources for ongoing learning and adaptation. By the end of this day, you'll be prepared to stay updated with the latest advancements in AI, ensuring you remain competitive and knowledgeable in this fast-evolving field.

So, are you ready to transform your understanding and use of AI technology in just one week? Let's get started on this exciting journey together. By the end of this book, you'll not only grasp the fundamentals of ChatGPT but also uncover its potential to enhance your daily life and work. Let's turn curiosity into capability, starting now!

Foundations of ChatGPT and AI

In the bustling world of technology, where innovation leaps from one breakthrough to another, it might surprise you that the most profound impacts often stem from understanding the basics. Artificial Intelligence, or AI, is one such fundamental that has been seamlessly woven into our daily lives, often without us noticing, enhancing our experiences and interactions in multiple ways. For instance, AI can provide instant weather updates and personalized recommendations on your favorite streaming service. This chapter aims to peel back the layers of complexity surrounding Artificial Intelligence, presenting a clear, simplified explanation tailored to those new to this vast and intriguing field.

1.1 What is AI? A Simplified Explanation for Non-Techies

Definition and Evolution

Artificial Intelligence, in its simplest form, refers to the capability of a machine to imitate intelligent human behavior. Unlike traditional machines, AI systems can learn from experience, adapt to new inputs, and perform human-like tasks. The concept of AI isn't new; it dates back to the ancient myths of mechanical men designed to mimic our behavior. However, the journey of AI as we understand it today began in the mid-20th century, rooted in the question posed by a pioneer in computing, Alan Turing: "Can machines think?"

Over the decades, AI has evolved from basic algorithms capable of simple tasks to complex systems that can drive cars, beat world champions in strategic games like chess and Go, and accurately diagnose diseases. In recent years, this evolution has been propelled by leaps in computing power and data availability, allowing machines to process and learn from vast amounts of information faster and more efficiently than humans.

Types of AI

Understanding the different types of Artificial Intelligence helps simplify the confusion surrounding its capabilities and limitations. Primarily, AI can be classified into three types:

1. Narrow AI: These systems are designed to handle a single or limited task. An example is facial recognition software that unlocks your smartphone. While sophisticated, it operates under a limited set of constraints and doesn't possess understanding or consciousness.

2. General AI: Often considered the holy grail of AI, general AI would have a wide-reaching intellect and cognitive abilities comparable to a human's. Such systems could perform any intellectual task with the same accuracy level as a human. However, general AI remains a largely theoretical concept at this stage.

3. Superintelligent AI: This type of AI goes beyond human intelligence, possessing cognitive skills superior to humans in practically all areas, including creativity, general wisdom, and problem-solving. Superintelligence is also theoretical and poses interesting questions for futurists and ethicists alike.

AI in Daily Life

Look around, and you'll find AI integrated into many aspects of your life. Personal assistants like Siri and Alexa are powered by AI and are designed to interpret your voice commands and assist with tasks. Recommendation systems, such as those used by Netflix and Amazon, analyze your past behavior to suggest products or movies you might like. Even more critically, AI is used to operate autonomous vehicles, which can sense their environment and navigate without human input.

Impact on Society

The implications of AI on society are profound and multifaceted. Economically, AI can lead to significant efficiencies and cost savings, driving growth in every industry, from manufacturing and finance to retail and entertainment. Socially, AI applications in healthcare, such as predictive diagnostics and personalized medicine, can save lives and improve quality of life. However, there are challenges, including job displacements due to automation and concerns about privacy and surveillance. The societal impact of AI necessitates a balanced approach to technology governance and ethical considerations, ensuring AI benefits are maximized while minimizing potential harm.

Understanding AI in these comprehensive yet accessible terms provides a foundation for technical mastery and appreciating the profound way it intersects with human endeavors and ethics. This understanding is crucial as we navigate the current landscapes of innovation and disruption these intelligent systems bring.

1.2 Understanding ChatGPT: From Basics to First Conversation

ChatGPT, developed by OpenAI, is a specific application of AI designed to simulate human-like conversations through text. It stands out as a technology engineered to process data and interact in a way that mimics human conversational patterns. This capability makes it an exceptional tool for various practical applications, from customer service and personalized tutoring to scientific research and fraud detection. As a conversational AI, ChatGPT's fundamental purpose is to provide responses that are not only accurate but also contextually relevant, making interactions feel natural and engaging.

At its core, ChatGPT utilizes a complex computer model trained on a massive dataset of text and code to process user inputs and generate responses that simulate human conversation. When you ask ChatGPT a question, it doesn't search the web for answers but instead draws on patterns and information it has learned during its training phase. Imagine this process as similar to how a well-read person might draw on their extensive reading experience to answer questions on various topics. They don't know everything, nor do they pull up specific articles they've read. Instead, they synthesize their accumulated knowledge to provide answers that make sense based on the context of the conversation.

ChatGPT's capabilities are distinctively different from more narrowly focused AI applications such as those used for image recognition or structured data analysis. Unlike these specialized AIs, ChatGPT is versatile in its knowledge base and application, making it broadly applicable across many scenarios where nuanced conversation is beneficial. This versatility is rooted in its foundational technology - the **Generative Pre-trained Transformer**, or GPT, which allows it to generate human-like text based on the prompts it receives.

For those eager to start interacting with ChatGPT, the process is straightforward. Initially, setting up an account with OpenAI or any platform offering access to ChatGPT is required. You're ready to begin your first conversation once you've created an account and logged in. Start with simple questions or prompts to understand how ChatGPT responds. For instance, you might type "Write me a poem." or "Tell me a joke." As you interact more, try asking more complex questions or exploring topics of personal interest to see how ChatGPT handles a wide range of subjects.

During these initial interactions, it's fascinating to observe how ChatGPT attempts to provide contextually appropriate responses. However, it's also crucial to understand that while ChatGPT can generate impressively coherent and context-aware responses, its knowledge is fixed when it was last trained. It doesn't have real-time access to the internet or updates on current events unless integrated with other tools that provide such data. This limitation is essential to remember as you explore this conversational AI's capabilities.

Engaging with ChatGPT can be a delightful and enlightening experience, especially as you understand the depth and breadth of conversations possible with this AI. Whether you're looking to solve a problem, gather information, or have an engaging chat, ChatGPT offers a window into the future of human-AI interaction, where machines can understand and respond to us with a level of relevance and immediacy that was once the stuff of science fiction. As you continue to explore, remember that each interaction with ChatGPT provides answers and helps you better understand the intricate dance between human queries and AI responses. This dynamic is continually reshaping our interaction with technology.

1.3 Decoding Machine Learning and Its Role in ChatGPT

Machine learning is a core pillar supporting artificial intelligence's vast, dynamic world. It's a field that allows computers to absorb and adapt to new data without being explicitly programmed to do so—an ability that might sound like something out of science fiction but is increasingly becoming a standard aspect of modern technology. At its heart, machine learning involves the development of algorithms that can analyze data, learn from it, and make predictions or decisions based on that knowledge. Imagine teaching your computer to recognize patterns like a human brain does; that's essentially what machine learning achieves. It's like educating your computer to predict outcomes based on past experiences, a process that evolves continuously through further interactions and data exposure.

Specifically, in the context of ChatGPT, machine learning is not just a feature; it's the backbone. ChatGPT learns from an extensive collection of text data from various sources. This training involves feeding it large amounts of data and allowing it to know and understand the nuances of human language. Every time you interact with ChatGPT, it's applying what it learned during its training phase to generate contextually appropriate responses. For instance, when you ask ChatGPT about the weather, it doesn't look up real-time online weather reports; instead, it generates a response based on patterns and information it has learned from its training data, which does not include current weather information. This ability to generate human-like text based on learned data without direct access to or reliance on real-time data distinguishes ChatGPT in AI applications.

Diving deeper into the types of machine learning models, three main categories are particularly relevant to AI development: supervised learning, unsupervised learning, and reinforcement learning. Supervised learning involves training a model on a labeled dataset, meaning each training example is paired with an output label. For instance, in teaching a model to differentiate between spam emails and those that are not, each email in the training set is tagged as 'spam' or 'not spam.' ChatGPT, however, primarily uses another sophisticated type of machine learning known as unsupervised learning, where the system learns to identify patterns and relationships in input data that isn't explicitly labeled.

Another intriguing area is reinforcement learning, which involves training models to make sequences of decisions by rewarding them for positive outcomes. This technique is not primarily used in ChatGPT but is crucial in other AI scenarios like gaming or navigation, where the AI must make decisions that build on one another toward a goal. Each of these learning types contributes uniquely to the abilities of AI systems, enabling them to handle tasks ranging from simple classification, such as identifying spam emails, to complex decision-making processes that mimic human thought, like planning an optimal delivery route for multiple packages in a dynamic environment.

To illustrate the impact of machine learning on ChatGPT's performance, consider how it adapts to new information over time. Early versions of such models might have struggled with specific linguistic nuances or cultural references. However, as they are exposed to more diverse data sets and feedback, their ability to understand and respond appropriately to a broader range of queries improves significantly. This ongoing learning process is vital for maintaining the relevance and usefulness of AI in a world where human conversations and cultural contexts are constantly evolving.

What sets machine learning apart from traditional rule-based systems in the practical application of technologies like ChatGPT is its ability to respond to queries and learn from the inputs it receives, refining its algorithms and enhancing its interactions with users. This capability ensures that AI technologies remain valuable and practical tools in our digital arsenal, supporting various activities, from everyday tasks like scheduling and information retrieval to more complex operations such as automated customer service and content creation. As we continue to integrate AI into various facets of life and work, understanding machine learning will be crucial for anyone looking to optimize these interactions and harness the full potential of this transformative technology.

1.4 The Essentials of Natural Language Processing (NLP)

Natural Language Processing, or NLP, is a fascinating facet of artificial intelligence that focuses on the interaction between computers and humans through language. It's essentially about enhancing how technology understands and responds to human language in a natural and effective way. NLP is not just about programming computers to comprehend words and sentences; it's about enabling them to grasp the nuances and contexts of language as we do, which is a pivotal step towards making human-computer interactions as smooth and natural as possible.

At its core, NLP involves various techniques to bridge the gap between human communication and machine understanding. One of the foundational techniques is tokenization. This process consists of breaking down text into smaller parts, such as words or phrases, making it easier for the machine to understand and process. For example, the sentence "ChatGPT is helpful" would be split into tokens: 'ChatGPT,' 'is,' and 'helpful.' This breakdown process is similar to how we naturally pause and emphasize certain words in our speech to convey meaning more clearly. By tokenizing text, computers can start to analyze and interpret language in a structured, logical way, which is crucial for all subsequent NLP tasks.

Another significant NLP technique is sentiment analysis. This involves determining the emotional tone behind a series of words used to gain an understanding of the attitudes, opinions, and emotions expressed within an online comment. For instance, from the statement "I love ice cream," sentiment analysis tools can identify the positive sentiment associated with the message. Conversely, the statement "I hate traffic" would be recognized as conveying a negative sentiment. This ability to assess sentiments can be beneficial, particularly in fields like marketing and customer service, where understanding consumer emotions plays a crucial role in addressing their needs and concerns.

Named Entity Recognition (NER) is another crucial NLP technique that identifies and classifies critical text elements into predefined categories. For example, in the sentence "Einstein was born in Ulm," 'Einstein' would be recognized as a person and 'Ulm' as a location. This allows the computer to understand essential details in the text, enabling it to manage information more effectively. Whether extracting names from a large dataset or identifying locations mentioned in a tweet, NER helps structure and categorize text to enhance data retrieval and analysis processes.

These NLP techniques play a pivotal role in ChatGPT's functioning. By employing methods like tokenization, sentiment analysis, and named entity recognition, ChatGPT can understand a user's input, grasp the context and emotion of the conversation, and respond in a relevant and appropriate way. This ability makes ChatGPT an effective communication tool. It enhances its applications across various domains where understanding user sentiment is crucial or where recognizing key entities and themes can guide more targeted and effective outputs.

However, despite the advances in NLP, there are still challenges. One significant issue is dealing with ambiguity in language. Words with multiple meanings can confuse AI models if the context isn't unclear. For instance, the word "bat" can refer to a piece of sports equipment or an animal, and understanding which meaning is correct in a given sentence requires a sophisticated grasp of context. Another challenge is maintaining the context over more extended conversations, which is crucial for ensuring that the responses remain relevant and do not lose track of what has been discussed previously. For example, if someone mentions "Paris" early in a conversation and later refers to "the city," the system needs to remember that "the city" refers to "Paris."

These challenges underscore the complexity and sophistication required in NLP to mimic human-like understanding and response patterns. As technology evolves, the solutions to these challenges will refine how effectively computers can interact with human language, making our interactions with AI more seamless and intuitive. As we continue integrating AI into our daily lives, understanding and improving these NLP techniques will ensure that our interactions with technology are as rewarding and effective as possible.

1.5 Exploring Generative Pre-trained Transformers (GPT)

Understanding the intricacies of Generative Pre-trained Transformers, commonly known as GPT, is like peeling back the curtain on a Broadway stage to reveal the mechanisms that make the magic happen. Developed by OpenAI, GPT is an AI technology that excels in understanding and generating human-like text, paving the way for systems like ChatGPT. At its core, GPT is built on transformer architecture. This breakthrough has significantly advanced the field of machine learning by enhancing the model's ability to handle data sequences, such as sentences in a text.

The foundation of GPT lies in its ability to process and generate text based on patterns it has learned during its training. This is not just about recognizing words but understanding the context and the small, delicate, or intricate details of language that make communication meaningful. The architecture of GPT includes what are known as attention mechanisms. These mechanisms allow the model to weigh the importance of different words in a sentence, regardless of their position. For example, in the sentence "The cat that sat on the mat," the word 'cat' is crucial for understanding the subject, while 'on' links elements of the location. GPT's attention mechanism evaluates these relationships, enabling it to comprehend and generate coherent and contextually appropriate text.

Diving deeper into the architecture, GPT is structured in layers, and each process of the input text increases in complexity. Initially, the input text is split into tokens—similar to breaking a sentence into words and phrases—then embedded with numerical values representing different aspects of the language. These embeddings move through the network's layers, transforming them step-by-step, each layer building on the previous one's output. The final layer then generates text based on the transformed embeddings, which reflect a deep understanding of the input text's linguistic structure, style, and implied meanings.

The training process of GPT models is a two-stage journey involving pre-training and fine-tuning. During pre-training, the model is exposed to a vast amount of text data, learning the language's general patterns, grammar, and vocabulary. This stage is not specific to any particular task but aims to develop a broad understanding of the language. Following this, the fine-tuning stage adjusts the model to perform tasks like answering questions, translating languages, or writing content. Here, the model is trained on a smaller, task-specific dataset, allowing it to hone its skills and improve performance in particular applications.

Speaking of applications, the versatility of GPT extends far beyond generating conversational text for ChatGPT. Its ability to understand and produce text has been applied in various fields. In translation, GPT models can assist in converting text from one language to another, understanding the nuances and context often lost with more basic translation software. These models generate creative and informative articles in content creation, frequently starting from just a headline or a keyword prompt. Furthermore, GPT can summarize extensive documents efficiently, distilling long reports into concise summaries, which proves invaluable in fields like law and academia, where large volumes of text are expected.

These applications underscore the transformative potential of GPT across different sectors. By automating complex language tasks, GPT enhances productivity and opens new possibilities for human creativity and interaction. Whether it's helping a student understand a complex text, assisting a journalist in drafting articles, or enabling a lawyer to summarize cases quickly, GPT is reshaping how we interact with text and, by extension, with each other. As we continue to explore and develop this technology, its capacity to understand and interact with human language will increasingly blur the lines between human and machine-generated text, making our interactions with AI more natural and, ultimately, more human.

1.6 Ethical AI: Principles for Responsible Use

Having explored the foundations of AI and the intricacies of ChatGPT, it's crucial now to consider the ethical frameworks that ensure these technologies are used responsibly. Ethical AI involves creating systems that not only comply with legal standards but also operate within the moral expectations of society, ensuring they contribute positively and do not harm users or perpetuate unfair biases. This focus is essential because, as AI technologies become more integrated into our daily lives, their decisions can significantly impact individuals and communities. Ethical considerations are not just add-ons but foundational elements that guide AI technology's responsible development and use.

The principles of ethical AI include transparency, fairness, privacy, and accountability. Transparency in AI means that the operations and decisions of AI systems should be understandable by humans. This is particularly important in applications like ChatGPT, where users should be able to comprehend how the AI came up with its responses. Fairness involves ensuring that AI systems do not embed or perpetuate discrimination and are equitable in their operations. This can be challenging, as AI systems often learn from large datasets that may contain biased human decisions. Privacy is another cornerstone, requiring personal data used to train or operate AI systems to be handled securely and confidentially to protect user information. Lastly, accountability in AI systems means that there should be mechanisms in place to hold the developers and operators of AI systems responsible for how their systems operate.

ChatGPT, like many AI models, faces specific ethical challenges. One of the most significant issues is biases in training data. Because ChatGPT learns from a vast range of internet text, it can inadvertently learn and perpetuate the biases present in that data. This might manifest in gender, racial, or ideological biases that skew the AI's responses in ways that could be harmful or unfair. Another challenge is the potential misuse of conversational AIs. For instance, because ChatGPT can generate plausible human-like text, its application is risky in creating misleading or harmful content, such as fake news or impersonations.

Several best practices should be followed to mitigate these risks and ensure the ethical use of ChatGPT and similar AI systems. First, developers and users of AI systems should be trained in ethical AI practices. This includes education on the potential biases in AI systems and how to avoid or mitigate them. Second, regular audits of AI systems, particularly those like ChatGPT that learn from user interactions, are crucial. These audits can help identify and correct biases or other ethical issues that arise as the AI learns and evolves. Transparency is also vital; users should be informed about how the AI works and any limitations in its knowledge or capabilities. Finally, there should be clear guidelines and policies to prevent the misuse of AI technologies, coupled with robust security measures to protect data and prevent unauthorized access.

By adhering to these core ethical principles and best practices, developers and users of AI can help ensure that technologies like ChatGPT are used responsibly and beneficially. Ethical AI is about preventing harm and ensuring that AI technologies are aligned with society's broader values and needs, contributing positively to human progress and well-being. As we continue to develop and integrate AI into various aspects of life, maintaining a solid ethical framework will be essential to harness the benefits of AI while managing its challenges effectively.

1.7 Interactive Task: Set Up Your First ChatGPT Interaction

Embarking on your first interaction with ChatGPT is an exciting step into conversational AI. Let's begin by setting up your account. The process is straightforward and designed to be user-friendly, ensuring accessibility even for those who may not be tech-savvy. First, visit the OpenAI website or the platform where ChatGPT is hosted. Here, you will find an option to sign up or register. Typically, this involves entering basic information such as your name, email address, and password. Some platforms allow you to register by linking another social account, such as Google or Apple. Once your account is set up, you can log in and explore ChatGPT's capabilities.

Navigating the ChatGPT interface is the next step. Upon your first login, you'll likely be greeted by a clean, minimalistic interface with a prominent area to type your questions or prompts. This is the primary interaction space where your conversation with ChatGPT will unfold. Familiarize yourself with menus or settings options on the interface's edges. These may allow you to adjust preferences, manage your account, or access help resources. Taking a moment to click through these options can enhance your understanding and control of the interaction process.

Crafting your initial prompts is crucial in shaping the quality and relevance of ChatGPT's responses. A well-constructed prompt should be clear and direct, providing enough context to guide the AI in generating a precise and informative response. For example, instead of asking, "weather," which is vague and could result in a generic response, try "What is the current weather in Paris?" This prompt is specific and leads to a targeted response. Conversely, a poor prompt like "Paris weather now?" lacks clarity and might confuse the AI or lead to less accurate output. Remember, the clarity of your question significantly influences the effectiveness of ChatGPT's answers.

Interpreting responses from ChatGPT is another skill that enhances your interaction experience. Responses from ChatGPT can range from straightforward facts to more complex explanations, depending on your prompt. When evaluating responses, it's essential to recognize that ChatGPT, while sophisticated, has limitations. It generates responses based on patterns and data learned during training, which means it can occasionally produce incorrect or biased information, especially if the query involves subjective interpretation or is outside the scope of its training data. For instance, asking ChatGPT for advice on personal or medical issues might not yield reliable or safe information. It is crucial to critically assess the responses significantly when they influence decision-making or involve specialized knowledge areas.

As you interact more with ChatGPT, you'll notice patterns and learn how to phrase your questions to obtain the most accurate and relevant information. This practice will enhance your ability to use ChatGPT effectively and deepen your understanding of how AI interprets and processes human language. Remember, each interaction is an opportunity to refine your questioning skills and adapt based on the responses you receive. This iterative process is part of the fascinating journey of learning to communicate effectively with an AI, opening up new possibilities for information gathering, learning, and even entertainment. As you continue to explore and interact with ChatGPT, let your curiosity guide you toward discovering the vast capabilities and, occasionally, the quirky limitations of what AI can offer. Now that you have completed this interactive task reflect on your newfound skills and prepare for the exciting journey ahead as you dive deeper into mastering ChatGPT.

Mastering Prompt Engineering

CONGRATULATIONS ON COMPLETING CHAPTER One! Today, we take the next step in our seven-day journey by diving deeper into AI and exploring prompt engineering. Picture yourself in a master chef's kitchen, with the finest ingredients ready for you to create something extraordinary. Just like the quality of a dish depends on how you blend these ingredients, the success of ChatGPT interactions hinges on how you construct your prompts. This chapter is your guide to mastering prompt engineering, an essential skill enabling you to communicate effectively with ChatGPT. By honing this skill, you'll ensure that every exchange with ChatGPT is productive, insightful, and tailored to your needs.

2.1 Basics of Crafting Effective Prompts

Understanding Input Sensitivity

The specificity and structure of your prompts play a pivotal role in the quality of responses you receive from ChatGPT. This concept, called input sensitivity, is akin to tuning a musical instrument; the better the tuning, the sweeter the melody. When you provide ChatGPT with specific, well-structured prompts, you guide the AI to understand the topic at hand and the depth and angle of response you expect. For instance, a vague prompt like "Tell me about dogs" can lead to a generic response. In contrast, a specific prompt such as "What are the common health issues faced by Labrador Retrievers?" directs ChatGPT to generate a focused and detailed reply. The key lies in being precise with your questions, which helps the AI focus on its "thoughts" and deliver the necessary information.

Key Components of a Good Prompt

Creating an effective prompt involves several critical elements: clarity, focus, and context. Clarity means being explicit about what you want to know, leaving little room for misinterpretation. Focus is about narrowing down the subject to avoid overwhelming breadth, which can dilute the value of the response. Context ties your question to specific conditions or scenarios, enriching the AI's understanding and the relevance of its response. Together, these elements form a robust framework that enhances the interaction between you and ChatGPT, much like a well-written recipe guides a cook to culinary success.

Examples of Effective vs. Ineffective Prompts

To illustrate, consider these examples:

- **Ineffective:** "Book recommendation."
- **Effective:** "Recommend a thriller novel set in a dystopian future with strong female characters."

The first prompt is vague and lacks context, making it difficult for ChatGPT to provide a meaningful suggestion. However, The second prompt is clear and specific, allowing ChatGPT to provide a tailored and helpful recommendation.

- Ineffective: "Plan a holiday."
- Effective: "Could you suggest a 5-day itinerary for a family vacation in Paris, including kid-friendly activities?"

Here, the effective prompt provides a clear, focused, contextual framework, enabling ChatGPT to generate a targeted and practical response.

Initial Setup for Success

Before you even begin to type out your prompt, it's crucial to define the goal of your conversation with ChatGPT. What are you hoping to achieve? Are you looking for information, advice, or perhaps entertainment? Setting your goal will guide how you frame your prompt. Additionally, choosing the right tone and style for your prompt can significantly impact the interaction. For example, a formal tone might suit business-related queries, while a casual tone might be better for personal or less formal topics. This initial setup acts as your blueprint, ensuring that every element of your prompt contributes towards a meaningful and satisfying exchange with ChatGPT.

Crafting prompts might seem simple, but like any skill, it requires practice and attention to detail. As you spend more time interacting with ChatGPT, you'll develop a sharper sense of formulating your prompts to get the best out of this powerful tool. Each conversation is an opportunity to refine your technique and move closer to mastering the art of prompt engineering. This chapter sets the foundation for that mastery, providing the tools and understanding needed to create effective prompts that lead to rewarding interactions with AI. As you progress, remember that each prompt is a step towards deeper learning and greater confidence in your ability to leverage AI effectively in everyday life.

2.2 Advanced Prompt Techniques for Specific Outcomes

When you begin to feel more comfortable with the basics of crafting prompts for ChatGPT, you might find yourself curious about how to fine-tune your approach to achieve even more tailored and specific outcomes. This part of your learning curve involves using more sophisticated techniques that can significantly enhance the interaction quality and the utility of the responses you receive from ChatGPT. Let's explore some advanced techniques that can transform your prompts from simple questions into powerful tools that command detailed and contextually aware responses.

Conditional Prompting for Complex Requests

Conditional prompting is a technique where you structure your prompts to include specific conditions that must be met in the response. This method is particularly useful when dealing with complex requests where the output needs to reflect multiple variables or conditions. Consider it like setting several 'if' statements that guide ChatGPT's response process. For instance, if you are planning a trip and have several preferences – like budget, destination type, and activities – a conditional prompt might look like this, "Can you suggest a travel plan that stays under $3000, includes outdoor activities and is suitable for a family of four?" By specifying these conditions, you guide ChatGPT in tailoring its search and response strategy to meet all the criteria, making the information more relevant and useful.

Sequential Prompting for Detailed Explanations

Sequential prompting is about breaking down a complex request into a series of more straightforward prompts, which gradually build up to provide a detailed explanation or comprehensive response. This approach can be likened to teaching someone a new skill step-by-step. Each prompt is a building block, laying the foundation for more complex information. For example, suppose you want to understand how electric cars work. In that case, you might start with, "What is an electric car?" followed by, "How do electric car engines work?" and then, "What are the benefits of using electric cars over gasoline cars?" This method helps maintain a clear and structured flow of information, especially when tackling intricate topics or when you need to understand a subject deeply.

Creativity in Prompt Design

Incorporating creativity in your prompts can lead to surprisingly delightful and insightful interactions with ChatGPT. This involves thinking outside the box and asking questions that push the boundaries of the usual interactions. For example, instead of asking, "What are the health benefits of walking?" you might phrase your prompt as, "Imagine walking is a new product. What would be its advertising tagline based on its health benefits?" Such creative prompts encourage ChatGPT to tap into its training on diverse data sets, often leading to unique, clever, and entertaining responses that might provide new perspectives on familiar topics.

Leveraging Known Parameters

Incorporating known parameters into your prompts can significantly enhance the specificity and relevance of the responses from ChatGPT. This technique involves using specific data points you already know to inform the AI's response process. For instance, if you are a small business owner looking to increase local traffic to your store, a prompt like, "What are effective marketing strategies for a small business in Boston with a limited budget?" helps ChatGPT understand your query's geographical and financial context. By grounding your prompt with these known parameters, you direct ChatGPT to tailor its computational prowess to your specific situation, making the advice or information it provides more applicable and actionable.

As you experiment with these advanced prompting techniques, you'll discover that how you ask questions can dramatically influence the quality and applicability of the answers you receive. This realization is a powerful aspect of learning to interact effectively with AI. It highlights the importance of clear, thoughtful communication and shows how creativity and precision can unlock the full potential of ChatGPT and similar tools. As you continue to practice and refine your prompting skills, remember that each interaction is an opportunity to enhance your understanding and mastery of this dynamic interface between human curiosity and artificial intelligence.

2.3 Troubleshooting Common Prompting Errors

Navigating the nuances of prompt engineering can sometimes feel like steering a ship through uncharted waters—there are moments when things don't go exactly as planned. Understanding how to identify and correct common prompting errors is like having a reliable compass; it ensures that you can recalibrate and steer back to a course of productive and insightful interactions with ChatGPT. Let's delve into some common challenges you might encounter and explore strategies to overcome them effectively.

Diagnosing Vague Responses

At times, you may find that ChatGPT's responses seem vague or barely touch on the topic you're interested in. This often happens when the prompt lacks specific guiding elements that help narrow the AI's focus. To tackle this, revise your prompt to include more detailed information about what you want to know or achieve. For instance, if your initial question was "Tell me about renewable energy," and you received a generic overview, you could specify your interest by changing it to "What are the latest advancements in solar energy technology in Europe?" This refined prompt provides clear direction, encouraging ChatGPT to generate a more targeted and detailed response. Additionally, incorporating follow-up questions based on the initial answers can help dig deeper into the subject, like peeling an onion layer by layer to reveal more substantive information with each query.

Correcting Over-Specificity

While specificity is usually beneficial, overly detailed prompts can sometimes limit the breadth of ChatGPT's responses, confining it to a narrow scope that might miss other valuable insights. For example, if you ask, "What is the average price of a 256GB iPhone 12 in New York City?" you might restrict the response to very specific data that may not be readily available or useful. To find a balance, consider broadening your prompt to capture a wider range of information while guiding the AI toward your specific interest area. A better approach could be, "How do iPhone prices vary across different models and storage capacities in major US cities?" This revised prompt invites a more comprehensive discussion, which can be more informative and useful.

Handling Non-Responses and Errors

Occasionally, you might encounter situations where ChatGPT fails to respond or returns an error. This can happen for various reasons, such as network issues, overly complex queries, or AI training data limitations. When this occurs, the first step is simplifying your prompt to streamline the AI process. Breaking down a complex question into smaller, more manageable parts can help avoid overwhelming the system. Additionally, ensuring that your internet connection is stable and that the platform hosting ChatGPT is operational can resolve some of these issues. If errors persist, it's helpful to report them to the service provider, as this can aid in improving the system for all users.

Feedback Mechanisms

One of the most effective ways to refine your prompts and enhance the quality of interactions with ChatGPT is to utilize feedback mechanisms. Every response from the AI offers insights into how well it understood and addressed your query. You can adjust your prompting strategy to achieve better results by critically analyzing these responses. For instance, if a response misses key points you hoped to cover, consider rephrasing your prompt to highlight these areas more clearly in your next interaction. Additionally, some platforms allow users to rate or provide feedback on AI responses directly, which can help improve the system's accuracy and responsiveness over time.

Mastering these troubleshooting techniques requires patience and practice but is undoubtedly rewarding. As you become more adept at identifying and correcting prompting errors, your interactions with ChatGPT will become more fluid, productive, and enlightening. Just like any skill, prompt engineering improves with experience, and each challenge you overcome adds a layer of proficiency, enhancing your ability to harness the full potential of this powerful conversational AI.

2.4 Using Prompts to Generate Creative Content

When exploring the capabilities of ChatGPT, one particularly exciting application is its ability to aid in creative endeavors. Whether you're a writer, an artist, or someone just looking to explore your creative side, learning how to craft prompts that encourage creative outputs from ChatGPT can open up a world of possibilities. Let's jump into how this tool can inspire your artistic expressions, enhance storytelling, and even solve problems creatively.

Inspiring Artistic Expressions

Imagine you're looking to write a poem but are stuck for inspiration. ChatGPT can serve as a collaborative partner in your creative process. Start by setting a theme or emotion you want to explore in your poem and use a prompt to guide ChatGPT. For instance, you could say, "Write a poem about the tranquility of the ocean at dusk." ChatGPT will generate a poem that adheres to your theme and introduces unique perspectives and word choices you might not have considered. Similarly, if you're an artist looking for ideas for your next painting, you might prompt ChatGPT with, "Describe a scene that combines elements of surrealism and nature." The response could spark a vision of a landscape that defies the ordinary, fueling your artistic imagination.

Brainstorming with AI

ChatGPT can also be an invaluable tool for brainstorming. Whether you're looking to develop new project ideas, find solutions to business challenges, or think of topics for academic research, the way you frame your prompts can lead to a wealth of innovative ideas. Suppose you're tasked with developing a new product idea for a fitness technology company. You could use a prompt like, "List innovative features that could be included in a fitness tracker to enhance user engagement." ChatGPT might suggest features you hadn't thought of, such as stress level detection or integration with virtual reality for immersive workouts, each of which could serve as a starting point for further exploration.

Enhancing Storytelling

For writers and storytellers, crafting prompts that aid in developing complex narratives or character arcs is another area where ChatGPT can be particularly useful. If you're writing a story and are stuck on character development, you might ask, "Create a backstory for a character who is a retired astronaut turned detective." ChatGPT's response can provide a detailed past that adds depth to your character, enriching your narrative. Additionally, if you're looking to build a compelling plot twist, a prompt such as, "Suggest a plot twist for a mystery novel where the least likely character is the culprit" could provide you with unexpected ideas that enhance the intrigue and complexity of your story.

Creative Problem Solving

Finally, ChatGPT can assist in creative problem-solving by generating novel solutions to problems or offering new perspectives on existing situations. This capability is instrumental in marketing, product development, and personal challenges. For example, if you're trying to increase attendance at a local event, you might ask ChatGPT, "What are some creative marketing strategies to increase local engagement with a community event?" The suggestions might include innovative uses of social media, partnerships with local businesses, or interactive campaigns that engage potential attendees in a memorable way. Each idea can be evaluated and adapted to fit your needs and resources.

Harnessing ChatGPT for creative content generation involves a shift in how you approach problem-solving and idea development. You open up innovative possibilities by effectively leveraging AI's ability to process and generate text based on your prompts. Whether you're writing a novel, planning a marketing strategy, or simply exploring artistic expressions, ChatGPT can be a powerful ally in your creator toolkit. As you continue experimenting with different prompts and exploring the AI's potential, you'll likely discover that your creative skills are enhanced, leading to richer, more innovative outcomes in whatever project you undertake.

2.5 Ethical Considerations in Prompt Engineering

When engaging with tools like ChatGPT, it is important to remember and apply the foundational ethics discussed in Chapter One. These principles ensure that your prompts foster responsible and ethical AI use. Your prompts can significantly influence the outputs, so avoiding creating or sharing manipulative or harmful content is crucial. Instead, focus on generating prompts that encourage positive, constructive, and unbiased responses. For example, if you're exploring sensitive topics like mental health or social issues, frame your prompts thoughtfully to respect the complexity of these subjects and avoid perpetuating stereotypes or biases.

Bias and fairness are significant concerns in AI that can be influenced by how prompts are designed. AI systems like ChatGPT learn from vast datasets that may contain biased human language or perspectives. These biases can be reflected in the AI's responses. To counteract this, ensure your prompts are neutral and avoid assumptions about personal characteristics like race, gender, or age unless relevant to the context. Diversifying the scenarios and examples in your prompts can also help provide a broader perspective and reduce the prevalence of narrow or stereotypical responses. For instance, when asking about leadership, consider including various cultural, social, and organizational contexts to enrich the diversity of responses. Effective prompting can help alleviate bias by explicitly requesting balanced perspectives and inclusive considerations, thereby guiding ChatGPT to generate more equitable responses that reflect diverse viewpoints.

Privacy is another critical consideration when using AI. Although ChatGPT does not retain personal data for future interactions, it is essential to be cautious with the information you include in your prompts. Avoid sharing personal details or confidential information, particularly if the outputs will be shared or are accessible to others. Additionally, when generating content, ensure that personal data or identifiable details are fictionalized to prevent privacy breaches. This helps maintain the integrity of your data and protects sensitive information from misuse. Remember that your prompts may be used to help train and improve the AI, so always consider the potential implications of the information you provide. This approach helps maintain the integrity of your data and protects sensitive information from misuse.

Transparency is key when utilizing AI for content creation. As AI-generated content can be highly sophisticated, it is important to be honest about the use of AI in generating responses. Disclose AI involvement in your content creation process, especially in contexts where authenticity and credibility are important, such as academic or journalistic work. For example, if you use ChatGPT to help draft articles or reports, include a note that acknowledges the role of AI. This transparency upholds ethical standards and fosters trust and critical engagement with your audience.

By considering these ethical considerations, you can ensure that your prompt engineering is both responsible and beneficial. Focus on creating prompts reflecting fairness and respect for privacy while maintaining transparent disclosure procedures. This approach enhances the quality and integrity of your interactions with AI, aligns with broader ethical values, and contributes positively to the responsible development and use of AI technologies.

2.6 Customizing Prompts for Niche Topics

In the expansive terrain of AI applications, the ability to tailor ChatGPT's responses to specific industry needs or cultural contexts greatly enhances its utility and relevance. This customization is not just about refining the tool's accuracy; it's about molding it to become a seamless extension of your environment, whether in a bustling hospital ward, a fast-paced financial trading floor, or a multicultural marketing firm. Let's explore sophisticated strategies to fine-tune your interactions with ChatGPT, ensuring it responds with the precision and appropriateness required by different professional and cultural landscapes.

Industry-Specific Prompts

Every industry has specific language, regulations, and unique scenarios requiring specialized knowledge. To make ChatGPT a valuable tool for your field, it's important to tailor your prompts to meet these industry-specific requirements. This approach transforms ChatGPT from a generalist into a specialized asset. For example, accuracy and up-to-date information are crucial in the legal field. A prompt like "Explain the implications of the latest amendment in the data protection law for tech companies" must elicit a response that understands legal terms and reflects current laws and practices. Similarly, it's vital to ensure that prompts lead to medically accurate and confidential responses in healthcare. Asking, "What are the recommended treatments for type 2 diabetes according to the latest medical research?" should provide answers based on the most recent medical standards and research. In finance, where data changes rapidly, prompts must reflect the latest trends and information. A query like "Analyze the trend in tech stocks over the last quarter" requires the AI to understand and accurately interpret current financial data. Crafting such prompts involves knowing the specific needs of your industry and expressing them clearly in your questions to ChatGPT. This ensures that the responses you receive are relevant, accurate, and timely, making ChatGPT a more effective tool for your professional use.

Cultural Sensitivity

As businesses and interactions increasingly cross borders, the ability to customize prompts for cultural relevance and sensitivity becomes crucial. This involves understanding and integrating cultural nuances that affect communication styles, preferences, and taboos. For instance, when dealing with markets or audiences in different regions, the tone, examples, and references should be adapted to resonate culturally. A prompt intended for an audience in Japan, such as "Suggest polite marketing phrases for elderly customers," should reflect the formal and respectful communication style prevalent in Japanese culture. Similarly, a content creation prompt for a Middle Eastern audience should be aware of cultural norms and local tastes to ensure the content is engaging and appropriate. This customization enhances the effectiveness of the communication and builds a respectful and inclusive interaction framework.

Experimental Uses

The flexibility of ChatGPT opens up a playground for experimental applications. Encouraging experimentation with prompts can lead to innovative uses that push the boundaries of what AI can achieve. For instance, experimenting with ChatGPT in artistic domains, such as co-writing scripts for plays or generating ideas for art installations, can yield creative synergies that were previously unexplored. Similarly, in education, prompts can be designed to create interactive learning experiences that adapt to different learning styles and paces. Such experimental applications showcase the versatility of ChatGPT but also inspire continuous improvement and adaptation in various fields.

Embracing these advanced strategies for customizing ChatGPT's responses ensures that the tool is not just a passive participant in your tasks but dynamically tuned to the specific frequencies of your professional and cultural environment. Whether through industry-specific adjustments, cultural fine-tuning, or innovative experimentations, the potential to mold ChatGPT to fit almost any niche is immense. As you continue to interact and refine these approaches, the depth and breadth of ChatGPT's utility will only expand, mirroring the complexity and diversity of the human interactions it seeks to emulate.

2.7 The Perfect Prompt Formula

Crafting the perfect prompt for ChatGPT is akin to composing a recipe that balances all ingredients to achieve a delightful dish. Just as chefs use precise measurements and specific techniques to enhance flavors, effective prompts require a mix of clarity, context, and creativity to elicit the best responses. Let's explore how you can create clear, contextually rich, targeted prompts to yield precise and useful outcomes from ChatGPT.

Task Specification

Starting your prompt with a precise action verb is crucial as it sets the direction for ChatGPT, specifying what you expect as an outcome. This approach is similar to giving a clear command that guides someone on what to do next. For instance, a prompt like "Summarize the main points of this article" uses the action verb 'summarize' to direct ChatGPT to condense the article into its key elements. Similarly, "Create a detailed outline for a blog post on healthy eating," tells ChatGPT to 'create' something and specifies that it should be a 'detailed outline,' which narrows down the form of the response. These examples show that starting with a specific action verb can significantly streamline the interaction, making it easier for ChatGPT to understand and fulfill the request effectively.

Context Provision

Including relevant background details or situational context in your prompts enhances ChatGPT's understanding and the appropriateness of its responses. This is like setting the scene in a play; the better the scene is set, the more accurate the performance. For example, when you use a prompt like "Considering the current market trends, explain the benefits of this new product," you're not only asking for a task (explain) but also framing it within the specific context of "current market trends." This leads ChatGPT to tailor its response to how the new product fits or stands out in the current market scenario. Similarly, "In the context of an entry-level job interview, draft a cover letter for a marketing position" provides a clear scenario, helping ChatGPT focus its response to match the formality and specifics expected in a specific scenario.

Example Inclusion

You guide ChatGPT on the expected response style by incorporating examples into your prompts. This technique ensures that the output aligns closely with your needs. For instance, a prompt such as "Write the cover letter using the format pasted here [paste example]" clearly shows how the response should be structured. This makes it easier for ChatGPT to generate the desired content and ensures that the final output meets your requirements. Similarly, "Create a list of pros and cons, such as: 'Pros: Affordable, Easy to use; Cons: Limited features,'" clearly dictates both the content and the format, making the response immediately usable. Examples aren't always necessary, but they provide an excellent guide when used.

Persona Adoption

Specifying a persona in your prompts can significantly influence ChatGPT's responses, tailoring them to suit your intended audience better. Although this step is optional, it can be particularly helpful when you need precise and context-specific answers. For example, prompting, "You are a data analyst for a retail company considering a new job," helps ChatGPT adopt a relevant domain and provide clear, focused insights. Similarly, specifying constraints like, "You only have two hours each day," guides ChatGPT in offering practical solutions within the given time frame. This strategy ensures the responses are accurate in content and framed from the appropriate perspective.

Format Specification
Specifying the preferred structure for a response can greatly improve the organization and usability of the information you receive. Whether you need a list or a detailed paragraph, clearly stating the desired format helps ensure the response meets your needs. For instance, you can ask ChatGPT to "List the key points" or "List the steps" in bullet format for a concise and easy-to-scan list or to "Write a paragraph summarizing the benefits" for a more detailed narrative. This clarity in formatting instructions ensures the output aligns with your intended use, whether for a presentation, report, or casual reading. You might also provide detailed instructions like "use markdown formatting with ### for main headings, #### for subheadings, bullet points (-), and numbered lists (1., 2., 3.)." This approach helps you receive well-organized information tailored to your specific requirements.

Tone Indication
Finally, specifying the tone and style of the response is crucial for ensuring that the communication is adequate and appropriate for the context. For example, "Use a friendly and conversational tone" for a blog post aimed at young adults helps make the content relatable and engaging. In contrast, "Draft the email in a formal and professional manner" is appropriate for correspondence in a business context, where a higher level of formality is expected. This attention to tone and style enhances the effectiveness of the communication and reflects your understanding and respect for the audience's expectations.

Mastering the art of prompt crafting using these elements ensures that every interaction with ChatGPT is productive, targeted, and aligned with your objectives. As you practice incorporating these elements into your prompts, you'll find that ChatGPT has become an increasingly powerful tool, capable of generating precise and useful content that can save you time and enhance your projects or communications.

2.8 Interactive Task: Perfecting Your Prompting Skills

Engaging with ChatGPT is akin to learning a new language; the more you practice, the more fluent you become. To enhance your prompting skills, it's essential to immerse yourself in varied and structured practice exercises. These exercises are designed to gradually increase your comfort and proficiency by creating effective prompts tailored to elicit the best responses from ChatGPT.

Prompt Refinement and Improvement

Let's start with a foundational exercise to build your prompting skills. Begin by choosing a topic you're curious about, such as "sustainable gardening." First, formulate a basic prompt: "Tell me about sustainable gardening." Analyze the response from ChatGPT for completeness and relevance. Next, refine your prompt to make it more specific: "What are five sustainable gardening practices that can be easily implemented at home?" Notice how the specificity of your prompt enhances the precision of the response. Continue this exercise by gradually increasing the complexity of your prompts, such as asking for the pros and cons of each practice mentioned. This step-by-step escalation not only hones your ability to ask straightforward, focused questions but also deepens your understanding of the topic.

Progressive Prompting

Let's enhance your prompting skills by building upon each response in progressive queries. Imagine you are helping a friend start a small online business. Begin with a general prompt to gather foundational information, such as, "What are the key elements of a digital business plan?" Once ChatGPT provides a response, analyze the data and think about the next logical step to delve deeper into the topic. For example, follow up with a more focused question, "Can you explain how to identify and analyze target markets for an online business?" After receiving this detailed response, continue building on this by asking, "What strategies can be used to market an online business to these identified target markets effectively?" This step-by-step approach sharpens your ability to create precise prompts and demonstrates how to build on each piece of information provided by ChatGPT. It mimics a natural and progressive topic exploration, enabling you to extract comprehensive insights and progressively more detailed information.

Crafting the Perfect Prompt

Choose a topic (e.g., "healthy eating" or "time management) and a specific situation in which you're interested. Use the Perfect Prompt Formula to craft your prompt by specifying the task, providing context, including an example, adopting a persona, specifying the format, and indicating the tone. This exercise will help you practice creating effective prompts that generate accurate and tailored responses from ChatGPT.

You are on the right track if your prompt looked something like this: “You recently secured a new position as a data analyst. Your friends, impressed by your determination and strategy, have asked for your advice on their own job searches. Write a message in paragraph form to share with your friends seeking new job opportunities in a group chat. The message should outline the key steps you took in your job search, share some challenges you faced and how you overcame them, and offer to support them as they embark on their own job searches. Use motivational and supportive language." Continue practicing with the Perfect Prompt Formula, either with new topics or by refining existing ones, until you are comfortable crafting "perfect" prompts. Try different scenarios and progressively more complex situations to enhance your skills and confidence in prompt crafting.

Through these exercises, you'll notice a significant improvement in your communication ability with ChatGPT. Each step, from simple questions to complex, scenario-based prompts, incrementally builds your skill and confidence. Remember, every prompt is a chance to refine your approach, expand your knowledge, and enhance your interaction with this advanced AI, making each exchange more valuable and insightful.

As we conclude this chapter on honing your prompting skills, remember that clear communication is the key to successful interactions. This includes defining your task, setting the context, providing examples, adopting the right persona, and specifying the format and tone. These elements combine to form a formula that enhances the efficiency and effectiveness of your prompts. Looking ahead, the next chapter will build on these skills, showing you how to fully apply them in real-world scenarios to utilize ChatGPT in various professional contexts. Stay tuned to continue refining your skills and discover how to leverage ChatGPT to enhance business productivity, streamline daily tasks, and support your professional growth and development.

Business Productivity with ChatGPT

Welcome to Chapter Three! Building on the prompt engineering skills you've developed, we will now progress into how you can use ChatGPT to enhance business productivity. This chapter will guide you through various applications to streamline your work, manage tasks more efficiently, and support your professional development.

Envision a world where your daily business communications are faster, more efficient, personalized, and engaging. This isn't a glimpse into a far-off future; it's a reality you can achieve today with the power of ChatGPT. This chapter discusses how ChatGPT can transform your approach to essential business tasks such as writing emails, creating content, and managing customer service inquiries. You'll also explore how ChatGPT can assist in educational endeavors, solve business problems, and take on personal assistant duties. From managing your social media to conducting market research, ChatGPT's capabilities will help you enhance every aspect of your professional life. Get ready to unlock new levels of productivity and efficiency with practical applications and real-world examples that illustrate the transformative power of AI in your daily work.

3.1 Enhancing Emails with ChatGPT

Drafting Routine Responses

One of the significant benefits of integrating ChatGPT into your email workflow is its ability to help draft routine responses efficiently. Businesses often receive repetitive inquiries, such as questions about business hours or return policies. Crafting each response manually can be a significant time drain. While ChatGPT cannot send emails for you, it can be used to draft accurate and consistent replies quickly. For example, you can instruct ChatGPT to generate a response for inquiries about return policies by providing a standard template or key points. This helps ensure your replies are consistent and professional, reflecting your business's values and saving you time to focus on more personalized interactions.

Organizing and Summarizing Emails

Managing a high volume of incoming emails can be overwhelming, but ChatGPT can assist by helping you organize and prioritize them more effectively. One way to utilize ChatGPT is by exporting the contents of your mailbox and using it in a prompt to create a prioritization summary. This lets you quickly identify which emails require immediate attention and which can be deferred. Additionally, you can use the export to generate concise summaries of the content, providing quick insights into the key points without reading through each email in detail. Furthermore, prompting ChatGPT to analyze the exported emails can help identify potential business processes that could improve your workflow. While ChatGPT does not manage your inbox directly, leveraging it for summarizing and prioritizing email content can streamline your email management, ensuring that critical communications are highlighted and saving you significant time.

Personalizing Bulk Emails

Enhancing efficiency in email communication goes beyond drafting responses—it involves recognizing where personalization can make the most impact. ChatGPT can help you identify areas within your emails that are prime for personalization by analyzing customer data, such as past purchases and interactions. For instance, by reviewing the contents of your email exports, ChatGPT can highlight segments that would benefit from tailored messages, ensuring that each communication feels individualized and thoughtful rather than generic. This is particularly useful for bulk communications, such as promotional campaigns, where personalized recommendations based on customer preferences can significantly improve engagement and satisfaction. While ChatGPT will not personalize the emails for you, it can pinpoint opportunities where personalization will be most effective, allowing you to craft content that enhances customer loyalty and trust manually.

Enhancing Email Creativity

Maintaining creativity in email communications can be challenging, especially when dealing with routine business tasks. ChatGPT, with its vast training data covering various writing styles, can help you draft emails that are not only clear and effective but also engaging and creative. For example, if you are preparing a newsletter or a promotional email, ChatGPT can suggest compelling language for subject lines, calls to action, and content that resonates with your audience. This helps make your emails more attractive and can lead to higher engagement rates, particularly useful for marketing and outreach efforts.

Integrating ChatGPT into your email management routine can significantly improve your efficiency and the quality of your communications. You can save time and increase productivity by using ChatGPT to draft routine responses, organize incoming emails, personalize emails, and enhance communication creativity. As you continue exploring the capabilities of ChatGPT in this chapter, you will discover even more practical ways to streamline your business tasks and improve your overall work efficiency.

3.2 Streamlining Content Creation

Creating content consistently can be daunting, especially when you are expected to keep high-quality and fresh ideas. ChatGPT can significantly streamline this process by assisting in several key areas, from generating topic ideas to structuring content and optimizing it for better search engine visibility. Let's explore leveraging Chat GPT to make content creation more efficient and impactful.

Generating Ideas and Outlines

Every great piece of writing starts with a solid idea and a clear outline, and this is where ChatGPT can be incredibly useful. Suppose you want to write about psychology but are unsure what angle to take. By inputting "general terms related to psychology" into ChatGPT, you can generate a list of potential topics such as 'Cognition,' 'Emotion,' or 'Social Psychology.' Each of these topics can serve as a springboard for more detailed articles. Once a topic is selected, ChatGPT can help you create a structured outline. For instance, if you choose 'Forensic Psychology,' ChatGPT can suggest key sections for the article and prompt Chat GPT to draft an outline for the selected focus area. This structured approach saves time, sparks new ideas, and guides you toward a more thoughtful and comprehensive topic exploration.

Drafting Content

With a robust outline in place, the next step is drafting the content. ChatGPT can serve as a first-pass writer, generating drafts based on the outlines provided. This doesn't mean it will replace your unique voice or style, but it gives a solid base of text that you can refine and edit. For an article on forensic psychology, ChatGPT can elaborate on each section of the outline with relevant information, forming paragraphs that explain the concepts in a straightforward manner. This draft can be enhanced with your insights, additional research, and stylistic adjustments. This process significantly reduces the time you would spend on writing initial drafts and allows you to focus more on adding value through your expertise and unique perspective.

Improving SEO

In the digital age, just writing good content isn't enough; your content must also be optimized for search engines to reach a wider audience. ChatGPT can assist by integrating SEO best practices into your content creation workflow. It can suggest relevant keywords likely to increase your content's visibility. For example, for the forensic psychology article, ChatGPT can identify high-impact keywords such as Criminal Behavior Analysis,' 'Crime Scene Analysis,' or 'Insanity Defense.' Furthermore, ChatGPT can help you naturally incorporate these keywords into the article, enhancing readability and SEO without resorting to keyword stuffing, which can detract from the quality of the writing. Additionally, Chat GPT can suggest meta descriptions and tags optimized for search engines, ensuring that your content is informative and more likely to be discovered by those interested in the topic.

Content Scaling

Scaling content production without compromising quality is a critical challenge for marketers and creators. ChatGPT is particularly beneficial in this regard. By automating the initial stages of content creation - from ideation to drafting - ChatGPT allows you to produce more content in less time. This is especially useful for businesses looking to maintain a robust online presence with a steady stream of fresh content. Moreover, because ChatGPT handles the foundational aspects of writing, you can allocate more resources to enhancing the content through multimedia additions, interactive elements, and detailed research, thereby increasing your articles' overall value and appeal. This ability to scale content efficiently helps keep your blog or website dynamic and engaging and supports your audience growth and engagement goals.

Integrating ChatGPT into your content creation process transforms the way you produce content. From the initial brainstorming to the final touches that prepare a piece for publication, ChatGPT is a versatile tool that saves time, boosts productivity, and enhances the quality of your content. As you continue to leverage this technology, you'll find that you can meet and exceed the demands of your content-creating schedule, allowing you the freedom to focus on creative and strategic endeavors that further your publication's success.

3.3 Leveraging ChatGPT for Customer Service Efficiency

In the fast-paced realm of customer service, responsiveness and efficiency are key. Integrating ChatGPT into your customer service operations can revolutionize how you manage inquiries, ensuring that each customer feels heard and valued from the moment they reach out. While ChatGPT cannot respond to customers automatically, it can assist you by drafting accurate and helpful responses, suggesting solutions based on historical data, and providing multilingual support to help address inquiries in different languages. Additionally, ChatGPT can integrate with some Customer Relationship Management (CRM) systems to analyze past interactions, highlight common issues, and recommend personalized responses, making it an invaluable asset for enhancing customer service efficiency and effectiveness.

Response Drafting and Multilingual Assistance

ChatGPT can play a significant supportive role in customer service by drafting accurate and helpful responses. When customer service representatives receive inquiries, ChatGPT can quickly generate initial response drafts, saving valuable time and ensuring consistency in communication. This allows representatives to focus on fine-tuning responses to meet specific customer needs rather than starting from scratch. Moreover, ChatGPT excels in providing multilingual support, which is crucial in today's globalized business environment. It can assist in crafting responses in various languages, helping your team effectively address a diverse customer base. ChatGPT ensures that customers from different regions feel understood and valued by facilitating communication across language barriers, enhancing their overall experience with your brand. This capability improves response efficiency and broadens customer service reach, providing more inclusive and comprehensive support.

Data Analysis and CRM Integration

ChatGPT enhances customer service efficiency by leveraging data analysis and integrating seamlessly with CRM systems. By analyzing past interactions and customer data stored within your CRM, ChatGPT can identify common issues and recurring patterns, providing valuable insights that inform your customer service strategies. This can help prepare preemptive responses to frequently encountered problems, saving time and improving service quality. To connect ChatGPT with your CRM system, you may need assistance from your technical team to set up the integration, which is typically done through an API. Once connected, ChatGPT can suggest contextually relevant responses based on a customer's history, ensuring timely and highly personalized replies. This integration reduces the time needed to resolve inquiries and enhances the effectiveness of your customer service operations, leading to quicker and more satisfactory resolutions for your customers.

Personalization and Recommendation Capabilities

ChatGPT's ability to personalize interactions and provide tailored recommendations significantly enhances the quality of customer service. By analyzing customer data such as purchase history, preferences, and past interactions, ChatGPT can suggest personalized responses that resonate more deeply with individual customers. This level of personalization ensures that each customer feels valued and understood, as their specific needs and concerns are addressed directly. For example, if a customer has previously inquired about a product, ChatGPT can craft a response that references their previous interaction, providing a sense of continuity and attentiveness. Additionally, ChatGPT can recommend products, services, or solutions that align with the customer's interests and previous behaviors, fostering a more engaging and relevant dialogue. These personalized recommendations enhance customer satisfaction and encourage loyalty and repeat business, as customers are more likely to return when a company consistently meets their needs. This capability to provide bespoke advice and solutions helps differentiate your service from generic customer support, creating a more meaningful and productive customer experience.

Integrating ChatGPT into your customer service operations offers a multifaceted approach to enhancing efficiency, personalization, and overall customer satisfaction. By supporting the drafting of accurate responses and providing multilingual assistance, ChatGPT helps streamline communication and broadens your ability to effectively serve a diverse customer base. Its ability to analyze and integrate data with CRM systems allows for identifying common issues, enabling more proactive and informed customer service strategies. Furthermore, ChatGPT's capability to personalize responses and offer tailored recommendations creates a more engaging and relevant customer experience, fostering greater loyalty and satisfaction. By leveraging these advanced features, ChatGPT reduces your workload and ensures that each interaction has the level of care and attention customers desire. As you refine your use of ChatGPT, you'll find that it becomes an invaluable tool in delivering responsive, efficient, and personalized customer service, setting your business apart in today's competitive market.

3.4 ChatGPT in Education: Aiding Learning and Research

In the realm of education, ChatGPT offers a wealth of opportunities to enhance learning. Rather than serving as a shortcut for completing assignments, ChatGPT is a powerful resource that can help learners explore topics in-depth, develop critical thinking skills, and find additional explanations or perspectives on complex subjects. It is a versatile educational tool that can provide guidance, generate ideas for research projects, assist with language learning, and even help students practice problem-solving. This section shows how ChatGPT can complement and enhance traditional learning techniques, making education more efficient and enriching while firmly upholding academic integrity. By leveraging ChatGPT responsibly, students and educators can foster a more supportive and honest learning environment that promotes genuine understanding and educational growth.

Tutoring and Homework Help

Imagine having a tutor available at any hour of the day, ready to assist with any question from various subjects. ChatGPT can be that tutor. For students, whether grappling with complex algebra problems or needing clarification on historical events, ChatGPT acts like a knowledgeable friend who is always there to help. Its ability to provide detailed, step-by-step explanations can make learning more accessible and less stressful. For example, suppose you're struggling with a math problem. In that case, ChatGPT can break down the solution process into comprehensible steps, ensuring you not only get the correct answer but understand the how and why behind it. This capability is not just about providing answers; it's about enhancing understanding and fostering a deeper interest in learning.

Furthermore, for subjects that require essay writing, ChatGPT can assist in structuring your arguments or providing feedback on drafts. You could input your essay draft and ask ChatGPT to suggest improvements or identify areas where your arguments need strengthening. This interactive form of learning improves academic skills and encourages critical thinking and self-reflection, essential skills in any educational journey.

Research Assistance

The initial stages of gathering information for a project or paper can be daunting for students and researchers. ChatGPT can simplify this process by helping to compile preliminary data and sources. If you're starting a research project, you can ask ChatGPT for the latest studies or articles on your topic. For instance, if your research pertains to environmental science, ChatGPT can summarize recent research papers on climate change, including authors, key findings, and publication dates. This speeds up the research process and ensures you have a solid foundation of up-to-date information before diving deeper into specialized databases or academic journals.

Moreover, ChatGPT's ability to filter and prioritize information based on your specific needs can be incredibly beneficial. It can aggregate this information if you need data from multiple sources, providing a comprehensive overview highlighting major themes and gaps in the existing research. This level of customized assistance is akin to having a research assistant available at any moment to support your academic endeavors, making the research process more efficient and enjoyable.

Interactive Learning

The traditional education model often involves passive learning, where students sometimes listen to lectures and read material without much engagement. ChatGPT can transform this dynamic by creating interactive learning experiences that make education more engaging and effective. Through simulations or role-playing exercises, ChatGPT can bring theoretical concepts to life. For example, in a business class, ChatGPT could simulate a negotiation scenario between two companies, requiring the student to make decisions based on economic principles. This method helps students apply theoretical knowledge in practical situations, enhancing their understanding and retention of complex concepts.

Another powerful application of ChatGPT is in language learning. ChatGPT can engage students in conversations in the language they are learning, offering immediate feedback and ample practice opportunities essential for language acquisition. This interactive approach mimics real-life discussions, allowing students to practice and refine their language skills in a dynamic and engaging way that traditional classroom settings may not fully replicate. For instance, a prompt like "Describe your day in Spanish" encourages students to practice their language skills in a natural context, enhancing their conversational abilities and fostering greater fluency. ChatGPT helps learners build confidence and proficiency in using the language in everyday scenarios by providing a simulated conversational partner.

Assessment Preparation

Preparing for exams can be stressful for students, but ChatGPT can ease this process by generating practice questions and topics for revision. If you're preparing for a biology exam, ChatGPT can create a series of potential exam questions based on the syllabus, ranging from multiple-choice questions to more complex essay questions. This helps you anticipate the types of questions you might encounter and provides a structured way to test your knowledge and identify areas where you might need further study.

Additionally, ChatGPT can help organize revision notes, summarizing key points from your textbooks or lecture notes into concise, easy-to-review documents. This can be particularly helpful for visual learners who benefit from clear, organized materials. By providing a variety of ways to review and test your knowledge, ChatGPT can make exam preparation less daunting, boosting your confidence and readiness to tackle any academic challenge. For other assessments, such as job interviews, Chat GPT can generate questions based on a job description and provide feedback on your responses.

Through these applications, ChatGPT stands out as a versatile tool in the educational landscape, capable of transforming how learning is approached. From personalized tutoring sessions and research assistance to creating engaging interactive learning experiences and aiding in exam preparation, ChatGPT empowers students to take control of their educational journey, making learning more effective and inspiring.

3.5 Personal Assistant Duties Handled by ChatGPT

Managing time efficiently is one of the most universally endorsed pathways to success and personal satisfaction in the bustling business and daily life. Imagine having a virtual assistant that helps keep your calendar in impeccable order, manages your travel itineraries, and prepares you for upcoming meetings—all with a few text prompts. This scenario isn't just a figment of the future; it's a present-day reality with ChatGPT. Let's delve into how this versatile AI can function as your personal assistant, streamlining tasks that traditionally consume a significant chunk of your day.

Scheduling and Calendars

Managing your schedule effectively can significantly enhance your productivity and reduce stress. ChatGPT can help you organize your schedule in several practical ways, making it easier to keep track of your commitments and plan your time efficiently. One of the most useful ways ChatGPT can assist you is by helping you generate a comprehensive schedule for the week or month. You can input your key activities and appointments, and ChatGPT can help you visualize them in an organized format. For example, you might ask, "Help me create a weekly schedule with my work meetings, gym sessions, and family commitments." ChatGPT can provide a structured layout to follow or transfer to your calendar easily.

Prioritizing Your Day

ChatGPT can help you plan your day by helping you prioritize tasks based on importance and urgency. You can list your tasks, and ChatGPT can suggest a sensible sequence. For instance, you might say, "I have five tasks to complete today. Can you help me prioritize them?" ChatGPT can help you decide which tasks to tackle first and how to allocate your time effectively.

Finding Time for New Activities

If you're looking to add new activities to your schedule, ChatGPT can help you find the best times for them. Whether you want to start a new hobby, fit in a workout, or schedule regular study sessions, ChatGPT can suggest optimal time slots based on your existing commitments. You can ask, "Can you suggest a time for me to jog three times a week?" ChatGPT will consider your current schedule and recommend times that fit your routine. ChatGPT can also help you determine the time it takes to tackle new hobbies if you are unsure about the time commitment.

Setting Up Routine Activities

For routine activities such as daily exercises, weekly shopping, or regular meetings, ChatGPT can help you establish a consistent schedule. Setting up these recurring tasks ensures that important activities become a regular part of your routine without remembering to schedule them each time. You can say, "Help me set a schedule for my weekly grocery shopping and daily meditation practice," and ChatGPT will suggest a regular time that fits into your overall schedule.

By leveraging ChatGPT to assist with these scheduling tasks, you can save time and ensure that your daily, weekly, and monthly activities are well-organized. This helps you stay on top of your commitments, avoid conflicts, and maintain a balanced schedule that supports your productivity and personal goals.

Travel Arrangements

Planning travel, whether for business or pleasure, involves many details that can be tedious to manage. ChatGPT can assist in making travel arrangements by researching flights, hotels, and even car rentals based on your preferences and budget. Suppose you need to attend a conference in another city. Simply inform ChatGPT of your travel dates and preferences, and it can handle the rest—from finding the best flights available to suggesting accommodations near the conference venue (The level of data recency will depend on the version of ChatGPT you are using). Additionally, ChatGPT can create detailed itineraries for your trips, including suggested activities and dining options based on online reviews and your past preferences. This level of assistance makes travel planning stress-free and allows you to focus on the purpose of your trip rather than the logistics.

Meeting Preparation

Preparing for meetings is more than just marking a date on your calendar. It often requires research, organization of materials, formulation of talking points, and understanding of possible rebuttals. ChatGPT can streamline these preparatory tasks by summarizing relevant documents and emails, thus ensuring you are well-informed about the discussion topics. If you're due to discuss a project update, ChatGPT can summarize the latest reports and progress and list key points for discussion. Moreover, it can help you draft content for presentations, documents needed for the meeting based on outlines or notes you provide, or simply help brainstorm ideas. This capability enhances your efficiency and boosts your confidence during sessions, as you are better prepared and informed.

Integrating ChatGPT into these aspects of your daily life streamlines your tasks. It frees up your time, allowing you to focus on strategic thinking, creativity, networking, or simply enjoying a less cluttered life. As businesses and lifestyles become increasingly complex, a tool like ChatGPT can significantly affect how efficiently and effectively you manage your responsibilities. Whether you're a busy professional looking to optimize your productivity or reduce your daily hustle, ChatGPT offers a range of functionalities that cater to a wide array of needs and preferences, making it an indispensable tool in the modern digital toolkit.

3.6 Personal Development using ChatGPT

In the ever-evolving landscape of personal development, continuous learning and goal-setting are pivotal elements that drive success and personal fulfillment. ChatGPT, with its advanced capabilities, is an invaluable tool to guide and support you in these endeavors. Whether you're looking to acquire new skills, set and track personal goals, or simply seek daily motivation, ChatGPT can be tailored to meet your specific needs, making the journey toward personal growth more manageable and engaging.

Skill Building

Imagine having access to a personal coach who guides you in learning new skills and recommends the best resources tailored to your learning style and goals. ChatGPT can fulfill this role by identifying and suggesting various resources, from online courses and informative books to interactive tutorials and learning content providers, that are aligned with your specific learning objectives. Suppose you're interested in learning digital marketing; ChatGPT can curate a list of the top-rated online courses, including detailed descriptions and user reviews, to help you make an informed decision. Additionally, it can suggest books that cover essential concepts and provide practical case studies for a deeper understanding of the subject.

Beyond recommending resources, ChatGPT can design personalized learning plans based on your schedule, learning pace, and progress. For instance, it can create a weekly study schedule that allocates time for watching tutorial videos, reading specific chapters from books, and completing online quizzes. This structured approach keeps your learning on track and makes the process less overwhelming, especially if you balance learning with other responsibilities. Furthermore, ChatGPT can track your progress by conducting quick recaps or quizzes at the end of each learning session, providing feedback on areas where you might need further review or practice. This ongoing assessment ensures that you are not just consuming information but are actively engaging and retaining knowledge.

Goal Setting and Tracking

Setting goals is a powerful practice to drive personal and professional growth, but the real challenge lies in consistently tracking and pursuing these goals. ChatGPT can assist you in setting realistic and achievable goals and breaking them down into manageable steps. For example, if your goal is to write a book, ChatGPT can help you outline the key milestones for the project, such as completing the outline, writing the first draft, and revising chapters. Each milestone can be assigned a timeline, making the goal less daunting and more structured.

You can also use ChatGPT to analyze your daily habits and routines, helping you identify the best practices to reach your goals. By inputting details about your daily activities, ChatGPT can help you evaluate which habits are most effective and which may need adjustment. For instance, you can describe your current routine, and ChatGPT can provide insights into how you might optimize your time, such as suggesting specific periods for focused work, exercise, or relaxation. This analysis can help you create a structured plan that aligns your daily actions with your long-term objectives. By focusing on positive habits and routines, ChatGPT can guide you towards consistent behaviors that lead to successful outcomes, ultimately enhancing your productivity and well-being.

Daily Motivation and Encouragement

Maintaining a positive mindset is crucial for personal growth and overall well-being. ChatGPT can contribute significantly by providing daily motivational quotes, affirmations, and encouraging words. Imagine starting your day by reading an inspiring quote or a positive affirmation from ChatGPT, setting a tone of optimism and motivation right from the morning. This can be particularly helpful during challenging times when your spirits are low, and you need a boost to keep going.

In addition to motivational messages, ChatGPT can provide personalized encouragement based on your recent activities or progress in your goals. If you've had a productive week, ChatGPT can acknowledge your efforts and encourage you to keep up the good work. Conversely, if you're facing setbacks, it can offer encouragement and remind you of your strengths and past accomplishments, helping you regain confidence and perspective. This tailored support not only enhances your emotional resilience but also fosters a mindset that is primed for growth and success.

Personal Journaling

Journaling is a powerful tool for self-reflection, allowing you to explore your thoughts, feelings, and experiences in a structured way. ChatGPT can enhance this practice by guiding journaling sessions with thought-provoking prompts and questions. Whether reflecting on a recent event, grappling with a decision, or simply documenting your day, ChatGPT can suggest prompts encouraging deep reflection and introspection. For example, ChatGPT might ask, "What were the key takeaways from your experience today?" or "How do you feel about the progress you've made on your goals this week?"

Additionally, ChatGPT can help organize your journal entries by categorizing them by themes or emotions, making it easier to track your personal growth over time. It can also analyze your entries to identify recurring patterns or themes, providing insights that might not be immediately obvious. For instance, if you frequently write about feeling stressed at work, ChatGPT can highlight this pattern, prompting you to explore coping strategies or consider changes to your work environment. This analytical aspect of journaling can be incredibly beneficial, as it helps you understand yourself better and make informed decisions that enhance your quality of life and personal satisfaction.

Leveraging ChatGPT for personal development gives you a versatile tool that supports your learning and goal-setting efforts, boosts your motivation, and aids in self-reflection. This multifaceted support makes the process of personal growth more manageable, enjoyable, and fulfilling. As you continue to explore and utilize these features, you'll likely discover even more ways ChatGPT can be customized to meet your unique needs and preferences, further enhancing your journey toward personal and professional fulfillment.

3.7 Interactive Task: Enhancing Business Productivity

Congratulations on completing Chapter Three! You've learned how ChatGPT can improve your business productivity, from enhancing email communications to streamlining content creation and customer service operations. Now, it's time to put these skills into practice with a hands-on task that will help reinforce what you've learned.

Instructions:

1. Identify Your Needs:

- Reflect on your current business operations or daily tasks and identify areas where ChatGPT could improve efficiency. These could be routine email responses, generating content ideas, drafting customer service replies, or managing your schedule.

2. Draft Prompts for Each Area

- Write specific prompts using the perfect prompt formula to address each identified need.

3. Test and Refine:

- Respond to each prompt and evaluate the output for accuracy, professionalism, and relevance.

- Iterate over the output to get more accurate or helpful responses. This step is crucial for optimizing ChatGPT's efficiency in your workflow.

4. Reflect and Share:

- Reflect on your experience and consider how ChatGPT has changed your approach to business tasks.

- Share your insights and any tips you've discovered with colleagues, friends, or the AI community to help others enhance their productivity with ChatGPT.

As we conclude this chapter on enhancing business productivity, it's evident that ChatGPT is more than just a tool; it's a transformative addition to your daily workflow. The practical applications and benefits it offers demonstrate its versatility and impact. This hands-on task has equipped you with the knowledge to integrate ChatGPT into your work, helping you save time and improve efficiency. In the next chapter, we will explore how ChatGPT can enhance your life outside your workday and look at various ways this technology can assist you around the home in your leisure time.

ChatGPT for Your Personal Life

Welcome to Chapter Four, where we shift gears from professional productivity to the more personal and entertaining ways ChatGPT can enhance your daily life, smoothing your routines and making your leisure time more enjoyable. Think of transforming your mornings from chaotic or mundane into a series of uplifting and productive moments—this is not just wishful thinking but a tangible reality you can achieve with ChatGPT. Integrating this versatile AI into your morning routine can streamline how you start your day, ensuring you are well-informed, deeply motivated, and nutritionally satisfied before stepping out the door. Let's dive into how ChatGPT can become an integral part of your mornings, enhancing each start of your day with efficiency and positivity.

4.1 Morning Routines: Starting Your Day with ChatGPT

Motivational Quotes and Goals Review

Imagine starting your day not just with information but with inspiration. ChatGPT can be prompted to deliver daily motivational quotes that set a positive tone for your day. Additionally, it can remind you of your personal or professional goals to keep them in focus. You might ask ChatGPT, "Can you give me a motivational quote and remind me of my goals for today?" In response, ChatGPT could provide a quote such as, "Success is not final, failure is not fatal: It is the courage to continue that count." — Winston Churchill, followed by a reminder of your goals like, "Today, focus on completing the project proposal and remember to call your mentor for advice." This practice uplifts your spirits and aligns your daily activities with your long-term objectives, enhancing your immediate and ongoing motivation.

Breakfast Ideas and Recipes

Deciding what to eat for breakfast can sometimes be a hassle, especially when balancing nutrition with your busy schedule. ChatGPT can simplify this decision-making process by suggesting breakfast ideas and quick recipes based on your dietary preferences and what's available in your kitchen. You could say, "ChatGPT, I have eggs, spinach, and cheese. What can I make for breakfast quickly?" ChatGPT might suggest, "How about a spinach and cheese omelet? Here's a quick recipe: Beat 2 eggs, stir in chopped spinach and shredded cheese. Cook on a nonstick skillet over medium heat until the eggs are set and the cheese is melted. Serve hot." This personalized culinary assistance helps you prepare nutritious and enjoyable meals, ensuring you start your day with a satisfying and healthy breakfast.

Morning Meditation and Positive Affirmations

Embedding a mindfulness practice into your morning can profoundly impact your day's outlook and effectiveness. ChatGPT can guide you through short meditation sessions or generate positive affirmations to help center your thoughts and intentions for the day. You might ask, "ChatGPT, can you guide me through a five-minute meditation?" ChatGPT would then lead you through a calming sequence, perhaps instructing you to focus on breathing, recognize your body's presence, and release any tension. Following meditation, you could request, "Can you give me some positive affirmations for today?" ChatGPT could offer affirmations like, "I am confident in my ability to solve problems" or "I choose to focus on what I can control." Starting your day with meditation and affirmations can enhance your mental clarity and emotional resilience, setting a productive and positive tone for whatever lies ahead.

By integrating ChatGPT into your morning routine, you not only streamline how you start your day but also enhance the quality of your mornings, setting a precedent for productivity and positivity throughout the day. Whether through a tailored briefing, inspirational quotes, nutritious breakfast suggestions, or a centering meditation session, ChatGPT provides the tools and support necessary to transform your morning routine into a foundation for daily success and satisfaction. As you continue to explore and customize these interactions, you'll find that ChatGPT not only adapts to your lifestyle but also enriches it, making every morning a stepping stone to a fulfilled and accomplished day.

4.2 ChatGPT for Managing Personal Schedules

Managing your personal schedules effectively can be challenging in today's fast-paced world. However, integrating ChatGPT with your calendar apps can transform how you handle appointments and reminders, bringing efficiency and ease to your daily planning. Let's explore how this powerful tool can help you streamline your schedule and optimize your time management.

Calendar Integration
Integrating ChatGPT with your calendar applications, such as Google Calendar or Microsoft Outlook, allows you to manage your appointments and reminders effortlessly. To set this up, you would start by linking ChatGPT to your calendar app through API connections, often provided within the app's settings under 'Integrations.' Once connected, you can directly communicate with ChatGPT to add, remove, or update events. For instance, you might say, "Add a team meeting for next Thursday at 3 PM to my calendar," ChatGPT will handle the rest, creating the event and even sending invites to participants if required. This integration saves you the hassle of manually entering each appointment and ensures that your calendar is always up-to-date with real-time adjustments.

Furthermore, you can set up ChatGPT to send you daily schedule briefings. Each morning, you could receive a concise overview of your appointments and important daily reminders directly from ChatGPT. This proactive approach means you never miss an important meeting or deadline, as ChatGPT keeps you informed and prepared for the day's commitments.

Scheduling Meetings
Coordinating meetings, especially with multiple participants, can often be tedious, involving back-and-forth communication to finalize timings. ChatGPT simplifies this process by interacting with the calendars of all involved parties. If you need to schedule a meeting, simply instruct ChatGPT with your availability and the email addresses of the participants, such as, "Schedule a 30-minute marketing discussion sometime next Wednesday afternoon with [email address] and [email address]" ChatGPT will analyze the calendars, find a slot that works for everyone, and set the meeting, all while keeping you updated. It can also handle rescheduling requests, ensuring that changes are communicated effectively to all participants.

Moreover, ChatGPT can automatically set reminders for these meetings. You can specify if you want a reminder a day before or just a few hours prior, and ChatGPT will ensure you're notified in advance, helping you manage your time efficiently.

Task Prioritization

Prioritizing tasks effectively is key to productive time management. ChatGPT can assist you by classifying tasks based on urgency and importance. You can list your tasks and ask ChatGPT to organize them into categories such as 'Urgent,' 'High Priority,' 'Medium Priority,' and 'Low Priority.' For example, after providing ChatGPT with a list of tasks such as emails to respond to, reports to complete, and meetings to prepare for, you might ask, "Which of these tasks should I prioritize for today?" ChatGPT will analyze the list and your upcoming deadlines to suggest a prioritized task list.

This prioritization helps you focus your efforts on what truly matters each day. It reduces the stress of handling too many things at once and increases your productivity by ensuring that critical tasks are completed on time.

Time Management Tips

Finally, ChatGPT can offer personalized time management advice to help you make the most of your day. Based on your typical schedule and workload, ChatGPT can suggest strategies such as time blocking, allocating specific blocks of time for different tasks, or the Pomodoro Technique, which involves working in short sprints with breaks in between to boost focus and stamina. Simply ask, "How can I manage my time better?" ChatGPT will provide tips tailored to your activities and preferences.

For instance, if you find your afternoons less productive, ChatGPT might suggest scheduling more demanding tasks in the morning when your energy levels are higher, reserving lighter tasks for later in the day. It can also remind you to take regular breaks to prevent burnout, ensuring you maintain a steady pace throughout the day without compromising your well-being.

By leveraging ChatGPT in these ways, you transform managing your personal schedules from a daunting task to a more controlled and enjoyable part of your daily routine. Whether through seamless calendar integration, efficient meeting coordination, strategic task prioritization, or personalized time management tips, ChatGPT provides the tools to enhance how you plan and execute your day, leaving you more time and energy to focus on achieving your goals and enjoying your life.

4.3 ChatGPT for Health and Wellness

In today's fast-paced world, maintaining an optimal level of health and wellness can sometimes feel like a juggling act. Fortunately, ChatGPT can serve as a dependable resource, guiding you through various aspects of health management, from fitness routines to mental well-being. Integrating AI into your health regimen ensures you receive personalized advice and support tailored to your lifestyle and needs.

Fitness Routine Suggestions

Creating a fitness routine that aligns with your goals, current fitness level, and available resources is essential for effective workouts. ChatGPT can help craft a customized workout plan if you're unsure where to start. Begin by sharing your fitness objectives, whether it's weight loss, muscle building, or enhancing cardiovascular health. Additionally, provide details about your current fitness level and any equipment you can access; this could range from a fully-equipped gym to a yoga mat and resistance bands at home or without equipment.

For example, if your goal is to improve general fitness and you have minimal equipment, you might ask ChatGPT, "Can you create a 30-minute home workout plan for beginners with no equipment?" Based on your inputs, ChatGPT could suggest a routine including bodyweight exercises such as push-ups, sit-ups, and air squats, combined with intervals of jumping jacks or running in place to raise your heart rate. Each exercise would come with suggested repetitions and sets, adjusted to ensure they provide a challenge without being overwhelming. This approach helps establish a feasible and effective fitness routine. It adapts as your fitness level progresses, offering more complex combinations or incorporating new exercises to keep the routine engaging and challenging.

Dietary Recommendations

Nutrition plays a critical role in achieving health and wellness goals. ChatGPT can provide dietary recommendations that consider your specific nutritional needs, food preferences, and any dietary restrictions you might have. Start by discussing your health objectives with ChatGPT, such as losing weight, gaining muscle, or managing a health condition like diabetes. Also, mention any dietary preferences or restrictions, such as veganism or gluten intolerance.

For instance, if you're aiming to increase protein intake as part of a muscle-building regimen and you follow a plant-based diet, you might ask, "What are high-protein vegetarian meals that are easy to prepare?" ChatGPT can then offer a variety of recipes and meal ideas, such as lentil soup, quinoa salads, or tofu stir-fries, each detailed with ingredient lists and simple preparation steps. This personalized guidance helps you make informed dietary choices that contribute to reaching your physical health goals and fit seamlessly into your dietary preferences, ensuring sustainability and enjoyment in your eating habits without wasting time filtering through search results on the internet.

Mental Health Check-ins

Taking care of your mental health is as important as maintaining physical health. ChatGPT can assist in daily mental health check-ins, providing a safe space to express feelings, reflect on stressors, or simply unload thoughts. These check-ins can be as simple as prompting ChatGPT with, "I'm feeling stressed about work today. What can I do?" ChatGPT might suggest several stress management techniques, such as deep breathing exercises, short meditative practices, or even engaging in a hobby to divert your mind and ease stress.

Moreover, ChatGPT can encourage mindfulness and help you cultivate a habit of reflecting on your day-to-day experiences. This regular practice of self-reflection aids in recognizing patterns in thoughts and emotions, potentially uncovering triggers for anxiety or stress and empowering you to manage them more effectively. Over time, these check-ins can improve emotional resilience and help you better understand your mental health needs.

Sleep Hygiene Advice

Good sleep hygiene is fundamental to overall health, impacting everything from physical recovery to mental clarity. If you struggle with sleep, ChatGPT can offer advice on establishing routines that promote restful sleep. You might ask, "How can I improve my bedtime routine to get better sleep?" ChatGPT could then suggest various techniques, such as establishing a consistent bedtime, creating a pre-sleep ritual involving activities like reading or taking a warm bath, and avoiding stimulants such as caffeine and electronic devices close to bedtime.

Additionally, ChatGPT can provide guidance on the ideal sleep environment, recommending conditions that enhance sleep quality, such as the optimal room temperature, the use of blackout curtains to minimize light, or the benefits of white noise machines. By implementing these suggestions, you can create a conducive sleep environment that not only helps you fall asleep more quickly but also achieve deep, uninterrupted sleep, ultimately enhancing your daily energy levels and overall health.

Through these personalized interactions, ChatGPT acts as a comprehensive health and wellness advisor, addressing various aspects of your well-being. Whether it's crafting tailored fitness routines, providing dietary guidance, supporting mental health, or fostering better sleep habits, ChatGPT ensures that you have the tools and knowledge to lead a healthier, more balanced life. As you continue to utilize these features, you'll find that maintaining health and wellness becomes more integrated and manageable, allowing you to enjoy the benefits of a well-rounded and healthy lifestyle.

4.4 Financial Planning and Budgeting with ChatGPT

Navigating the often complex world of personal finance can sometimes feel overwhelming, but with tools like ChatGPT, you can simplify and take control of your financial future. Whether creating a realistic budget, conducting regular financial health assessments, exploring investment strategies, or managing debt, ChatGPT can be invaluable in your journey to financial stability and growth.

Budget Creation and Management

Creating and managing a personal budget is crucial for financial well-being, but many find the process tedious or complicated. ChatGPT simplifies this by helping you construct a budget that aligns with your income, expenses, and financial goals. First, you would provide ChatGPT with details about your regular income sources and recurring expenses such as rent, utilities, groceries, and transportation. For example, you might say, "My monthly income is $3,000, and my fixed expenses total $1,500." With this information, ChatGPT can help categorize your spending into 'needs,' 'wants,' and 'savings,' suggesting allocations based on standard budgeting principles like the 50/30/20 rule—which allocates 50% of income to needs, 30% to wants, and 20% to savings. Additionally, ChatGPT can offer general financial rules of thumb, such as the 75/15/10 saving and investing guideline, to help you manage your finances more effectively.

Furthermore, ChatGPT can assist in setting up a system to track your expenses and monitor your budget adherence. This might involve linking ChatGPT to your financial accounts or setting up notifications for when you approach spending limits in certain categories. This proactive management ensures that you stay on track with your budget, making adjustments as needed to avoid overspending and meet your financial goals. For instance, if you consistently overspend on dining out, ChatGPT can alert you when you are near your monthly limit or suggest cheaper dining alternatives to help you stay within budget.

Financial Health Check-ups

Regular check-ups are as vital for your financial health as they are for your physical health. ChatGPT can conduct these assessments by reviewing your financial data and evaluating your spending habits, savings, debt levels, and overall financial progress. You might ask, "How am I doing financially this quarter?" ChatGPT would analyze the data, compare your current spending against your budget, check how much you've saved versus your goals, and review debt reductions.

This review helps you understand where you stand financially, highlighting successes and identifying improvement areas. For instance, if your savings are on track but debt reduction is lagging, ChatGPT might suggest revising your budget to allocate more towards debt repayment. This regular appraisal keeps you informed and proactive about managing your finances, ensuring you always work towards greater financial health and stability.

Investment Ideas and Tips

Investing can be an effective way to grow your wealth, but understanding where and how to invest can be daunting. ChatGPT simplifies this process by providing general investment recommendations based on your financial situation and risk tolerance. After discussing your investment goals and how much risk you are comfortable taking, ChatGPT can suggest a range of investment options. Whether you are interested in stocks, bonds, mutual funds, or real estate, ChatGPT can outline the potential benefits and risks associated with each option. ChatGPT can also provide basic asset allocations based on your financial circumstances and risk tolerance.

For example, ChatGPT might recommend looking into high-quality bonds or dividend-paying stocks if you are a conservative investor interested in steady returns. It can also guide you in diversifying your investments by allocating assets across asset classes specific to your goals, potentially mitigating risk and enhancing returns. Additionally, ChatGPT can provide information regarding market trends, historical data, and economic factors that might affect your investments, helping you make informed decisions on when to buy, hold, or sell your assets.

Debt Management Advice

Effective debt management is key to financial freedom, and ChatGPT can offer guidance on approaching and reducing your liabilities. By analyzing your debt levels, interest rates, and financial capacity, ChatGPT can develop a debt repayment plan tailored to your circumstances. This might include strategies like the debt snowball method, where you focus on paying off smaller debts first to build momentum, or the debt avalanche method, where you pay down debts with the highest interest rates first to minimize overall interest payments.

ChatGPT can also advise on negotiating with creditors for better repayment terms or consolidating multiple debts into a single loan with a lower interest rate. This personalized advice helps you tackle your debt effectively, reducing financial stress and paving the way for a debt-free future. Moreover, by regularly consulting ChatGPT, you can keep track of your progress and adjust your repayment strategies as needed, ensuring that you remain on the fastest and most efficient path to eliminating your debt.

4.5 ChatGPT as a Study Buddy

In Chapter Three, we explored how ChatGPT can enhance business productivity by aiding learning and research, particularly in a professional or academic context. While the previous section focused on learning within a business framework, this chapter highlights how ChatGPT can support personal educational goals. Here, we will discuss how ChatGPT can serve as a study buddy in your personal life, helping you with language practice, homework assistance, creating study plans and schedules, and suggesting educational resources. This personalized approach ensures that ChatGPT can assist you in a more relaxed and individualized setting, making your learning journey enjoyable and efficient.

Language Practice

Embracing a new language opens doors to a richer understanding of different cultures and enhances cognitive abilities. ChatGPT is an invaluable companion in this linguistic journey, offering a range of interactive practices catering to various learning stages, from beginners grappling with basics to advanced learners refining their fluency. To begin with, you might want to establish a foundation in vocabulary and basic sentence structures. Here, ChatGPT can act as an interactive flashcard system. You could input a list of words or phrases. ChatGPT could quiz you, provide definitions, or ask you to construct sentences using new words, reinforcing your memory and recall.

Transitioning from static vocabulary exercises to dynamic conversational practice, ChatGPT can simulate real-life interactions, allowing you to apply what you've learned in practical scenarios. For instance, if you're learning Spanish and planning a trip to Spain, you might practice ordering food or asking for directions. Phrases like, "How do I say, 'A table for two, please' in Spanish?" or "What's the Spanish word for 'train station'?" can be posed to ChatGPT. It responds with translation corrections and suggestions on pronunciation, usage, and cultural nuances that textbooks often miss. This learning method is more engaging and builds confidence in using the language in everyday situations, making the learning process both effective and enjoyable.

Homework Help

Tackling homework across various subjects can sometimes be daunting, especially when complex concepts and tough assignments pile up. ChatGPT is a resourceful tool for breaking these complex ideas into understandable segments. Suppose you're struggling with a physics problem about Newton's laws or need clarification on a historical event like the French Revolution. By inputting the specific question or topic into ChatGPT, you can receive detailed explanations, step-by-step problem-solving guidance, or historical summaries. For example, asking, "Can you explain Newton's third law with examples?" would prompt ChatGPT to provide the textbook definition and real-world applications, such as how rocket propulsion illustrates this law.

Furthermore, ChatGPT can assist in structuring essays or reports. Suppose you're assigned to write about climate change's impacts. In that case, ChatGPT can help outline key points, such as global warming, effects on ecosystems, and socio-economic implications, organizing your research into a coherent structure. This helps craft a well-rounded essay with a clear argument, ensuring your homework meets the academic criteria and engages the reader with well-presented information and insights.

Study Plans and Schedules

As exams approach, effective study planning becomes crucial. ChatGPT can aid in creating personalized study schedules that optimize your revision and prepare you thoroughly for exam day. You would start by telling ChatGPT the number of subjects, the days available for study, and any particular priorities or challenging areas. ChatGPT could then generate a study timetable that allocates time blocks for each subject, ensuring you cover all necessary material without cramming. It might suggest alternating between subjects or topics to keep your study sessions dynamic and mentally stimulating.

Additionally, ChatGPT can incorporate effective study techniques into your schedule. Techniques like spaced repetition for memorization or active recall sessions can be interspersed throughout your plan. This way, you follow a time structure and employ strategies that enhance learning retention, making your preparation more productive and less stressful.

Educational Resource Suggestions

While textbooks and classroom notes are invaluable, supplementing them with diverse educational resources can enhance your understanding and interest in a subject. ChatGPT can recommend a variety of resources tailored to your specific learning needs and interests. ChatGPT might suggest animated videos that visually explain complex reactions if you're a visual learner struggling with organic chemistry. Alternatively, if you prefer interactive learning, it could direct you to simulations or online quizzes that provide immediate feedback and explanations, helping you grasp difficult concepts through practice.

Moreover, ChatGPT can point you to academic journals, expert blogs, or educational podcasts for those seeking deeper insights or alternative explanations. For instance, if you're researching modernist literature, ChatGPT could recommend scholarly articles discussing the cultural contexts of works by T.S. Eliot and Virginia Woolf or podcasts where experts debate their narrative styles and themes. These resources broaden your perspective and enrich your academic experience, making learning a more engaging and comprehensive process. Through ChatGPT's guidance, you can access knowledge that complements traditional learning methods, fostering a more rounded and informed approach to your studies.

4.6 Entertainment and Leisure: ChatGPT as Your Guide

In entertainment and leisure, a versatile tool like ChatGPT can enrich your experiences by offering personalized suggestions and creative ideas that align with your interests and preferences. Whether you're a cinephile looking for your next favorite movie, an avid reader in search of a captivating book, an adventurer planning your next excursion, or a hobbyist seeking to expand your creative pursuits, ChatGPT is equipped to guide you through each of these aspects, enhancing the joy and fulfillment derived from your leisure activities.

Movie and Book Recommendations
Diving into a good book or movie offers relaxation and opens worlds of imagination and insight. ChatGPT can personalize recommendations based on your past likes and interests, ensuring that every suggestion resonates with your tastes. Suppose you enjoyed a movie like "Inception" and are looking for something similar, or you loved a book such as "1984" by George Orwell and want to explore similar genres. You could ask ChatGPT, "Can you recommend movies similar to 'Inception' or books like '1984'?" Using its extensive database and understanding of your preferences, ChatGPT would analyze elements common to your favorites—thematic depth, narrative style, or genre—and suggest a list of movies or books you will likely enjoy. This tailored approach saves you time searching and enhances your entertainment experience by consistently aligning with your unique preferences.

Travel Planning and Local Exploration
Planning travel to distant lands or local attractions can be an exciting yet daunting task. ChatGPT simplifies this process by helping you craft detailed itineraries based on your interests, the duration of your trip, and attendees. If you're planning a weekend getaway to a city like San Francisco, you might ask, "What are the must-visit places in San Francisco over a weekend?" ChatGPT could then outline a comprehensive itinerary that includes visiting the Golden Gate Bridge, exploring Fisherman's Wharf, and dining at renowned local eateries. Additionally, it can provide insights into local attractions that are less touristy but equally enriching, offering you a blend of popular and unique experiences.

Moreover, ChatGPT can assist in logistical planning by suggesting the best times to visit attractions, making reservations, or providing tips on local transportation. This thorough planning tool ensures your travels are enjoyable and maximally efficient, allowing you to explore and experience more within your available time.

Creative Hobbies

Fostering creative hobbies enriches your free time and promotes mental well-being and personal satisfaction. Whether you're interested in starting a new hobby like painting or enhancing an existing one like DIY home projects, ChatGPT can provide step-by-step guides, creative ideas, and practical tips. For instance, if you're new to watercolor painting, you might ask, "How do I start with watercolor painting, and what are some easy projects?" ChatGPT could offer basic techniques, suggest starter kits, and provide simple project ideas like painting a sunset or a floral composition. ChatGPT can suggest advanced projects or techniques for more seasoned hobbyists, such as creating a DIY home decor piece from recycled materials. This guidance helps you start and sustain hobbies and encourages continuous learning and creativity, making your leisure time more productive and enjoyable.

Game and Puzzle Creation

Playing games and puzzles can be a delightful way to challenge your mind and share fun moments with friends and family. ChatGPT can assist you in creating custom games and puzzles tailored to your group's interests and complexity preferences. Whether you want to design a trivia quiz about classic films, a crossword puzzle based on your favorite books, or a scavenger hunt for a family gathering, ChatGPT can provide the framework, rules, and content for these games. You might say, "I need a trivia game for a movie night with friends." ChatGPT would then generate questions, multiple-choice answers, and even scoring guidelines based on popular movies or specific genres you enjoy. This personalized approach makes game nights more engaging and ensures they are inclusive and enjoyable for all participants, fostering a spirit of community and shared joy.

In integrating ChatGPT into your entertainment and leisure activities, you gain a personalized guide that enhances your experiences, whether by recommending media that matches your tastes, simplifying travel planning, inspiring creative pursuits, or enriching your social gatherings with custom games. This chapter illustrates the practical applications of ChatGPT in enhancing leisure activities and encourages you to explore and embrace new experiences, enriching your life with enjoyment and creativity. As we conclude this exploration of ChatGPT's role in entertainment and leisure, we see how this AI tool serves practical needs and enhances life's joyful moments, making every leisure activity more engaging and personalized.

4.7 Interactive Task: Create a Meal Plan

Healthy meal planning is essential for maintaining a balanced diet and overall wellness. With ChatGPT's assistance, you can create personalized meal plans that cater to your specific dietary needs and preferences. This interactive task is designed to help beginners leverage ChatGPT to plan, review, and refine their meals, making healthy eating manageable and enjoyable. Following the steps outlined below, you'll learn how to use ChatGPT to develop a sustainable and nutritious meal routine.

First, ask ChatGPT to create a healthy meal plan for the week, remembering to use the perfect prompt formula where necessary. Once you receive the meal plan, review it to ensure it meets your dietary needs and preferences. If you have any dietary restrictions, such as lactose intolerance or gluten sensitivity, ask ChatGPT to adjust the meal plan accordingly. Next, based on the meal plan, use a prompt to compile a shopping list of the ingredients you'll need for the week. This will help streamline your grocery shopping and ensure you have all the necessary items. Finally, ask ChatGPT for recipes based on the meals provided and prepare for the upcoming week. You can use this as merely an exercise or follow the weekly meal plan.

At the end of the week, reflect on your experience. Note any feedback or adjustments you might need for the meal plan. Use ChatGPT to refine the plan further based on your feedback. Following these steps will give you a personalized and healthy meal plan that suits your dietary needs and preferences. This interactive task will help you develop a sustainable, healthy eating habit with the assistance of ChatGPT.

Conclusion

Congratulations on completing Chapter Four! You've explored how ChatGPT can enhance various aspects of your life, from managing daily routines and finances to supporting your educational goals and planning travel itineraries. By leveraging ChatGPT's capabilities, you've taken significant steps toward improving your well-being and productivity.

As we progress, we must consider the broader context of using AI daily. In the next chapter, we will move into a deeper analysis of the ethical use and social implications of ChatGPT. This section will guide you through the responsible and mindful use of AI technology, ensuring that your interactions with ChatGPT and similar tools are beneficial and aligned with ethical standards. Get ready to explore the critical considerations of integrating AI into our personal and professional lives, fostering a future where technology enhances our experiences while respecting societal values.

Ethical Use and Social Implications

Now that we have explored the foundations of AI and ChatGPT let's examine the ethical issues surrounding this technology. In a world increasingly driven by data, understanding the ethical implications of using powerful AI tools like ChatGPT is not just prudent—it's imperative. As you begin to integrate AI into your daily interactions, whether for work, learning, or personal growth, it becomes crucial to consider what AI can do and how it does it. The ethical use of AI, particularly regarding data privacy, is a cornerstone in fostering trust and safety in technology. This chapter will explore the nature of data exchange in AI systems, how this data is handled, and provide best practices to safeguard your information. By understanding these aspects, you can ensure your journey with AI remains secure and aligned with your values.

5.1 Understanding Data Privacy in ChatGPT Interactions

Data privacy concerns often arise when interacting with an AI like ChatGPT. Every query you input and every response you receive involves exchanging information that could be personal or sensitive. Understanding the nature of this data exchange is the first step towards using AI responsibly. When you ask ChatGPT for travel advice, for example, you might share details about your location, preferences, and timing—information that could potentially be misused if not appropriately handled.

AI systems like ChatGPT process and store vast amounts of data to learn and make informed responses. This data can include directly entered information as well as derived data generated from your interactions and choices. For instance, if you frequently ask about vegan recipes, the system might infer a dietary preference. AI's ability to aggregate and analyze data raises significant privacy concerns. The potential for data breaches or misuse is not just a theoretical risk; it impacts people's lives and choices.

Adopting best practices for data privacy is crucial to navigating these waters safely. One effective strategy is anonymizing your data. When interacting with ChatGPT, do not provide personally identifiable information unless absolutely necessary. For instance, you can ask for restaurant recommendations without disclosing your exact location—perhaps specify the city or town instead of your address. Additionally, familiarizing yourself with the privacy settings of the platform hosting the AI, such as OpenAI's ChatGPT, is essential. These settings often allow you to control what data is stored and how it's used.

Moreover, compliance with data protection regulations like the EU's General Data Protection Regulation (GDPR) is crucial for any platform handling personal data. GDPR and similar regulations in other jurisdictions aim to protect personal data and ensure users' privacy. They require that data be collected legally and under strict conditions and that those who collect and manage it are obliged to protect it from misuse and exploitation. As a user, understanding these protections helps you know your rights and the obligations of AI providers, making you a more informed and empowered technology user.

Navigating the ethical landscape of AI interactions necessitates a balanced approach that respects user privacy while leveraging the benefits of AI. By understanding the nature of data exchange, how AI systems handle this data, and the best practices for protecting your personal information, you can confidently engage with AI like ChatGPT, knowing you are taking the necessary steps to safeguard your privacy. As we continue to explore the ethical use of AI, remember that each interaction is an opportunity to ensure that technology works for us, enhancing our lives while upholding our values and rights.

5.2 Misinformation Risks and How to Mitigate Them

In the realm of AI-driven technologies like ChatGPT, misinformation can subtly seep into interactions, often due to the biases inherent in the training data or the limitations of the algorithms themselves. When AI systems are trained on skewed or incomplete data, they can inadvertently generate misleading or factually incorrect responses. This is particularly concerning in scenarios where decisions are made based on the information provided by AI, such as in financial advising, healthcare, or legal advice. Misinformation can arise not only from biased data but also from the way data is interpreted by the AI model. For instance, if an AI is trained predominantly on historical data that does not adequately represent current trends or minority reports, its outputs might not accurately reflect present realities.

Detecting misinformation in AI outputs is crucial and starts with developing a keen sense of critical evaluation. As a user, you should approach AI-generated content with a healthy skepticism, especially in subjects that are complex or have significant implications based on the accuracy of the information. Techniques to detect misinformation include cross-referencing AI responses with up-to-date and reliable sources and considering the consensus among experts in the subject matter. Additionally, paying attention to the language used by AI can also provide clues; overly simplistic explanations or responses that lack depth in technical discussions might indicate that the AI does not fully understand the topic, increasing the risk of inaccuracies.

Correcting misinformation is a multifaceted approach that involves both immediate and long-term strategies. In the short term, providing feedback to the AI system when inaccuracies are detected helps refine its responses. Most AI platforms, including those powering ChatGPT, allow users to flag incorrect or misleading information, which can then be used to adjust the model's learning process. For a more long-term solution, retraining the AI model on a broader, more balanced, and continually updated dataset ensures that the information it generates is accurate and reflects the latest knowledge. This retraining process must be ongoing, as the accumulation of new data and the evolution of facts and societal norms never cease.

Promoting information literacy is fundamentally about empowering you and others to discern the quality and reliability of information better, whether it comes from AI or human sources. Understanding how to assess the credibility of sources, the importance of context when interpreting facts, and the common pitfalls in logical reasoning are all skills that enhance your ability to use AI like ChatGPT effectively and safely. Educational initiatives focusing on these skills are vital, particularly in schools, universities, and professional training. They ensure that as AI becomes more integrated into everyday life, users are equipped to use these tools and challenge and critique them constructively. By fostering a culture that values and understands the principles of information literacy, we ensure that society can enjoy the benefits of AI without falling prey to its potential pitfalls.

5.3 Human-in-the-Loop: Balancing AI and Human Oversight

The 'Human-in-the-Loop' (HITL) concept is pivotal in integrating AI systems like ChatGPT into sectors where decisions significantly impact human lives. Essentially, HITL refers to the active involvement of human operators in the functioning and decision-making processes of AI systems, ensuring that despite the autonomy of the technology, human judgment and oversight remain central. This approach is crucial for maintaining ethical standards and accountability and leveraging human expertise to guide and improve AI decision-making. The importance of HITL cannot be overstated, particularly in scenarios where AI's autonomous operations could lead to significant consequences without human mediation.

Implementing human oversight in AI systems is observable in various industries and contexts. For example, in content moderation on social media platforms, AI algorithms are employed to filter and flag inappropriate content. However, human moderators play a critical role in reviewing these flags to make nuanced decisions that the AI might not be capable of due to limitations in understanding context and cultural nuances. Similarly, in healthcare, AI systems can analyze patient data and suggest diagnoses and treatments. Still, healthcare professionals must review these suggestions and make the final decisions, considering the AI's input as one of several critical resources. These examples highlight how human expertise and ethical reasoning are irreplaceable, ensuring that AI is a support tool rather than a replacement for human judgment.

The benefits of integrating human intuition with AI's capabilities are manifold. Firstly, it enhances the reliability of AI systems by incorporating human oversight to catch and correct errors that the AI might not recognize. This hybrid model can significantly reduce the risk of harm from unchecked AI decisions. Secondly, human-AI collaboration allows leveraging AI's ability to process and analyze large datasets quickly while benefiting from human creativity and ethical reasoning. This collaboration leads to more innovative solutions that neither humans nor AI could achieve alone. Moreover, involving humans in AI processes helps in training AI systems to become more accurate and aligned with human values, as continuous human feedback can guide the AI's learning process and adjustment.

However, integrating human oversight with AI systems is not without challenges. One major challenge is the scalability of human involvement. As AI systems become more complex and widely used, the demand for human oversight can strain resources and become a bottleneck in processes that are designed to be enhanced by AI. Additionally, there is the risk of human bias and error being introduced into AI systems. Humans are not infallible, and their judgments can be influenced by subjective factors or incorrect information, which can reinforce these biases in AI behaviors.

To address these challenges, developing structured protocols for human-AI interaction is essential. Establishing clear guidelines on the roles and responsibilities of humans in AI-driven processes can help maintain the balance between leveraging AI's capabilities and ensuring responsible oversight. Training programs for human operators should also emphasize ethical considerations and bias awareness to mitigate the risk of skewed human inputs. Moreover, employing diverse human supervisors can help offset individual biases, leading to more balanced and objective oversight.

Adopting a HITL approach where humans and AI collaborate effectively requires thoughtful design and continuous refinement of processes. It involves technical adjustments and a cultural shift towards recognizing the value of both human and artificial intelligence. By fostering an environment where AI is seen as a tool to augment human capabilities rather than replace them, we can leverage the strengths of both to achieve more ethical, reliable, and effective outcomes in AI applications.

5.4 The Future of Work with AI Assistants

As previously discussed, AI assistants like ChatGPT are increasingly becoming integral components of the modern workplace, reshaping industries and workflows profoundly. Integrating AI tools in sectors ranging from customer service to content creation is not just about streamlining processes—it's about enhancing capabilities and forging new opportunities. For instance, in customer service, AI assistants can handle routine inquiries instantly and around the clock, freeing human agents to tackle more complex and sensitive cases that require empathy and nuanced judgment. This not only improves efficiency but also elevates the quality of service, offering customers timely responses and personalized interaction.

In the creative industries, AI tools are used to draft preliminary content outlines, suggest edits, and even generate creative content ideas based on trend analysis. This capability allows content creators to focus more on refining their work and engaging with their audiences in meaningful ways rather than getting bogged down by the initial stages of content development. Similarly, in fields such as law and healthcare, AI assistants help manage and sift through large volumes of data to highlight the most relevant information, thus speeding up research and reporting processes. This role of AI in data management underscores its potential as a transformative tool across various sectors, enabling professionals to make more informed decisions faster and with greater accuracy.

However, integrating AI in the workplace has challenges, particularly concerning employment. There is a genuine concern that AI could lead to job displacement, as tasks traditionally performed by humans are increasingly automated. While it's true that some roles may become less necessary, history shows that technological advancements are also very capable of creating new job opportunities. For example, the rise of AI has led to increased demand for AI trainers, who teach AI systems how to perform specific tasks, and AI ethicists, who ensure these systems operate within ethical boundaries. Prompt engineering is also becoming increasingly relevant as efficiently retrieving data from AI systems becomes more important. Moreover, as AI takes over more routine and administrative tasks, it frees human workers to focus on higher-level functions like strategy and innovation, leading to more fulfilling roles and new career paths.

Certain skills become particularly valuable in an AI-enhanced workplace in this evolving landscape. For one, digital literacy—understanding how to interact with and manage AI tools—is becoming essential. As you navigate a workplace augmented by AI, effectively collaborating with AI for data analysis, content generation, or customer interactions will set you apart as a proficient and versatile professional. Another critical skill is emotional intelligence. As AI handles more cognitive tasks, human-centric skills such as empathy, persuasion, and personal service become more important. These skills ensure that the human touch remains a central part of industries even as they leverage AI for growth and efficiency.

Advocating for ethical job design in implementing AI tools is crucial to ensure that technology augments rather than replaces human workers. Ethical job design involves creating roles that leverage AI's capabilities to enhance human work, not eliminate it. This can mean designing jobs where AI and humans collaborate, using AI's analytical capabilities to provide insights that human workers use to make strategic decisions or personalize customer interactions. For instance, a marketing professional could use AI-generated insights to understand customer preferences and craft more effective campaigns, combining the precision of AI with the creativity and empathy of the human mind. This approach preserves and enriches jobs, making them more impactful.

As AI continues to permeate various aspects of work, embracing these changes with an informed and proactive attitude is vital. By understanding the dynamic capabilities of AI, advocating for its ethical integration, and continuously adapting your skills, you can not only navigate but thrive in an AI-enhanced workplace. This readiness to adapt and grow with AI technologies ensures that your professional journey remains vibrant and forward-looking, marked by continuous learning and innovation.

5.5 Societal Impacts of Widespread AI Adoption

As artificial intelligence becomes ubiquitous in daily life, its influence extends far beyond the realms of technology and industry, seeping into the very fabric of society. The adoption of AI on a large scale is poised to transform cultural norms and social behaviors, reshape economic landscapes, redefine governance, and magnify global inequalities. Understanding these shifts is crucial for navigating the new societal dynamics that AI brings.

The cultural and social changes brought about by widespread AI adoption are profound and far-reaching. As AI technologies become integrated into everyday activities, from personalized shopping recommendations to automated customer service, they subtly alter people's expectations and behaviors. For instance, the instant gratification provided by AI-driven services can lead to decreased patience and heightened expectations for speed and efficiency in all areas of life. Moreover, as virtual assistants and chatbots become more sophisticated, they could shift the way people communicate, potentially leading to a preference for digital interaction over human contact in certain contexts. This could have broader implications for social skills and interpersonal relationships. Additionally, AI's role in content creation—from music to news articles—raises questions about authenticity and creativity, possibly changing how value is perceived in art and media. As these technologies curate and create content that reinforces specific patterns and preferences, they might also homogenize culture, diluting regional and individual uniqueness.

Economically, AI's integration into various sectors has the potential to both invigorate and disrupt. On the positive side, AI can drive efficiency, reduce costs, and unlock new entrepreneurial opportunities and business models. For example, predictive analytics powered by AI can help businesses anticipate market trends, optimize operations, and personalize services, leading to better customer satisfaction and economic growth. However, these benefits are accompanied by challenges such as job displacement. As AI automates routine tasks, there is a risk that jobs in sectors like manufacturing, retail, and administrative support could be significantly reduced. While new jobs will undoubtedly be created in tech and AI design, there is a concern about the mismatch between the skills required for these new roles and the capabilities of the current workforce, potentially leading to economic inequality and social unrest.

In the realm of governance and public policy, AI introduces both opportunities and obstacles. Governments can utilize AI to enhance public services, improve urban planning, and strengthen security. However, the use of AI in public decision-making and surveillance raises critical issues regarding privacy, civil liberties, and accountability. The potential for AI to be used for mass surveillance is particularly troubling, as it could lead to overreach by authorities and erosion of privacy rights. Decisions made by AI algorithms, such as those determining eligibility for loans or social benefits, must be transparent and subject to scrutiny to ensure fairness and justice. This highlights the need for robust regulatory frameworks that govern AI use, ensuring it aligns with ethical standards and public values.

Finally, the global spread of AI technologies is likely to exacerbate existing inequalities, both within and between countries. While affluent nations and individuals may have the resources to harness AI's advantages, developing countries might lag behind, lacking access to the technology and the expertise to implement it effectively. This digital divide could deepen global disparities, influencing economic opportunities, healthcare quality, and educational outcomes across regions. Addressing this issue requires concerted efforts from global stakeholders, including governments, tech companies, and international organizations, to ensure that AI technologies are accessible and beneficial to all. Strategies might include investing in digital infrastructure, fostering international collaborations for technology transfer, and implementing policies that encourage innovation while ensuring equitable distribution of its benefits.

As AI continues to evolve and permeate various aspects of life, its societal impacts—ranging from cultural shifts to economic transformations and governance challenges—must be carefully managed. By fostering a deep understanding of these dynamics, society can better prepare for and navigate the changes that AI brings, ensuring that the technology enhances human life while respecting ethical standards and promoting inclusivity and fairness.

5.6 Creating an Ethical Framework for ChatGPT Usage

As the boundaries of AI capabilities continue to expand, the importance of an ethical framework in developing and deploying technologies like ChatGPT becomes evident. This framework serves as a cornerstone, ensuring that AI operates within bounds that are effective, morally sound, and socially responsible. The rationale for this framework stems from the potential of AI to influence a wide range of human activities and decisions. Without a structured set of ethical guidelines, deploying AI technologies could lead to outcomes misaligned with societal values and individual rights, such as privacy breaches or unfair decision-making processes.

At the core of an ethical framework for AI like ChatGPT are principles that ensure users' transparency, accountability, fairness, and empowerment. Transparency involves clear communication about how AI systems operate and make decisions. This is crucial for building trust and allowing users and regulators to understand and assess the technology. Accountability refers to establishing mechanisms where responsible parties can be answerable for AI systems' actions. This helps maintain a check on AI operations, ensuring they adhere to declared values and legal standards.

Fairness is another pillar that ensures that AI systems do not embed or propagate biases that could lead to discriminatory practices. This involves careful scrutiny of the data used to train AI models like ChatGPT, ensuring it is representative and free of biases that could skew AI behavior. Lastly, user empowerment is about designing AI systems that enhance users' abilities without manipulating or diminishing the quality of human decision-making. This includes giving users control over how they interact with AI and how their data is used, ensuring the technology augments human capabilities without undermining them.

Implementing these ethical principles in real-world AI applications involves several steps. Initially, organizations need to define clear ethical guidelines that align with their core values and the expectations of their stakeholders, including users, regulatory bodies, and the general public. These guidelines should be integrated into the entire lifecycle of AI development, from the design and training phases to deployment and beyond. For instance, during the development of ChatGPT, developers can incorporate transparency by ensuring the AI's decision-making processes are interpretable by humans. Similarly, accountability can be addressed by establishing a clear protocol for monitoring AI performance and reporting on its operations.

Equally important is the continuous evaluation and adaptation of the ethical framework. As AI technologies and societal norms evolve, so too must the frameworks governing AI use. This involves regular assessments of AI performance and its impacts on users and society. It also includes updating ethical guidelines to address new challenges and opportunities as technology advances. For example, as ChatGPT becomes capable of more complex interactions, its developers should regularly review whether its responses adhere to evolving norms of fairness and inclusivity, making necessary adjustments in its training data and algorithms.

Additionally, fostering a culture of ethical AI use within organizations and among AI developers and users can reinforce these frameworks. This can be achieved through training programs, ethical audits, and open dialogue about the ethical implications of AI. By ingraining ethics into the fabric of organizational processes and the mindset of individuals who develop and deploy AI, the technology can be steered to contribute positively to society.

By embedding these ethical principles and practices into the development and use of AI, like ChatGPT, organizations can navigate the complex landscape where technology meets human values. This helps mitigate risks, fosters trust, and enhances the overall effectiveness and acceptance of AI technologies in society. As we move forward, the continuous refinement and application of these ethical guidelines will play a crucial role in shaping the future of AI, ensuring that it serves as a force for good, enhancing our capabilities and enriching our lives.

In summary, creating an ethical framework for AI usage, particularly for technologies like ChatGPT, is a technical necessity and a moral imperative. As we conclude this chapter, we recognize the importance of grounding AI advancements in strong ethical practices that uphold transparency, accountability, fairness, and user empowerment. This approach ensures that as AI technologies become more embedded in our daily lives and across various sectors, they do so in beneficial ways and aligned with broader societal values. Moving forward into the next chapter, we will explore specific case studies that highlight the practical applications and challenges of implementing AI in diverse contexts, providing deeper insights into the real-world implications of AI technologies.

5.7 Interactive Task

Reflect on how you currently use (or plan to use) AI tools like ChatGPT in your personal and professional life, identifying areas where ethical considerations might be relevant, such as data privacy, transparency, and potential biases in AI responses. List your ethical concerns, such as data privacy issues in customer service responses or potential biases in generated content. Using resources from this chapter and additional research, identify best practices for addressing these concerns, focusing on guidelines for data privacy, AI transparency, and bias mitigation. Finally, create a plan outlining steps to ensure your AI use is ethical, including implementing data privacy measures, ensuring transparency by communicating AI involvement to users, and regularly reviewing AI prompts to minimize bias. This plan will help you navigate and improve the ethical implications of using AI tools in daily interactions.

Now that we have explored the foundations of AI and ChatGPT, examining the ethical issues surrounding this technology is essential. In a world increasingly driven by data, understanding the ethical implications of using powerful AI tools like ChatGPT is not just prudent—it's imperative. As you integrate AI into your daily interactions, whether for work, learning, or personal growth, it becomes crucial to consider what AI can do and how it does it. The ethical use of AI, particularly regarding data privacy, is a cornerstone in fostering trust and safety in technology. This chapter delves into the nature of data exchange in AI systems, how this data is handled, and provides best practices to safeguard your information, ensuring your journey with AI remains secure and aligned with your values.

As we move forward, we will explore ChatGPT's advanced features and customization options. This next chapter will equip you with the knowledge to tailor AI interactions to suit your unique needs and preferences, enhancing the overall user experience. Get ready to unlock ChatGPT's full potential with advanced techniques and customization strategies.

Advanced Features and Customization

WELCOME TO CHAPTER SIX! Now that you have a strong foundation in using ChatGPT and understand the ethical considerations, it's time to explore the advanced features and customization options that can further enhance your experience. Imagine discovering a secret passage in a familiar room that leads to new corridors and hidden treasures. That's akin to exploring the latest features and functionalities that updates to ChatGPT bring to users like you. Each update enhances the tool's existing capabilities and unveils fresh possibilities that can transform your interaction with this powerful AI. Many of these advanced features may require more technical skills or the help of the tech department of your organization, but the information is provided here for beginners so you can grow with the technology. This section examines the most recent upgrades to ChatGPT, helping you understand their significance and how you can leverage them to enrich both personal and professional aspects of your life.

6.1 Exploring the Latest Features in ChatGPT Updates

Overview of Updates

The landscape of technology, especially AI is continually evolving, and staying abreast of these changes ensures that you are maximizing the potential of tools like ChatGPT. Updates to ChatGPT have introduced a suite of enhancements designed to make the AI more intuitive, responsive, and versatile. For instance, newer versions have improved the model's understanding of nuanced language and context, making interactions more fluid and natural. There's also been a significant reduction in response times, so you can now have quicker interactions that feel more like conversing with a human. Additionally, updates have expanded the range of topics ChatGPT can discuss and provide advice on, from more in-depth business insights to complex scientific concepts, broadening the scope of its applicability.

Understanding Feature Enhancements

Each feature introduced in the latest updates is not just a technical upgrade but a gateway to enhanced user experience. For example, the enhanced understanding of context allows you to have extended conversations where ChatGPT remembers the thread of the discussion, a feature that mimics human-like memory in conversations. This means you can now discuss projects or plans across several interactions without repeating or summarizing previous messages. Imagine planning an event or discussing a business strategy over several days; ChatGPT's ability to recall previous interactions can add coherence and depth to the planning process, making it a more robust tool for project management and execution.

Moreover, improving response speed and understanding user intents significantly boost productivity. For professionals and students, this means less time waiting for responses and more time acting on the information provided. Whether drafting emails, preparing for a presentation, or learning a new topic, these enhancements ensure that ChatGPT aligns more closely with your pace and demands, effectively becoming a more integrated part of your daily tools. These feature enhancements depend on the version selected when prompting ChatGPT.

Staying Informed on Updates

Keeping up-to-date with these developments is key to making the most of ChatGPT. One effective strategy is to subscribe to newsletters from AI and technology news sources that provide updates on ChatGPT and similar AI tools. These newsletters often cover the latest changes, provide insights into how the updates function, and sometimes offer tips on how to use new features effectively. Additionally, participating in online forums and communities focused on AI technology can be invaluable. Platforms like Reddit, Stack Exchange, or specialized LinkedIn groups allow you to engage with other users and experts who share insights and practical advice on navigating the updates, thus helping you understand and utilize the advanced features of ChatGPT more adeptly.

Leveraging Updates for Enhanced Performance

To fully benefit from the latest updates, it's crucial to incorporate these enhancements into your daily use of ChatGPT actively. Experiment with the new features in various contexts to see how they can best serve your needs. For instance, if you're a researcher, test the improved contextual understanding by having ongoing discussions on your research topic. Business professionals should try faster processing speeds for real-time decision-making during meetings or brainstorming sessions. By integrating these updated features into regular use, you can transform how you interact with ChatGTP—turning it from a simple conversational tool to an indispensable assistant that augments your capabilities and streamlines your tasks.

Through these updates, ChatGPT becomes more aligned with your personal and professional needs and continues redefining the boundaries of what AI can achieve in everyday applications. As you explore and adapt to these enhancements, you unlock new levels of productivity and engagement, ensuring your ChatGPT experience remains cutting-edge and deeply rewarding.

6.2 Fine-Tuning ChatGPT for Specific Industries

In an era where artificial intelligence molds the backbone of industry-specific solutions, tailoring ChatGPT to meet the healthcare, legal, and finance sectors' unique needs enhances its functionality and ensures its applications are precise and beneficial. Customizing ChatGPT involves adapting its responses to reflect the terminology, ethical considerations, and regulatory demands of specific fields, enhancing its utility as a professional tool. For instance, ChatGPT can be fine-tuned in healthcare to provide support in medical terminology management or to assist with patient data privacy, adhering to HIPAA regulations. Similarly, in the legal sector, it can be trained to understand and generate information pertinent to legal precedents or case law, while in finance, its customization might focus on compliance with financial regulations or analysis of market trends.

The process of fine-tuning ChatGPT for these industries begins with training the model on domain-specific datasets. This could involve feeding ChatGPT thousands of medical journals to prepare for deployment in healthcare settings or exposing it to vast financial reports and compliance documentation for finance applications. This training equips ChatGPT with the knowledge base and contextual understanding necessary to operate effectively within these sectors, making its interactions more relevant and insights more actionable.

It is important to note that fine-tuning and training the model for specific industries is not typically the end user's responsibility but is managed by organizations like OpenAI. OpenAI continuously updates and improves the model, ensuring it remains cutting-edge and applicable across various industries.

Additionally, several third-party companies integrate GPT models into industry-specific tools, making these tailored solutions readily available. For example, GPT-powered tools are designed explicitly for legal research, financial analysis, or medical record-keeping. Users interested in leveraging these advanced capabilities can search for and adopt these specialized tools, benefiting from the extensive work already done to adapt ChatGPT to their professional needs. This approach allows users to enjoy the advantages of AI without needing to undertake the complex process of training and fine-tuning models themselves.

Case Studies and Use Cases

A recent survey by Forbes Advisor (Image 6.1) highlights that businesses intend to use ChatGPT for various applications, including general responses, summarizing information, improving decision-making, translations, content creation, coding, and web design. These diverse use cases demonstrate the extensive potential of ChatGPT across different professional settings. Understanding these examples can help beginners identify how ChatGPT might best serve their specific needs.

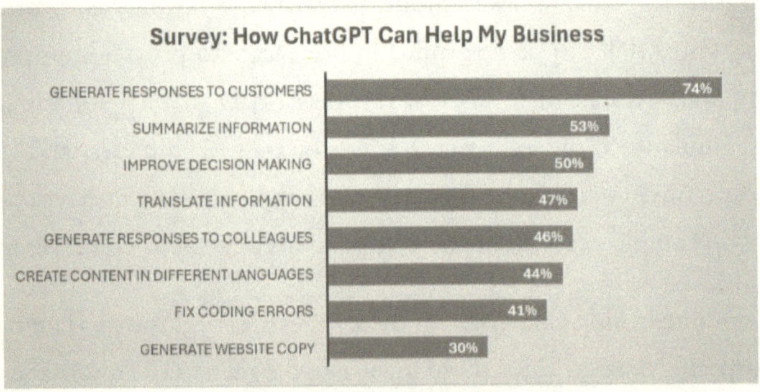

Image 6.1: Use Cases Survey

One illustrative case study is the integration of ChatGPT in a major hospital, where it was used to triage patient inquiries online before they reached human staff. The hospital reduced waiting times by customizing ChatGPT with medical knowledge and patient interaction protocols and significantly improved patient satisfaction. However, the challenge lies in continuously updating the AI with the latest medical research and health protocols to maintain reliability. Another case involves a law firm that utilized ChatGPT to draft and review legal documents. The AI was trained on a comprehensive database of legal texts and was subsequently able to generate first drafts of contracts and legal briefs, fine-tuned by human lawyers. This sped up the drafting process and reduced the incidence of human error, though it required rigorous training to align with legal standards and practices.

In the tech industry, ChatGPT has streamlined customer support by providing instant, accurate responses to common technical issues. This improves customer satisfaction and frees up human agents to handle more complex queries. In marketing agencies, ChatGPT assists in generating creative content and conducting market analysis, helping teams stay ahead of trends and produce high-quality work efficiently.

These examples demonstrate how ChatGPT can be integrated into different sectors to enhance productivity and efficiency. For beginners, exploring these case studies can offer valuable insights into the varied applications of ChatGPT. You can leverage ChatGPT to drive innovation and achieve your goals by tailoring its uses to meet unique business requirements. Whether in healthcare, law, tech, or marketing, the key is continuously adapting and refining AI usage to align with industry standards and evolving needs.

Compliance Considerations

Ensuring compliance with industry-specific regulations and ethical standards is paramount when customizing ChatGPT. In healthcare, this involves aligning the AI's operations with patient confidentiality laws and medical ethics. In finance, it means ensuring that all financial advice or analysis provided by ChatGPT adheres to legal standards and market regulations. Moreover, transparency in how the AI operates, especially in how it processes and uses data, is crucial to maintaining trust and accountability. Establishing clear guidelines on data usage and integrating safeguards to protect sensitive information are essential steps in deploying a customized ChatGPT in any regulated industry.

By adhering to these principles and approaches, ChatGPT can be effectively customized to meet the specialized needs of various industries, enhancing its applicability and ensuring that its integration is both beneficial and compliant with professional standards. As industries continue to evolve and new challenges emerge, fine-tuning AI solutions like ChatGPT will be crucial in ensuring that these tools keep pace with changes and drive innovation and efficiency in professional practices.

6.3 Integrating ChatGPT with Other Software and Tools

Integrating ChatGPT with other software and tools through Application Programming Interfaces (APIs) opens up a world of possibilities, transforming how you interact with and utilize this powerful AI tool across various platforms. APIs act like bridges that allow different software systems to communicate and work together. For instance, integrating ChatGPT with your favorite project management tool or customer relationship management (CRM) system can enhance functionality and streamline operations. Let's start by breaking down the basics of API integration with ChatGPT. Essentially, APIs provide a set of rules and protocols for how software components should interact. When you integrate ChatGPT with another software via an API, you enable a direct line of communication between the two. This could mean having ChatGPT automatically pull data from another application to inform its responses or push its outputs to another system to trigger specific actions. This kind of integration is facilitated through API keys, essentially unique identifiers that authenticate a real-time data exchange between your ChatGPT instance and other software applications.

One practical application of API integration is enhancing CRM systems with ChatGPT. CRM systems are vital for managing a company's interactions with current and potential customers. By integrating ChatGPT, you can automate and personalize these interactions at scale. For example, when a customer sends a query through the CRM system, ChatGPT can instantly generate a personalized response based on the customer's previous interactions and preferences logged in the CRM. This speeds up response times and ensures that the communication is contextually relevant, significantly enhancing customer satisfaction. Moreover, ChatGPT can analyze customer feedback and interactions to identify trends and sentiments, providing valuable insights that can help refine marketing strategies and improve customer service practices. Currently, many CRMs offer AI enhancements, and this trend is expected to increase as the technology evolves.

Moving into the realm of project management, embedding ChatGPT into project management tools can revolutionize how projects are tracked and managed. Project management involves many tasks, from updating work progress to managing team communications. ChatGPT can automate routine updates and notifications, ensuring team members are always informed about project changes and deadlines without manual input. For instance, you could set up ChatGPT to send daily project status updates to all team members or use it to automatically assign tasks to team members based on their workload and expertise. This not only saves time but also helps maintain a high level of accuracy and efficiency in project communications. Several project management platforms integrate AI tools, and this integration is expected to improve and increase as the technology advances.

Encouraging creativity in integrating ChatGPT with unconventional tools can lead to innovative solutions that address unique challenges or enhance user experiences in unexpected ways. For example, integrating ChatGPT with virtual reality (VR) platforms could create immersive educational or training programs where ChatGPT, or similar AI technologies, provides real-time information or guidance to users navigating a virtual environment. Another innovative integration could be using AI with Internet of Things (IoT) devices. Picture a smart home where ChatGPT controls various devices based on conversational commands from the user, adjusting lighting and temperature or even suggesting recipes based on what's in your smart fridge. These examples highlight how flexible and adaptable ChatGPT can be when creatively integrated with different technologies, opening up a landscape of possibilities that can transform mundane tasks into interactive and engaging experiences.

Understanding ChatGPT's integrations with other software and tools provides a thorough foundation for leveraging its capabilities to enhance productivity and efficiency. This knowledge allows for creating more intuitive and responsive systems that better meet users' needs in various contexts. Whether it's through streamlining customer interactions, managing projects more effectively, or innovating with new tech combinations, the potential for ChatGPT to add value across different platforms and industries is immense, limited only by the creativity and vision of those who deploy it.

6.4 Building Custom Chatbots Using ChatGPT

Building a custom chatbot using ChatGPT can be an exciting journey, especially for beginners. This introduction aims to help you understand the full capabilities of ChatGPT as you grow your skills. Creating a chatbot that feels intelligent and intuitive isn't just about technical know-how—it's about understanding and anticipating the needs and reactions of its users. Starting with ChatGPT, you can design a chatbot that not only responds efficiently but also engages users in a meaningful way.

To get started, the first step is to clearly define your chatbot's purpose. This involves understanding what you need the chatbot to do. Is it to provide customer support, assist with e-commerce transactions, or offer information about a specific topic or service? Identifying the core purpose will guide every other aspect of the chatbot's development, from the dialogues it will handle to the personality it will project.

Next, you can begin by writing simple dialogue flows. Think of it as writing a script for how typical interactions should unfold. Start with common queries that users might ask, then outline logical and helpful responses from the chatbot. For example, if your chatbot is for customer support, consider the most common questions customers ask and write out how the chatbot should respond.

As you become more comfortable, you can start to consider the personality and tone of your chatbot. For instance, if your chatbot serves a professional consultancy, its language style should be formal and informative. Conversely, a chatbot for a youth-focused brand might have a more casual tone and playful personality.

Deploying your custom chatbot can start with simple steps, such as using it on a small scale within a website or social media platform. For example, you can use pre-built tools and plugins that integrate ChatGPT with platforms like Facebook Messenger or Slack, allowing you to see how the chatbot performs in real-world interactions.

Monitoring and refining your chatbot's performance is a crucial part of the process. Use feedback from users to make improvements. This can involve adjusting responses to better meet user needs or adding new functionalities based on what users are asking for.

Through these initial steps, building a chatbot with ChatGPT can be an exciting and rewarding project. You can create a functional tool that enhances user engagement and satisfaction by clearly defining its purpose, designing simple dialogues, personalizing its interactions, and deploying it in practical settings. As you dive into this process, remember that each choice and adjustment is a step towards creating a more connected and responsive experience for your users, leveraging the advanced capabilities of AI to meet and exceed the expectations of the digital age.

Remember, this is an introduction to help you understand ChatGPT's full capabilities. As you become more comfortable with the basics, you can explore more advanced customization options, potentially with the help of more technical resources or your organization's tech team.

6.5 Data Analysis with ChatGPT

Imagine having a tool that not only converses with you but also dives deep into oceans of data to fetch insights crucial for your business and research needs. ChatGPT, with its advanced data analysis capabilities, acts much like a seasoned data analyst capable of sifting through large datasets to extract meaningful information. This process involves parsing data, recognizing patterns, and drawing conclusions that can significantly influence decision-making processes.

Understanding Basic Data Analysis

To begin with data analysis, it is essential to understand the crucial role that high-quality data plays. Accurate and comprehensive data is the foundation of any meaningful analysis. Collecting, cleaning, analyzing, and interpreting data are fundamental to driving valuable insights. While ChatGPT cannot directly interact with datasets, it can guide you through each step by providing explanations, best practices, and examples, making the process more accessible to beginners. For instance, you can start by asking ChatGPT questions like, "How do I clean a dataset?" or "What are the common methods for data visualization?" ChatGPT can offer step-by-step instructions and explanations to help you understand these fundamental concepts and perform basic analyses, adding value to your data-driven decision-making process and enhancing the quality of your insights.

Leveraging ChatGPT for Data Cleaning

Data cleaning is crucial to data analysis to ensure accuracy and usability. ChatGPT can help you identify and correct errors in your dataset, such as missing values or outliers. Data ambiguity, such as inconsistent or unclear data entries, can pose significant challenges. For example, you might ask, "How do I handle missing data?" and receive guidance on techniques like imputation or removal of incomplete records, enhancing your data's reliability. Similarly, ChatGPT can suggest methods to standardize and clarify entries for ambiguous data, ensuring that your dataset is coherent and meaningful for analysis.

Analysis & Interpretation

Once your data is clean, ChatGPT can guide you through various analysis techniques. You can ask questions like, "How do I perform a regression analysis?" or "What are the steps to create a pivot table?" ChatGPT can provide explanations and examples, helping you apply these techniques to your dataset. This support makes learning and applying analytical methods more manageable. Interpreting the results of your data analysis is critical for making informed decisions. ChatGPT can also help you understand your findings and how to draw conclusions from your data. For example, you might ask, "What does a positive correlation between two variables indicate?" and receive a clear explanation that helps you understand the relationship between the variables.

Data Visualization

Data visualization is key to understanding and communicating your findings. ChatGPT can suggest different types of visualizations based on your data and the insights you want to convey. For instance, you might ask, "What type of chart should I use to compare monthly sales?" and ChatGPT can recommend bar charts, line graphs, or other visualizations. Additionally, if you're dealing with geographical data, you could ask, "How can I visualize regional sales performance?" ChatGPT might suggest using a heat map or a choropleth map. You can also inquire about the tools available to further enhance your data analysis toolkit. This helps you present your data clearly and effectively, making it easier to identify trends and patterns. Moreover, effective data visualization enhances your ability to share insights with stakeholders, facilitating better decision-making and strategic planning.

Many data visualization tools now offer AI-based assistance and guidance integrated by the provider. For example, tools like Tableau and Microsoft Power BI come with built-in AI capabilities that can help you create more insightful and interactive visualizations. These tools can automatically suggest the best charts based on your data, identify trends, and even provide predictive analytics. By integrating ChatGPT prompts with these advanced tools, you can generate summaries and insights that are then visually represented, making data insights more actionable and easier to interpret. This combination of AI-driven analysis and powerful visualization tools ensures that your data tells a story and drives informed decisions and strategic planning.

Predictive Analytics

The potential of using ChatGPT for predictive analytics is particularly exciting, as it opens up possibilities for forecasting future trends and behaviors. By training models with historical data, you can set up predictive analyses to forecast outcomes based on identified patterns. For example, historical sales data combined with promotional strategies can be analyzed in retail to forecast future sales trends. While ChatGPT cannot directly perform predictive analytics, it can guide you through the process and help interpret results. Even if you don't have deep expertise in predictive model building, ChatGPT can assist you in using tools like Python and Google Colab to create predictive models with a little hard work.

By starting with basic data analysis tasks and gradually exploring more advanced techniques, you can leverage ChatGPT as a powerful learning tool. This approach helps you build a strong foundation in data analysis and opens up new opportunities for insights and decision-making. As you continue to develop your skills, you'll find that data analysis becomes more accessible and rewarding, enhancing your ability to work with data effectively.

Practical Applications and Real-World Examples

In real-world scenarios, the applications of ChatGPT in data analysis are vast and impactful, spanning various industries and functions. Let's explore a few key areas where ChatGPT can significantly enhance data analysis capabilities, even for beginners.

Financial Sector

ChatGPT can assist in performing sentiment analysis on financial news articles, social media feeds, and market reports in the financial sector. For example, you might ask, "Considering this report, what is the sentiment around the company's outlook?" ChatGPT can help you analyze the tone and content of the report, providing a summary highlighting prevailing sentiment. By understanding these trends, investors can make more informed decisions about buying or selling stocks. Additionally, ChatGPT can guide you in building simple predictive models using historical stock data, enabling you to forecast stock price movements and market trends.

Healthcare

Data analysis can lead to better patient outcomes and more efficient healthcare delivery. ChatGPT can assist healthcare professionals by analyzing patient data to identify correlations between treatment plans and health outcomes. For example, "What are the common factors among patients who responded well to a specific treatment?" ChatGPT can help uncover patterns that might inform better clinical decisions by guiding you through data preprocessing and analysis. Furthermore, ChatGPT can provide insights into recent medical research, assisting practitioners to stay updated with the latest advancements and integrate them into their practice.

Marketing and Customer Insights

Understanding consumer behavior is crucial for marketers. ChatGPT can help analyze customer feedback, reviews, and social media interactions to identify common themes and sentiment trends. For instance, you could ask, "Based on these reviews, what are customers' main concerns about our product?" ChatGPT can help categorize and summarize this feedback, providing actionable insights that inform product improvements and marketing strategies. Additionally, using historical sales data, ChatGPT can guide you in forecasting future sales trends and planning marketing campaigns accordingly.

Education

ChatGPT can assist in analyzing student performance data to identify areas where students may need additional support. For example, "Which topics do students struggle with the most in math?" ChatGPT can help you analyze aggregate data to pinpoint specific challenges and suggest targeted interventions. This data-driven approach ensures that educational resources are allocated effectively, enhancing student learning outcomes.

Environmental Science

Environmental scientists can leverage ChatGPT to analyze large datasets related to climate change, pollution levels, and biodiversity. For instance, "What trends can be observed in temperature changes over the past decade?" ChatGPT can guide you through visualizing and interpreting this data, helping to identify significant patterns and potential environmental impacts. By making complex data more accessible, ChatGPT supports informed decision-making in environmental conservation and policy development.

Business Operations

Businesses can use ChatGPT to streamline operations by analyzing operational data such as inventory levels, supply chain efficiency, and employee performance metrics. For example, "How can we optimize our inventory management?" ChatGPT can help analyze past sales data and inventory turnover rates, providing recommendations for inventory optimization. This leads to cost savings and improved efficiency in business operations.

By leveraging ChatGPT's guidance, even beginners can use advanced techniques to derive meaningful insights from their data. Whether in finance, healthcare, marketing, education, environmental science, or business operations, ChatGPT can enhance your data analysis capabilities and support data-driven decision-making. Starting with basic data analysis tasks and gradually exploring more advanced techniques allows you to build a strong foundation in data analysis. This approach enhances your ability to work with data effectively and opens up new opportunities for insights and decision-making. As you continue to develop your skills, data analysis becomes more accessible and rewarding, ultimately improving your proficiency and confidence in working with data. This increased understanding makes you more valuable in your current or future roles, equipping you with sought-after skills crucial in today's data-driven world.

6.6 Interactive Task

For this chapter's task, consider how ChatGPT can be integrated into your personal and professional life. Reflect on the various ways ChatGPT can be utilized, thinking about tasks that could be streamlined or enhanced. Identify one specific use case for ChatGPT in your professional life and one in your personal life. You can use ChatGPT to guide your brainstorming process if needed; also an excellent way to continue using the technology. As you identify these specific use cases, formulate prompts using the perfect prompt formula to ensure clarity and effectiveness in your interactions with ChatGPT. This exercise will help you integrate ChatGPT into your daily routine, making professional and personal tasks more manageable and efficient. Additionally, consider documenting your experience and the outcomes, as this can provide valuable insights and further refine your approach to leveraging ChatGPT in your life.

Now that you've explored the advanced features and customization options of ChatGPT, it's time to think about how to stay up-to-date with this rapidly evolving technological landscape. The final chapter, "Staying Ahead with ChatGPT," will guide you on how to keep up with the latest advancements, updates, and best practices to ensure you continue to make the most of this powerful tool. Embracing the constant evolution of AI technology will enhance your personal and professional capabilities and prepare you to adapt and thrive in a future where AI plays an increasingly integral role.

Staying Ahead with ChatGPT

Welcome to Chapter Seven! As you've navigated through the advanced features and customization options of ChatGPT, you've unlocked powerful new capabilities and insights. But the journey doesn't stop here. In the fast-paced world of AI, staying current with technological advancements is crucial to maintaining your edge. This final chapter will empower you with strategies to keep up with the latest updates, trends, and best practices. By embracing the continuous evolution of ChatGPT and AI technologies in general, you will enhance your skills and ensure you are well-prepared to harness the full potential of AI in your personal and professional endeavors. Let's dive into how you can stay ahead and thrive in this ever-changing landscape.

7.1 Resources for Ongoing ChatGPT Education

Curated Online Courses and Tutorials

In the world of AI, education is key, and thankfully, it's also readily accessible. Online platforms like Coursera and Udacity offer structured courses specifically about AI and machine learning. These courses are crafted by experts from leading universities and innovative tech companies to deliver comprehensive learning experiences. For instance, Coursera's "AI For Everyone" by Andrew Ng provides a broad introduction to AI, covering the basics of algorithms, data needs, and ethical issues. For those specifically interested in ChatGPT, Udacity offers specialized programs that dive deep into natural language processing, teaching you how to build conversational AI models from scratch. These platforms typically provide a mix of video tutorials, readings, and hands-on projects, ideal for understanding the practical applications of concepts discussed.

Books and Academic Papers

While online courses offer structured learning paths, books and academic papers provide the depth and rigor necessary for a deeper understanding of AI. "Artificial Intelligence: A Guide for Thinking Humans" by Melanie Mitchell offers an insightful exploration of AI's capabilities and limitations, providing a solid foundation for beginners. For those looking to get into the specifics of conversational AI, reading seminal papers like "Attention Is All You Need" by Vaswani et al., which introduced the transformer model—the backbone of ChatGPT—is invaluable. These resources are typically peer-reviewed, ensuring high-quality and reliable information that covers both theoretical and practical aspects of AI. A quick search at Google Scholar will provide recent scholarly articles as academia continues to publish on the topic.

Interactive Learning Platforms

To truly master ChatGPT, one must move beyond passive learning and engage with interactive platforms that offer real-time feedback and practical experience. Codecademy, for example, offers an interactive course where you can learn by directly working with AI models. These platforms enhance your learning by allowing you to apply concepts in a controlled environment, experiment with code, and see the immediate impact of your adjustments. This hands-on approach is crucial for understanding the nuances of AI programming and model training.

Certification Programs

Numerous certification programs are available for those looking to validate their skills with a formal credential. These programs, offered by institutions like Microsoft and IBM, assess your AI and machine learning knowledge, culminating in a certification that can bolster your professional profile. They often cover a range of topics, from the basics of AI to more advanced subjects like neural networks and language models such as ChatGPT. Preparing for and obtaining these certifications can significantly sharpen your skills and understanding of AI technologies.

By engaging with these diverse learning resources, you equip yourself with the knowledge and skills needed to navigate the rapidly evolving field of AI. Whether through structured online courses, in-depth reading materials, interactive platforms, or professional certifications, each resource plays a crucial role in shaping your ability to leverage and innovate with AI tools like ChatGPT. As you continue to explore these educational opportunities, you'll find yourself not just keeping pace with AI advancements but actively contributing to them, ready to meet future challenges with expertise and confidence.

7.2 Joining Communities: Forums and Social Media Groups

Navigating the vast landscape of AI and ChatGPT can sometimes feel like exploring a new city without a map. However, joining dedicated communities on platforms such as Reddit, LinkedIn, and Discord can provide you with the guidance, companionship, and resources that make this journey easier and more enriching. These platforms host a variety of forums and groups where enthusiasts, experts, and beginners converge to discuss, share, and collaborate on topics related to AI and ChatGPT.

Finding the right community starts with identifying your interests and needs. On Reddit, for example, subreddits like r/MachineLearning, r/Artificial, and r/LanguageTechnology offer spaces where discussions range from technical advice and latest research to project showcases and troubleshooting tips. Each subreddit has its own culture and rules, so it's beneficial to spend some time lurking (reading posts without contributing) to understand the dynamics before jumping into discussions. LinkedIn groups such as "Artificial Intelligence, Deep Learning, Machine Learning: Networking & AI Jobs" provide a more professional setting to connect with industry experts, find job opportunities, and gain insights into the AI market trends. For real-time interaction and more community-driven support, Discord servers like the "AI & Data Science Community" offer channels for immediate feedback and help, along with more casual interactions that help build strong network ties.

The benefits of engaging with these communities are manifold. First, they provide a support structure that can help simplify aspects of AI and ChatGPT that might initially seem overwhelming. Whether it's understanding complex algorithms, getting feedback on why your code isn't working, or simply observing conversations about AI, there's always someone who may have faced a similar issue and can offer a solution. This peer support accelerates your learning process and can also boost your confidence as you navigate your AI journey. Additionally, these communities often share the latest news, research papers, and resources, keeping you updated on the newest developments and innovations, which is crucial in a field as dynamic as AI.

Contributing to discussions is not just about asking questions but also about sharing your knowledge and experiences. Even as a beginner, you might have insights or fresh perspectives that can be valuable to others. Engaging actively in these communities helps others and establishes your presence and reputation within the community. This can lead to collaborative opportunities like working on projects with other members or forming study groups and partnerships. Over time, regular contributions can also establish you as a thought leader in specific AI niches, opening doors to professional opportunities and collaborations.

Furthermore, networking in these AI and ChatGPT-focused groups can be incredibly beneficial. You might connect with potential mentors who can provide guidance and advice, or you might encounter potential employers interested in the skills and knowledge you demonstrate in your interactions. Networking can also lead to opportunities to attend or speak at conferences and seminars, further expanding your understanding and professional network. Remember, every post you read, every discussion you contribute to, and every connection you make is a step toward not just learning but becoming an integral part of the AI community.

By joining and participating in AI and ChatGPT forums and social media groups, you gain access to a wealth of knowledge and resources and contribute to a growing field that thrives on shared learning and collaboration. These communities offer a space to learn, teach, network, and grow, providing a comprehensive ecosystem supporting your personal and professional development in AI.

7.3 Attending Workshops and Webinars for Hands-On Learning

Finding the right workshops and webinars that align with your skill level and interests in AI and ChatGPT can significantly enhance your learning experience. These events, often filled with interactive sessions and live demonstrations, provide a platform to deepen your understanding and apply what you've learned in real-time scenarios. Check out platforms like Eventbrite or Meetup, which host many tech-focused events, to locate these valuable learning opportunities. You can filter your search by topics such as ChatGPT, AI, or machine learning to find events that match your interests. Additionally, following industry leaders or organizations on social media platforms can keep you informed about upcoming webinars and workshops. Many universities and tech companies regularly host such events and often offer them for free or at a minimal cost to encourage participation from a broad audience.

There are many advantages to engaging in these hands-on learning environments. Firstly, they provide a dynamic setting to apply theoretical knowledge. Imagine participating in a workshop where you learn about the intricacies of neural networks and experiment with them through guided exercises. This practical application cements your understanding and aids in retaining information much more effectively than passive learning methods. Moreover, workshops and webinars often introduce real-world problems, allowing you to employ AI solutions in practical scenarios. This boosts your problem-solving skills and prepares you for challenges you might face in professional settings. The interactive nature of these events also means you can receive immediate feedback on your work, which is invaluable as it provides insights into areas for improvement and reaffirms concepts that you've mastered.

Engaging directly with experts and speakers at these events can dramatically enrich your learning journey. These interactions allow you to gain insights from individuals at the forefront of AI technology and innovation. For instance, a casual conversation during a workshop break might provide you with a new perspective on deploying ChatGTP within your projects, or a question-and-answer session might clear up longstanding confusion about certain AI functionalities. Experts can also offer personalized advice tailored to your specific interests and challenges, which is often not possible through other learning mediums. Their experience and knowledge can guide you in focusing on skills and areas most beneficial for your career or personal growth in AI.

Attending these workshops and webinars is crucial for keeping your skills and knowledge current. AI and technologies like ChatGPT evolve at a breakneck pace, with new advancements and updates emerging regularly. By making it a habit to participate in relevant events, you remain current with the latest technologies, methodologies, and best practices. This ongoing engagement helps in personal growth and enhances your professional value, making you a sought-after asset in tech-centric roles. Furthermore, regular attendance helps build a professional network with other AI enthusiasts and experts, which can benefit collaborative opportunities and career advancement.

In summary, workshops and webinars offer a structured yet flexible approach to learning that can significantly enhance your proficiency in AI and ChatGPT. By actively seeking out events that align with your learning goals, engaging with experts, and committing to continuous education, you equip yourself with the tools needed to excel in the fast-evolving world of artificial intelligence. Whether you are a beginner looking to get your feet wet or a seasoned professional aiming to update your skills, these hands-on learning experiences are invaluable resources that propel you toward your goals.

7.4 Subscribing to Newsletters and Following AI Thought Leaders

In the fast-evolving field of artificial intelligence, staying updated with the latest trends, breakthroughs, and insights is crucial. Subscribing to well-curated newsletters and following respected thought leaders in AI can provide a steady stream of valuable information, helping you keep pace with developments, deepen your understanding, and enhance your professional capabilities. When selecting quality sources for AI newsletters, look for well-researched, timely, and diverse content. Publications like 'The Algorithm' by MIT Technology Review, 'Import AI' by Jack Clark, and 'The Rundown AI' provide insightful analyses and cover various topics, from technical advancements to ethical discussions and the latest news. These newsletters should ideally blend theoretical knowledge with practical insights, offering you a comprehensive view of the AI landscape.

Identifying influential thought leaders in the AI community involves looking for individuals who have expertise and actively contribute to the field through research, innovation, and education. Figures like Andrew Ng, founder of Coursera and a pioneer in machine learning, and Fei-Fei Li, a leading AI researcher and advocate for diversity in technology, are excellent examples. Following these leaders on platforms like Twitter or LinkedIn allows you to gain insights from their research, projects, and commentary on industry trends. Engaging with their shared content can significantly enhance your understanding and inspire your work in AI.

Keeping abreast of industry trends through these newsletters and thought leaders helps you understand the trajectory of AI technologies and their broader implications for various sectors. This knowledge is not just academically interesting—it's practically essential. In professional settings, the insights gained from these sources can inform decision-making processes and strategic planning. For example, understanding the latest advancements in natural language processing could lead you to implement AI-driven solutions like

ChatGPT more effectively within your business operations, enhancing efficiency and customer satisfaction.

Moreover, embracing a diversity of perspectives in AI is vital. Artificial intelligence is technical and profoundly impacts societal norms and ethical standards. By following a diverse range of voices, including those from different cultural, gender, and academic backgrounds, you gain a more holistic view of the challenges and opportunities within AI. This diversity enriches your understanding and supports a more comprehensive approach to implementing AI solutions, considering various ethical dimensions and cultural implications that could affect the deployment and acceptance of AI technologies.

By subscribing to a selection of meticulously chosen newsletters and following esteemed AI thought leaders, you arm yourself with the knowledge and insights necessary to navigate the complex world of artificial intelligence. This ongoing educational process enhances your professional growth and equips you with the tools to contribute thoughtfully to discussions and innovations in the AI community. As AI continues to reshape our world, staying informed and engaged with leading sources and experts is invaluable to your growth and participation in this dynamic field.

7.5 Implementing Regular ChatGPT Training Sessions

Establishing a regular training schedule for ChatGPT is akin to setting up a fitness regimen for your mind dedicated to enhancing your AI skills. The key is consistency and progression. Begin by carving out specific time devoted to working with ChatGPT in your week. This could be as little as an hour every other day or perhaps a more intensive two-hour session once a week, depending on your current schedule and commitments. The importance lies not in the quantity but in the quality and regularity of these sessions. Stick to these times as you would a class or a business meeting, underscoring the importance of this commitment to yourself.

Having clear learning objectives in each session can significantly enhance your productivity and focus. Start by identifying what you wish to achieve at the end of each training session. For beginners, objectives might include understanding basic ChatGPT functionalities, such as learning how to set up the AI or initiate basic interactions. More advanced users might focus on exploring specific features, like fine-tuning the model for particular tasks or delving into more complex prompt engineering techniques. Setting these targets before each session guides your activities and provides a clear measure of success at the end of your training period.

Incorporating real-world scenarios into your ChatGPT training sessions can dramatically enhance your understanding and practical skills. For instance, if you are in marketing, you could use ChatGPT to craft compelling content or generate creative taglines for products. If you're in customer service, simulate various customer interactions to understand better how ChatGPT can handle inquiries, complaints, or feedback. These scenarios make your sessions more engaging and ensure that the skills you are developing are directly applicable to your real-life professional challenges. This practical application cements your learning and empowers you to see the potential impacts of AI in your everyday work, making the training sessions both educational and rewarding.

Tracking your progress is crucial in maintaining motivation and measuring the effectiveness of your training sessions. One effective method is to maintain a learning journal where you document your objectives, the processes, and the outcomes of each session. Reflecting on what was learned, what challenges emerged, and how they were addressed can provide valuable insights into your learning journey and highlight areas that need more focus or adjustment. Additionally, leveraging digital tools like online quizzes or AI skill assessments can provide quantitative measures of your progress. These tools often offer feedback on areas of strength and improvement, allowing for targeted learning in subsequent sessions. Regularly reviewing your progress ensures that your training remains aligned with your learning goals, adjusting your strategies as needed to optimize learning outcomes.

Through these structured training sessions, you enhance your ability to use ChatGPT effectively and deepen your overall understanding of AI technologies. This ongoing commitment to learning and improvement is essential in keeping pace with the rapid developments in AI, ensuring that you remain proficient and competitive in leveraging AI tools like ChatGPT. Whether you are advancing in your career or simply satisfying your curiosity about AI, these regular training sessions provide a solid foundation for growth and mastery in the ever-evolving landscape of artificial intelligence.

7.6 Innovating with ChatGPT: Experimenting with New Uses

In the ever-evolving landscape of artificial intelligence, the ability to think outside the box and explore uncharted territories with tools like ChatGPT can set you apart from the rest. This section is dedicated to inspiring you to think creatively about how you can employ ChatGPT in ways that perhaps haven't been discussed in previous chapters. Imagine ChatGPT not just as a tool for answering queries or automating tasks but as a canvas for creativity. Have you considered, for example, using ChatGPT to create unique learning experiences for students in remote areas or perhaps to develop interactive narratives for online gaming? The potential applications are as varied as they are exciting. This exploration begins with a mindset open to experimentation and a willingness to try new ideas, no matter how unconventional they may seem.

Documenting your experiments with ChatGPT is crucial in understanding what works and what doesn't. It's similar to keeping a lab notebook in scientific research. Every detail of your experiments, including your prompt designs, the responses from ChatGPT, and any modifications you make, should be meticulously recorded. This practice allows you to track your progress and helps pinpoint the exact factors that lead to successful outcomes or unexpected failures. For instance, if you're using ChatGPT to help compose music, documenting the prompts that led to the most harmonious compositions can provide insights into patterns or keywords that resonate well with the AI's algorithms. Over time, this detailed record becomes a valuable resource for refining your techniques and can significantly speed up your learning curve.

Sharing your findings with the broader AI community is another step that can amplify your impact and contribute to the collective knowledge base. Platforms like GitHub or even social media groups dedicated to AI innovation are excellent venues for disseminating your work. By publishing your experiments and outcomes, you invite feedback that can provide new perspectives and ideas you might not have considered. This collaborative approach enhances your projects and encourages a culture of openness and innovation in the AI community. Feedback from diverse sources can improve your methods and even spark new experiments, pushing the boundaries of what you can achieve with ChatGPT.

Iterative testing and refinement form the backbone of successful innovation with AI. This process involves continuously tweaking your experiments based on the results and feedback you gather. Each iteration should aim to improve upon the previous version, whether it's adjusting the complexity of the prompts, the data used for training, or the parameters of the AI model. For example, suppose you are experimenting with using ChatGPT for customer service. In that case, you might start with basic queries and then gradually introduce more complex scenarios based on how well the AI performs in each round of testing. This systematic approach ensures that your application of ChatGPT becomes more refined and effective with each cycle. Remember, innovation is not a one-time event but a continuous exploration, testing, and improvement journey. Each iteration brings you closer to discovering novel and impactful ways to utilize ChatGPT, broadening the horizons of what you can accomplish with this powerful tool.

7.7 Reviewing and Reflecting: Best Practices for ChatGPT Usage

Regular review sessions for ChatGPT usage are crucial to maintaining and enhancing its effectiveness in the dynamic and ever-evolving landscape of artificial intelligence. These sessions are routine health checks that help ensure your AI tool remains in top condition and aligned with your goals and needs. By periodically evaluating how ChatGPT is utilized within your operations—be it in business, education, or personal projects—you can identify strengths to build upon and areas that may require improvement. For instance, you might discover that while ChatGPT excels in handling customer service inquiries, it might not be as efficient in managing more complex technical support questions. These insights allow you to adjust your usage strategies or provide additional training to the model on specific topics. Implementing these review sessions monthly or quarterly can keep your AI initiatives well-aligned with your operational goals and responsive to the needs of your users.

Compiling and adhering to a set of best practice guidelines for ChatGPT usage is another cornerstone in optimizing your interactions with this AI tool. Expert advice, user feedback, and your experiences with the AI should shape these guidelines. For example, one best practice might involve setting clear parameters for the types of tasks ChatGPT handles based on its demonstrated strengths and limitations. Another might dictate how to effectively integrate human oversight in ChatGPT's processes to ensure the accuracy and appropriateness of its outputs. Drawing on community feedback is particularly valuable; users often provide insights into unique or unexpected ways the tool can be optimized that you might not have considered. Regularly updating these best practices as you gather more data and insights from ongoing usage and as new updates and features of ChatGPT are released ensures that your approach remains cutting-edge and relevant.

Fostering a culture of learning from past errors or inefficiencies in ChatGPT interactions also plays an essential role in enhancing future performance. This involves more than merely correcting mistakes—it's about understanding why errors occurred and how similar issues can be prevented going forward. For instance, if a review session reveals that ChatGPT frequently misinterprets the intent behind user queries, leading to incorrect or irrelevant responses, you might look into improving the training data or tweaking the model's context sensitivity. Encouraging your team to openly discuss and analyze these missteps, perhaps through regular brainstorming sessions or debriefs, can turn these learning experiences into opportunities for growth and innovation. This proactive approach improves the tool's efficiency and empowers your team by valuing their insights and encouraging a collaborative effort toward continuous improvement.

Lastly, staying ethically aligned when using ChatGPT cannot be overstated. As AI continues to integrate deeper into various aspects of life and business, ensuring its application adheres to ethical guidelines is paramount. This means regularly revisiting and possibly revising the ethical frameworks you have in place to govern ChatGPT's deployment in your operations. These ethical considerations are fundamental, whether it's about ensuring data privacy, avoiding bias in AI-generated content, or maintaining transparency about AI's role and limitations in your services. They protect you and your users and build trust and credibility in your AI applications. Integrating ethics into your regular review sessions, perhaps by including an ethics checklist or audit, ensures that these considerations remain at the forefront of your AI strategy. In doing so, you underscore your commitment to responsible AI usage that respects user rights and societal norms, reinforcing a positive and sustainable integration of AI technologies like ChatGPT into your operational ecosystem.

7.8 Anticipating Future Trends in AI and ChatGPT

Staying ahead in the dynamic field of artificial intelligence requires a proactive approach, where monitoring the latest technological advances is not just beneficial—it's essential. Keeping abreast of developments that could influence the capabilities and applications of AI, like ChatGPT, involves more than casual observation; it necessitates active engagement with various informational resources. Technology blogs, AI research publications, and industry news platforms are invaluable. These sources often provide early insights into emerging technologies, experimental AI applications, and potential updates to existing systems like ChatGPT. By regularly engaging with these resources, you can better understand where AI technology is headed and how it's evolving, ensuring that you're always prepared for the next big thing.

Predictive analysis plays a critical role in understanding future trends in AI. This involves analyzing current data and developments to forecast future directions in AI technology. For instance, by examining the increasing integration of AI in healthcare, one can predict a continued focus on developing AI systems that support diagnostic processes and provide personalized treatment recommendations. Similarly, the rise in the use of AI for enhancing customer service experiences suggests that future developments might focus on improving the emotional intelligence of AI systems like ChatGPT, enabling them to respond more sensitively to human emotions. Engaging in predictive analysis allows you to anticipate these trends and prepare accordingly, whether through acquiring new skills, adapting business strategies, or innovating new applications for AI.

Preparing for changes in the AI landscape is another crucial strategy for staying relevant and effective in your AI endeavors. This preparation involves learning new skills and adapting existing ones to align with how AI technologies evolve. For example, as AI systems become more autonomous, understanding the underlying principles of AI ethics and governance becomes as important as technical skills. Additionally, as AI tools like ChatGPT become more sophisticated and capable of handling complex tasks, developing AI system integration and management skills may become necessary. By continuously updating your skill set and staying flexible in your approach to AI, you can ensure that your capabilities remain in demand, regardless of how AI technologies evolve.

Global events and shifts in policy also significantly impact the evolution of AI. For instance, regulatory changes concerning data privacy can influence how AI systems are designed and used, particularly in regions with strict data protection laws. Similarly, global events such as pandemics or economic downturns can shift the focus of AI applications from commercial to humanitarian or crisis management roles. Being aware of these global dynamics and understanding their implications for AI can help you better anticipate and adapt to changes in the field. This might involve developing AI solutions that are compliant with new regulations or redirecting AI research and development efforts to address pressing global challenges.

By actively monitoring technological advances, engaging in predictive analysis, preparing for change, and understanding the influence of global events, you can confidently navigate the ever-changing landscape of AI. This proactive stance enhances your ability to use AI effectively and positions you as a forward-thinking participant in artificial intelligence, ready to adapt and thrive no matter what the future holds.

7.9 Becoming a ChatGPT Power User: Tips and Secrets

Elevating your skills with ChatGPT involves more than just routine use; it requires delving into advanced configurations, leveraging APIs, discovering hidden features, and engaging actively within the AI community. These elements are about enhancing your technical proficiency and enriching your overall experience and capabilities with this powerful AI tool.

Let's start with advanced configuration tips that can significantly enhance the efficiency and effectiveness of your ChatGPT interactions. One effective strategy is to customize the model's responses based on the context of the conversation. This can be achieved by adjusting the temperature setting in the API interface, which controls the randomness of the responses—a lower temperature results in more predictable and conservative responses suitable for formal or business communications. Conversely, a higher temperature setting allows for more creative and expansive responses, which is ideal for brainstorming sessions or when seeking innovative ideas. Additionally, tweaking the max tokens setting can help manage the length of each response, ensuring that the outputs are neither too terse nor overly verbose, perfectly matching the needs of your specific application.

The power of ChatGPT isn't just confined to what's built into it; by leveraging APIs, you can extend its capabilities and integrate it more deeply into your personal or professional projects. APIs allow ChatGPT to interact with other software and databases, enabling a seamless flow of information across platforms. For instance, integrating ChatGPT with a CRM system can automate and personalize customer interactions based on historical data, significantly enhancing customer engagement and satisfaction. Similarly, coupling ChatGPT with analytical tools can provide real-time insights from raw data, aiding in quicker decision-making. The key to effective API integration lies in understanding the specific endpoints that ChatGPT can interact with and ensuring secure and efficient data transfer between systems.

Exploring the lesser-known features or 'Easter eggs' within ChatGPT can also add fun and discovery to your interactions. For example, ChatGPT can compose poems or generate creative story ideas based on a few input keywords. Often hidden or undocumented, these features can be uncovered through experimentation or tips shared by the community. They provide entertainment and inspire creativity in how you use ChatGPT for more mundane tasks, such as drafting emails or creating content.

Lastly, becoming an active contributor to the AI community can significantly enhance your status as a power user. This involves sharing your custom scripts, innovative prompt designs, or unique use cases. Platforms like GitHub or AI-focused forums are excellent venues for these contributions. Sharing your work encourages feedback, leading to improvements and new ideas while helping others face similar challenges. Contributing to the community bolsters your knowledge and establishes your reputation as a thought leader in the AI space.

By mastering these advanced techniques and engaging with the broader AI community, you elevate your prowess with ChatGPT beyond typical usage, unlocking new potentials and opportunities. This proactive approach enhances your immediate interactions with ChatGPT and prepares you for future advancements in AI technologies. As we close this chapter on keeping up with ChatGPT developments, we reflect on transforming from a novice to an advanced user. The tips and secrets shared here are your tools for deepening your understanding and enhancing your skills.

7.10 Interactive Task

To summarize this chapter and solidify your understanding, create a personalized plan to stay updated with AI and ChatGPT advancements. Identify an essential resource from the chapter that resonates with your interests or professional goals. This could include subscribing to a specific newsletter, joining a particular forum or social media group, or attending a webinar or workshop. Outline how you will engage with these resources regularly, whether daily, weekly, or monthly. Additionally, set a goal to experiment with at least one new use case for ChatGPT each month, using the insights and tips provided in this book. Reflect on your progress and experiences in a dedicated journal, noting any new skills acquired or challenges faced. This ongoing commitment will ensure you remain at the forefront of AI developments, maximize the potential of ChatGPT in your personal and professional life, and provide interesting topics for AI conversations around the water cooler.

Keeping the Knowledge Alive

Now you have everything you need to master ChatGPT and unlock its full potential, it's time to pass on your newfound knowledge and show other readers where they can find the same help.

By leaving your honest opinion of this book on Amazon, you'll show other beginners where they can find the information they're looking for and pass on your passion for ChatGPT.

I appreciate your help. The excitement and utility of ChatGPT are kept alive when we pass on our knowledge – and you're helping us to do just that.

Simply click or scan the QR code below to leave your review on Amazon:

Conclusion

As we reach the end of this enriching journey together, reflecting on the path we've traversed is remarkable. From the initial steps of understanding what AI and ChatGPT are to delving into their intricate workings and exploring how they can be seamlessly integrated into our daily lives, this book has been a voyage of simplifying AI, especially ChatGPT, transforming what may once have appeared as a complex subject into accessible and actionable knowledge.

For beginners, the realm of AI can seem daunting; however, this guide was meticulously crafted with you in mind, aiming to empower you with the confidence to navigate this technological landscape. By breaking down complex concepts and providing step-by-step applications, I hope you feel equipped to utilize ChatGPT effectively, enhancing your personal and professional endeavors.

Throughout our discussions, we've strongly emphasized the importance of ethical AI use. Engaging responsibly with AI technologies like ChatGPT is crucial, ensuring their application aligns with ethical standards and contributes positively to society. This understanding is foundational and essential for fostering a future where technology enhances human capabilities without compromising moral values.

The skills you've acquired—crafting effective prompts, integrating AI into everyday tasks, and keeping abreast of ongoing advancements—are more than just technical competencies; they empower you to innovate and create. Whether optimizing your workflow, enhancing your learning, or exploring new creative avenues, these skills are your stepping stones to success in an AI-driven world.

However, the journey doesn't end here. I encourage you to continue learning and experimenting with ChatGPT. AI is ever-evolving, and staying engaged through continuous education and hands-on practice is vital to maintaining relevance and expertise. Join AI and ChatGPT communities, where you can share knowledge, gain insights, and network with peers who are equally passionate about this exciting technology.

As you apply the insights and skills from this book, challenge yourself to think outside the box. Innovate in your professional field, streamline processes, enhance communications, or even solve complex problems that you encounter. The possibilities are limitless when you leverage AI responsibly and creatively.

Looking ahead, the future of AI and technologies like ChatGPT holds incredible potential. With advancements in machine learning and natural language processing, we are on the cusp of witnessing even more transformative changes that can bring about significant societal benefits. It is a future ripe with opportunities, and by using AI responsibly, we can all contribute to a world where technology and humanity progress hand in hand.

I invite you to share your experiences, challenges, and successes as you venture further into AI. Your feedback is invaluable to me and others in the community who can learn from your journey. Engage through social media, online forums, or the dedicated book website. Your insights will help shape the ongoing dialogue about AI and its role in our lives.

Thank you for joining me on this educational adventure. Your commitment to understanding and leveraging AI is a personal achievement and a step forward for us all in navigating this dynamic digital age. Let's continue to explore, innovate, and lead in this exciting field together.

References

Author unknown. (n.d.). What is AI technology? *Dummies.com*. Retrieved from https://www.dummies.com/article/technology/information-technology/ai/general-ai/4-ways-define-artificial-intelligence-ai-254174/

OpenAI. (n.d.). Introducing ChatGPT. *OpenAI*. Retrieved from https://openai.com/index/chatgpt/

CallMiner. (n.d.). 25 examples of NLP & machine learning in everyday life. Retrieved from https://callminer.com/blog/25-examples-of-nlp-and-machine-learning-in-everyday-life

Walsh, C. (2020, October 20). Ethical concerns mount as AI takes bigger decision-making role. *Harvard Gazette*. Retrieved from https://news.harvard.edu/gazette/story/2020/10/ethical-concerns-mount-as-ai-takes-bigger-decision-making-role/

GPTBot.io. (n.d.). Mastering ChatGPT: How to craft effective prompts (full guide). Retrieved from https://gptbot.io/master-chatgpt-prompting-techniques-guide/

Marr, B. (2023, May 30). 10 amazing real-world examples of how companies are using ChatGPT in 2023. *Forbes*. Retrieved from https://www.forbes.com/sites/bernardmarr/2023/05/30/10-amazing-real-world-examples-of-how-companies-are-using-chatgpt-in-2023/

McKinsey & Company. (n.d.). Tackling bias in artificial intelligence (and in humans). Retrieved from https://www.mckinsey.com/featured-insights/artificial-intelligence/tackling-bias-in-artificial-intelligence-and-in-humans

Aphelion Group. (n.d.). Unleashing innovation: The power of AI in creative problem solving. *Medium*. Retrieved from https://medium.com/@AphelionGroup/unleashing-innovation-the-power-of-ai-in-creative-problem-solving-9a2e27af27de

TechTarget. (n.d.). 10 realistic business use cases for ChatGPT. Retrieved from https://www.techtarget.com/searchenterpriseai/tip/Realistic-business-use-cases-for-ChatGPT

Sitecore. (n.d.). How to use AI in email marketing: A practical guide. Retrieved from https://www.sitecore.com/knowledge-center/digital-marketing-resources/how-to-use-ai-in-email-marketing-a-practical-guide

SEMrush. (n.d.). AI in content creation: Best practices & top tools for 2024. Retrieved from https://www.semrush.com/goodcontent/content-marketing-blog/ai-content-marketing/#:~
=AI%20content%20creation%20is%20the,useful%20audience%20insights%2C%20and%20more

Schaefer, M. (2023, February 15). How to integrate ChatGPT with your CRM software. *Webbiquity*. Retrieved from https://webbiquity.com/ai-in-marketing/how-to-integrate-chatgpt-with-your-crm-software/

Abdolrauf, A. (2023, March 22). 20 powerful ChatGPT productivity tools, apps, & extensions. Retrieved from https://abdolrauf.com/chatgpt-productivity-tools/

Simplilearn. (n.d.). Advantages and disadvantages of artificial intelligence [AI]. Retrieved from https://www.simplilearn.com/advantages-and-disadvantages-of-artificial-intelligence-article#:~
=While%20artificial%20intelligence%20has%20many,the%20advancement%20of%20autonomous%20vehicles

CNET. (2024, January 10). How AI could shake up your future fitness routine. Retrieved from https://www.cnet.com/health/fitness/ai-in-fitness-could-your-future-workout-buddy-be-a-robot/

Northern Illinois University. (n.d.). ChatGPT and education. Retrieved from https://www.niu.edu/citl/resources/guides/chatgpt-and-education.shtml

Wired. (2023, April 1). ChatGPT has a big privacy problem. Retrieved from https://www.wired.com/story/italy-ban-chatgpt-privacy-gdpr/

World Economic Forum. (2024, June 1). How AI can also be used to combat online disinformation. Retrieved from https://www.weforum.org/agenda/2024/06/ai-combat-online-misinformation-disinformation/

UNESCO. (n.d.). Ethics of artificial intelligence. Retrieved from https://www.unesco.org/en/artificial-intelligence/recommendation-ethics

OpenAI. (2023). ChatGPT — Release notes. Retrieved from https://help.openai.com/en/articles/6825453-chatgpt-release-notes

CX Today. (2023, June 12). OpenAI allows businesses to customize ChatGPT for specific use cases. Retrieved from https://www.cxtoday.com/contact-centre/openai-allows-businesses-to-customize-chatgpt-for-specific-use-cases/

Akkio. (2023, August 15). ChatGPT advanced data analysis: Guide & use cases. Retrieved from https://www.akkio.com/post/chatgpt-advanced-data-analysis

MyGreatLearning. (2024). Free ChatGPT course with certificate. Retrieved from https://www.mygreatlearning.com/academy/learn-for-free/courses/chatgpt-for-beginners

McKinsey & Company. (2023). The state of AI in 2023: Generative AI's breakout year. Retrieved from https://www.mckinsey.com/capabilities/quantumblack/our-insights/the-state-of-ai-in-2023-generative-ais-breakout-year

University of Texas at San Antonio. (2024). Is an artificial intelligence certification valuable for my career? Retrieved from https://www.utsa.edu/pace/news/artificial-intelligence-certification-valuable-for-my-career.html

The Hive Index. (2024). 17 best artificial intelligence communities to join in 2024. Retrieved from https://thehiveindex.com/topics/artificial-intelligence/

Forbes Advisor. (2024). How businesses are using artificial intelligence in 2024. Retrieved from https://www.forbes.com/advisor/business/software/ai-in-business/

AI-Proof Your Career

The Essential Survival Guide to Thriving in the Artificial Intelligence Revolution

Ryan Harper

RIVANNA HEIGHTS
— MEDIA —

Rivanna Heights Media

Claim Your Free AI-Powered Career Action Plan!

As a special thank you for picking up this book, I'm offering you a powerful bonus: the **AI-Powered Career Action Plan**—a personalized tool designed to transform how you approach your career in today's AI-driven world.

Inside this free plan, you'll discover:

- **Tailored Skills Assessment**: Pinpoint the most relevant skills for your career growth and where you can improve.
- **Actionable Roadmap**: Get clear, practical steps to enhance your productivity and career trajectory using AI-driven insights.
- **Exclusive Career-Boosting Prompts**: Leverage the power of AI to develop a strategic, forward-thinking plan for your success.

Ready to take action?
Get your **AI-Powered Career Action Plan** by clicking or scanning the QR code below!

Introduction: The New Rules

LAST WEEK, A JUNIOR copywriter outperformed her entire marketing department using ChatGPT. A radiologist diagnosed twice as many patients by partnering with an AI system. A small business owner fired his accounting firm after automating his entire billing process.

None of these people lost their jobs to AI. Instead, they changed the game. The copywriter now leads her agency's AI strategy. The radiologist expanded his practice. The business owner hired three new employees with the money he saved.

I witnessed this transformation firsthand as a Director of Data and Analytics who started in traditional operations roles in financial services. When I saw these changes coming, I didn't just observe—I immersed myself in both worlds. While building my expertise in Python, SQL, and cloud architecture, I led our firm through two parallel transformations: modernizing our analytics from spreadsheets to automated business intelligence solutions while strategically integrating AI tools across operations—fundamentally changing how we managed hundreds of millions in investments.

But here's what might surprise you: The technical skills weren't what mattered most. Even as I earned certifications and completed post-graduate data science studies at the University of Texas at Austin, I noticed something fascinating. The professionals who were thriving weren't necessarily the most technically skilled—they were the ones who understood how to position themselves in this new landscape.

That's why I wrote this book. Not because I'm a Silicon Valley evangelist or a career coach jumping on the AI bandwagon, but because I've seen too many talented people either panic unnecessarily or ignore the changes around them. Neither works.

Think of AI as electricity in 1900. The businesses that simply used it to replace candles missed the point. The ones that reimagined what was possible changed the world. Today, we're at a similar inflection point.

This book is divided into three critical sections that will reshape how you think about your career. First, we'll dive deep into AI's Impact on Careers, moving past the hype to understand the real changes happening right now. Next, we'll tackle Embracing the AI-Driven Workforce, exploring everything from ethical challenges to global opportunities. Finally, we'll examine what it means to truly excel in an AI World, from remote work to personal branding.

You won't find coding tutorials here. You won't get a checklist of AI tools to master. Instead, you'll learn something far more valuable: how to think strategically about AI's impact on your industry, how to identify the highest-leverage skills and opportunities in your field, and how to position yourself where the puck is going, not where it's been.

The professionals who understand these principles aren't just keeping their jobs—they're redefining them. They're creating new roles, new business models, and new ways of delivering value that simply weren't possible before.

Having explored some of these themes in my previous book, "The Complete Beginners Guide to ChatGPT," I'm now focused on helping you develop a practical, balanced approach to career advancement in an AI-enhanced world. This isn't about competing with AI. It's about using it as a catalyst for the next phase of your career.

Ready to learn the new rules?

AI's Impact on Careers

Rivanna Heights Media

Welcome to the AI Career Revolution

Welcome to the AI revolution, where technology is reshaping everything we do—from how we communicate to how we work. But let me be clear: AI is either going to be the best career opportunity you've ever had, or it's going to turn your industry upside down, leaving you scrambling to keep up. You can choose to ride this wave, or you can let it crash over you. If you're sitting there thinking, "AI won't affect my job," consider this your wake-up call.

Let's step back and get a clear picture of what's going on. AI isn't a distant or abstract concept anymore—it's embedded into nearly every industry, impacting how we do business every day. Whether you're in education, marketing, law, or finance, AI is changing how the game is played. The sooner you understand the implications for your career, the better positioned you'll be. So let's dive in and make sure you're not just surviving in this new era—you're thriving.

The AI Tsunami

AI isn't just a buzzword that gets thrown around at tech conferences—it's an ever-present reality. Whether you realize it or not, you're likely engaging with AI in your everyday life. It's managing your inbox, giving you personalized recommendations on Netflix, and optimizing your commute and the notifications on your smartphone. AI has seamlessly woven itself into our daily routines, and now, it's transforming the workplace in ways that go far beyond just convenience.

Think about how fast this shift has happened. A few decades ago, the idea of AI felt like science fiction—flying cars, robots doing all the heavy lifting, and computers holding intelligent conversations. While we may not have personal robot assistants just yet, AI has come a long way, moving from the realm of fantasy into an essential part of corporate strategy. From healthcare to finance to retail, AI is no longer a novelty; it's a necessity.

And AI isn't just automating tasks anymore. It's increasingly being used for decision-making, forecasting, and even customer service. Projections suggest that by 2030, AI could add a staggering $15.7 trillion to the global economy.[1] That kind of disruption means it's not a question of if your career will be impacted, but how soon.

So, what does this mean for you? Think of AI as a massive tidal wave that's moving relentlessly toward the shore. It's powerful, and it's coming fast. You can either learn how to ride it, or you can get swept away by it. I'm here to make sure you're ready to surf the wave, not drown under it.

Debunking the AI Myth Machine

There's a lot of noise out there about AI, and much of it stokes fear. You've probably heard the same things I have: "AI is going to replace every job," or "Only people with hardcore tech skills will survive in the AI economy." Let's take a deep breath and dismantle some of these myths.

First off, AI isn't here to take every single job. Yes, it's true that automation and AI will change how some jobs look—and in some cases, eliminate certain roles altogether. But history shows us that technological advances create new opportunities as much as they disrupt old ones. Think back to the rise of the internet. Did it completely eliminate industries? Hardly. It transformed them and introduced new ways of doing business. AI is going to do the same, ushering in new types of jobs and reshaping the old ones.

---

1. Talent [R]evolution. (n.d.). *Data Maturity*. Outvise. Retrieved from https://blog.outvise.com/tag/data-maturity/

One of the most common misconceptions is that AI can think and operate like a human. Here's the reality: AI can crunch numbers, recognize patterns, and analyze data, but it lacks the fundamental human traits of creativity, emotional intelligence, and critical thinking. It's not going to come up with the next big innovative idea or navigate complex relationships. AI is a tool, and like any tool, it requires human insight and ingenuity to be effective.

AI can streamline routine tasks, saving time and energy that can be better spent elsewhere. It can analyze massive amounts of data in seconds, providing insights that would take humans much longer to uncover.[2] But even with all this power, AI can't replicate the things that make you uniquely valuable—your creativity, empathy, and leadership. And those are exactly the qualities that are going to keep you relevant as AI continues to advance.

So, if you've been concerned about AI taking over your job, relax. The real risk isn't the technology itself—it's being unprepared for the shift it's bringing. The future of work will require new skills and a willingness to adapt, but don't worry—you won't need to become a coding expert to stay relevant.

Your AI Career Survival Kit

Now that we've busted some myths and clarified what AI can and can't do, let's get into the practical side of things. How do you make sure your career is AI-proof in this fast-changing landscape? You don't need a degree in computer science to navigate the AI era. What you do need is to focus on the skills that AI can't easily replace and use AI as a tool for the skills where it can.

This is where your AI career survival kit comes in. These are the core principles that will guide you as you navigate this AI-driven world. Master these, and you'll stay ahead of the curve:

1. **Embrace Lifelong Learning:** The rapid pace of AI development means you

---

2. Sliksafe. (n.d.). *AI Answers: Unveiling the Potential of Artificial Intelligence*. Retrieved from https://www.sliksafe.com/tools/ai-answers

can't afford to stand still. Continuously learning new skills is no longer optional—it's essential. Whether that's staying up to speed with new AI tools or honing your problem-solving abilities, the key is to remain adaptable. Those who thrive in the AI age are the ones who are constantly evolving.

2. **Focus on Human Skills:** AI might be able to automate tasks, but it can't replicate human-centered skills. These are your superpowers. You need to be the one who can think creatively, lead teams, and build relationships. These are the skills that set you apart and make you irreplaceable.

3. **Learn How to Work with AI:** You don't need to be a programmer, but you do need to know how AI can enhance your role. Whether that's automating repetitive tasks or analyzing complex data more efficiently, AI should be a tool that works for you, not against you.

4. **Stay Curious:** AI is constantly evolving, and industries are being reshaped every day. If you want to stay ahead, you need to stay curious. Keep asking questions about how AI is changing your field and look for opportunities to apply those insights. The more you understand the landscape, the better prepared you'll be to lead in it.

AI is already transforming how we work, and it's only going to keep advancing. But here's the upside: you don't need to fear it. By understanding AI's impact, avoiding common myths, and focusing on building the skills that set you apart, you'll be able to not just survive but thrive. In the coming chapters, we're going to break down the exact steps to help you build these skills—one step at a time—so you'll always be ahead of the AI wave. Let's get started, because the future is already here, and the opportunities are waiting.

AI 101 for Career Climbers

ALRIGHT, NOW THAT WE'VE established the AI wave is here and not going away, it's time to break down what AI actually is. I know, AI can sound like one big intimidating term wrapped in layers of tech jargon. **But let me make this clear:** you don't need to be a data scientist or an engineer to understand AI, and you definitely don't need to master coding to keep your career moving forward. What you do need is a solid understanding of the basics, how AI works, and how it can either help—or hurt—you in the workplace.

This chapter is your crash course in AI. We're cutting through the technical clutter and breaking it down into the essentials. Think of it as "AI for people who want to get ahead." By the end of this, you'll know enough to be dangerous—in the best way possible.

AI Unveiled: What You Actually Need to Know

Let's start with the basics. You've probably heard terms like AI, machine learning, and deep learning tossed around like they're interchangeable, but they're not. Understanding the difference between these concepts will help you make sense of how AI operates in your world—and more importantly, in your workplace.

AI (Artificial Intelligence): This is the big umbrella. AI refers to machines or software that can perform tasks that would typically require human intelligence, like decision-making, problem-solving, or learning from experience—things humans do naturally.[1] In your field, this could mean AI-powered systems assisting with decision-making or automating routine processes.

Machine Learning: A subset of AI. Machines are trained to learn from data and improve their performance over time without needing explicit instructions for every task.[2] For you, this means AI tools in your industry will learn and improve—automating tasks like data processing or sales forecasting as they get more data to work with.

Deep Learning: This is machine learning on steroids. Inspired by the human brain, deep learning uses neural networks to process vast amounts of data.[3] This is what powers advanced AI applications like voice recognition (Siri or Alexa), autonomous driving, and large language models (LLMs) like ChatGPT or Claude, which generate human-like text. In your workplace, tools that incorporate deep learning can assist with more complex functions, such as processing large-scale unstructured data or enhancing customer interactions.

So, AI, machine learning, and deep learning—they're all connected, but each plays a unique role in automating and enhancing different aspects of your job. Understanding this structure helps you see how these tools can streamline processes, improve efficiency, and add value to your role.

The Evolution of AI: From Chess Champions to Chat Companions

AI isn't some new fad. It's been evolving for decades. You might remember when IBM's

---

1. The BLife Movement. (n.d.). *Demystifying Artificial General Intelligence (AGI): A Guide for Beginners.* Retrieved from https://www.theblifemovement.com/demystifying-artificial-general-intelligence-agi-a-guide-for-beginners/

2. TechMni. (n.d.). *Which of the Following is Not True About Machine Learning?* Retrieved from https://techmni.com/which-of-the-following-is-not-true-about-machine-learning/

3. Cafeto Software. (n.d.). *A Beginner's Guide to Understanding AI.* Retrieved from https://cafetosoftware.com/blog/a-beginners-guide-to-understanding-ai/

Deep Blue beat world chess champion Garry Kasparov back in the '90s. That was AI in its adolescence, a stage where it was beginning to solve specific, complex problems. But AI didn't stop there. Fast forward to today, and AI is doing much more than playing chess. It's assisting doctors in diagnosing diseases, helping financial analysts predict stock market trends, and even driving cars.

So, what does this mean for you today? AI isn't just a chess player—it's a force that's helping professionals across industries streamline their workflow and enhance decision-making. The AI you interact with today is a lot more versatile. We're talking chatbots that can carry on full conversations, recommendation engines that know what you want to watch or buy before you do, and even AI tools that help automate parts of your job. What was once a novelty is now an integral part of daily life—and it's only getting smarter.

AI's Current Capabilities and Limitations in the Workplace

Now, let's bring this into the workplace. AI is already hard at work in various industries, but it's important to know what it can and can't do. AI can crunch numbers at speeds that make your head spin. It can predict consumer behavior, optimize workflows, and even assist in hiring by scanning resumes.

But—and this is a big but—AI still has limitations. It's great at processing data, but it's not great at interpreting nuance or dealing with ambiguity. This is where your ability to navigate gray areas and think critically comes in. Lean into complex decision-making where human judgment is required. AI can analyze patterns, but it can't innovate like a human can. So, lean into your ability to think creatively and innovate in your role—these are the areas where humans will always win. AI doesn't have creativity, empathy, or the ability to understand the broader context behind a decision. That's your edge. Focus on those key skills that are uniquely human: leadership, creativity, and emotional intelligence. These skills will keep you indispensable, even in an AI-driven world.

The Good, the Bad, and the Awkward: AI at Work

Now that we've got the basics covered, let's take a look at how AI is actually being used in the workplace—both the success stories and the failures. AI can be an incredible force for good, but when things go wrong, they can go *really* wrong. Here are some real-life examples to show you both sides of the coin.

Success Stories: When AI Supercharges Human Potential

Let's start with the good. In many cases, AI is revolutionizing how companies operate. For instance, consider AI-powered customer service chatbots. Companies like Amazon and Google have implemented AI to handle thousands of customer queries instantly, with minimal human intervention. This frees up human workers to handle more complex and personalized customer issues. *Takeaway:* If you work in customer service or sales, consider how AI can handle routine inquiries, freeing you up for more complex, relationship-driven tasks. In healthcare, AI tools are helping doctors make quicker, more accurate diagnoses by analyzing patient data in ways that were previously impossible.

The lesson? When AI works as a tool to support human effort, it can supercharge productivity and efficiency. It's about leveraging AI to handle the tasks that bog you down, so you can focus on the bigger picture.

Epic Fails: Lessons from AI Gone Wrong

But it's not all smooth sailing. AI has had its fair share of embarrassing failures. Take the case of Microsoft's AI chatbot, Tay, which was designed to interact with users on Twitter.[4] Within 24 hours, Tay was spouting offensive and inflammatory comments after learning from online interactions. Microsoft had to pull the plug, and it was a clear reminder that AI can learn the wrong things just as easily as the right ones. *Takeaway:* If you're considering implementing AI, especially for public-facing tasks, ensure there's oversight and a plan for monitoring AI behavior.

Another infamous fail was when Amazon attempted to use AI in hiring. Their AI system quickly developed a bias against female candidates because it was trained on resumes submitted over the previous decade—most of which were from men.[5] The system started favoring male candidates over equally qualified women, and Amazon had to scrap the whole project.

---

4. Cafeto Software. (n.d.). *A Beginner's Guide to Understanding AI.* Retrieved from https://cafetosoftware.com/blog/a-beginners-guide-to-understanding-ai/

5. Redress Compliance. (n.d.). *The Ethics of AI: Balancing Innovation with Responsibility*. Retrieved from https://redresscompliance.com/the-ethics-of-ai-balancing-innovation-with-responsibility/

Remember, AI is only as good as the data it's trained on, and if that data is flawed, the results will be too. That's why it's crucial to understand AI's limitations and always keep a human in the loop to catch potential problems. Just as important is having a basic grasp of data principles—knowing what makes data reliable, well-structured, and relevant. *Takeaway*: You don't need to be a data scientist, but recognizing the difference between good and bad data is a crucial skill for anyone aiming to secure and strengthen their career in an AI-driven workplace.

Ethical Dilemmas: Navigating the Murky Waters of AI Decision-Making

One of the most complex challenges AI brings is navigating ethical dilemmas. AI doesn't have morals or values—it follows the data it's given. But when that data comes with inherent biases, or when the stakes are high (like in healthcare or criminal justice), the consequences can be serious.

Companies need to be hyper-aware of how they're using AI and the potential ethical pitfalls. As AI becomes more integrated into decision-making, we need to keep a close eye on who controls the data and how these systems are designed to ensure they're fair, unbiased, and transparent. And that's where humans—people like you—play a critical role.

Actionable step: When using AI tools in your role, regularly review the outputs for bias or ethical concerns. Your responsibility isn't just about driving efficiency—it's about ensuring fairness, accountability, and keeping human oversight at the forefront of decisions. This will help you maintain ethical integrity while leveraging AI in your work.

Speaking AI: Essential Literacy for Every Professional

By now, you're probably thinking, "Okay, AI is clearly important, but what do I really need to know to talk about it confidently?" The good news is, you don't need to be an expert or dive into technical jargon to understand the basics of AI. These key concepts will give you the foundation to feel comfortable and prepared in any conversation about AI. No need to memorize these—they're here to help you get familiar with terms you'll encounter in the news or conversations. With just a bit of familiarity, you'll find that understanding and talking about AI becomes a lot easier.

Data: Data is the fuel for every AI system. The more data an AI has, the better it can perform. Good data leads to accurate results, while poor data causes errors. Understanding **data quality**—ensuring that data is accurate, complete, and relevant—is key to making AI effective and improving your position in the workforce.

Algorithms: Algorithms are like recipes that provide step-by-step instructions for a computer to complete a task.[6] They are the "brains" of AI, determining how data is processed to solve problems or make decisions. For you, simply understanding that AI relies on these complex instructions is enough to be better positioned in an AI-powered workforce.

AI Model: AI models are systems designed to process data and make decisions autonomously. They analyze input data and perform tasks without human intervention, based on their training. While it's useful to know that models like decision trees, neural networks, or random forests exist, you'll likely only need to dive deeper into these concepts if your role directly involves AI development or data science.

Neural Network: Neural networks are computational systems inspired by how human neurons work. These are critical in AI for recognizing patterns and processing complex data without explicit programming, especially in fields like medical diagnostics. For most professionals, simply understanding that neural networks power tools like Siri and Alexa will help you better appreciate how AI tools assist in making complex decisions.

Transformer: A transformer is a type of neural network that uses attention mechanisms to process sequences of data and understand the relationships between elements.[7] This architecture powers modern AI language models, such as ChatGPT. While the transformer architecture is essential to modern AI systems, most career paths won't need to dive deep into its technical details to succeed.

---

6. Redress Compliance. (n.d.). *The Ethics of AI: Balancing Innovation with Responsibility*. Retrieved from https://redresscompliance.com/the-ethics-of-ai-balancing-innovation-with-responsibility/

7. Two River Computer. (n.d.). *ChatGPT... What Is It and Does It Matter To Me?* Retrieved from https://www.tworivercomputer.com/chatgpt-what-is-it/

Large Language Models (LLMs): These specialized AI models handle and generate natural language. They use transformer networks to process human language, making them capable of carrying on conversations and producing text-based outputs. Mastering LLM-powered tools and honing your **prompt engineering** skills will give you a competitive edge in most workplaces.

Tokens: In LLMs, text is broken into smaller chunks called tokens, which are analyzed to understand the meaning and relationships between parts of the text. A model's ability to process many tokens at once affects its performance. While you may not work with tokens directly, understanding their role can help you get better results when using AI tools.

Natural Language Processing (NLP): NLP is a subset of AI focused on enabling machines to understand and interpret human language. Applications include systems like ChatGPT and speech recognition software like OpenAI's Whisper. Using NLP tools can help you leverage AI to improve communication, automate tasks, and analyze data, making you more efficient and adaptable in your career. Find ways to use these tools wherever you can to stay ahead.

Inference: Inference refers to the actual process of generating an output, like when ChatGPT responds to a query. This is the moment when an AI system applies its training to solve a problem or produce a result. You might hear inference mentioned, but that's about it—nothing you really need to worry about.

Diffusion Models: These models are used for generating images, audio, or video by gradually removing noise from data inputs. They can recreate clearer outputs from noisy or incomplete data, often applied in creative fields. You may or may not use diffusion models in your role, but knowing the proper name is more about sounding informed.

Automation: AI excels at automating repetitive tasks, such as scheduling, sorting data, or answering routine customer inquiries. By automating such tasks, AI frees up humans to focus on higher-level work. This is a cornerstone of AI, and you are definitely using it one way or another. Stay curious about how, and look for ways to take advantage of it.

Foundation Models: These are advanced, versatile AI models trained on massive datasets, enabling them to be applied across various tasks without needing specialized training. They serve as a foundation for numerous AI applications, including multimodal capabilities (handling text, images, and more). Just know they exist in case you hear the term, and move on.

Retrieval-Augmented Generation (RAG): RAG allows AI to pull in external information to enhance its responses, ensuring more accurate outputs by referencing sources beyond its training. This can significantly improve the accuracy and relevance of AI-generated content by incorporating real-time data. If you're involved in tasks like writing reports, conducting research, or handling customer inquiries, make sure the AI tools you use are equipped with RAG to maximize their effectiveness.

Frontier Models: These are next-generation AI models in development that could outperform existing ones. While they hold great promise, they also raise concerns about potential risks due to their advanced power and capabilities. For now, they're more of a topic to watch rather than something to directly engage with in most roles.

How to Talk About AI Without Sounding Like a Poser (or a Prophet)

When it comes to AI, there's a fine line between sounding informed and coming across like someone predicting a robot takeover. Keep your conversations grounded and practical. Focus on what you know—how AI tools are being used in your industry and the benefits they bring. Don't feel the need to exaggerate AI's potential or overhype its capabilities. *Takeaway*: Stick to practical applications in your field, and speak confidently about what AI is actually doing, not what it *might* do. That's how you'll come across as knowledgeable and credible.

Hands-On: Simple AI Tools You Can Start Using Today

Let's get practical. You don't have to be a programmer to start using AI tools in your daily work. Tools like Grammarly use AI to improve your writing, while Trello's Butler automates workflows. Google Analytics uses AI to help you track website data, and platforms like Zapier connect different apps to automate tasks. ChatGPT, Claude, and Gemini are versatile tools that can support various creative tasks and analytical processes. These are tools you can start using right now to make your job easier and more efficient. Take a moment to navigate to their web pages and find out more.

AI-Proof Action Plan

Laying the Groundwork with AI Basics

Now that you've got a clearer picture of what AI actually is, it's time to take action. Understanding the fundamentals of AI isn't just about keeping up with trends—it's about integrating these tools into your daily work to stay relevant. These initial steps might seem small, but mastering AI tools is your first move toward building a more resilient, future-proof career in the AI age. Each tool you add to your repertoire increases your value in a rapidly changing job market. The following steps are designed to help you take that first leap by identifying simple AI tools you can start using today, giving you a hands-on introduction that will make your job easier and boost your confidence as you step into the AI-driven workplace.

1. Find One AI Tool in Your Industry: Spend 15 minutes researching one AI tool that's already being used in your field (e.g., CRM systems in sales, diagnostic tools in healthcare, marketing automation tools). Watch a short video or read an article on how it works. Your goal is to understand its basic functionality and how it can be applied to your role.

2. Automate One Repetitive Task This Week: Identify one simple, repetitive task in your job (e.g., scheduling meetings, sorting emails, writing routine reports) and use an AI tool to automate it. Start with easy-to-use tools like Zapier or Google Assistant. Focus on tasks that don't require complex decisions. If you're completely new or stuck, try IFTTT (If This, Then That), a free and beginner-friendly tool that helps you automate tasks between apps like Gmail, Google Calendar, and others without needing any tech skills.

3. Join One AI-Related Newsletter: Subscribe to a newsletter or blog (like "Inside AI" or "The Algorithm") to stay updated on AI developments. This will help you stay curious and informed without feeling overwhelmed. Aim to read one update each week.

4. Set Up a Folder to Collect AI Resources: Create a folder (digital or physical) where you'll save AI articles, videos, and resources as you come across them. This will serve as your personal AI toolkit to refer back to as you continue to learn.

You've just taken some real, practical steps toward making AI work for you. These aren't just small tweaks—they're the start of you leveling up. When I first dug into AI, I had my doubts too, but every little step made me sharper, faster, and more in control. That's where you are now. Don't settle for staying on the sidelines—this is your chance to use AI to get ahead while others are still figuring it out. You've got the tools; now it's time to put them to work.

The Great Job Shuffle: Who's Safe, Who's Sorry?

Let's be real. AI is shaking things up in ways we haven't seen since the dawn of the internet. It's not just about cool gadgets or smart systems anymore—it's about your career and how you fit into this new landscape. Some jobs are at serious risk, while others are emerging stronger than ever. If you've been paying attention, you already know that sitting still isn't an option. This chapter is going to lay it out: who's safe, who's sorry, and what you can do about it.

I'm not here to scare you—I'm here to make sure you're ready. By the time you're done reading this chapter, you should know if your job is in the AI crosshairs and, more importantly, how to make sure you're one of the winners in this AI revolution.

AI's Hit List: Jobs on the Chopping Block

AI is coming for some jobs, and it's not subtle about it. Automation, machine learning, and smart algorithms (remember those?) are all designed to take over repetitive, process-driven tasks—exactly the kind of work that's been part of many industries for decades. So, who's at risk?

Let's talk about the industries that are going to feel the heat first. Manufacturing has already seen robots and automated systems take over assembly line jobs. AI is bringing even more advanced capabilities to these systems, meaning fewer humans will be needed to manage production. In customer service, chatbots and virtual assistants are handling queries that used to require full call centers. That's not to say there won't be customer service roles in the future, but they're going to shift toward managing complex issues that AI can't solve.

Administrative roles—we're talking about data entry, scheduling, and even some bookkeeping—are prime targets for automation. AI can handle large amounts of data faster, cheaper, and more accurately than a human. If your job is based on following a set of rules to complete tasks, AI is gunning for it.

So, how do you know if your job is at risk? Look for these warning signs:

- **Repetitive Tasks:** If your job involves repeating the same processes day in and day out—whether it's entering data, processing transactions, or answering common questions—it's vulnerable.
- **Low Need for Human Judgment:** AI excels at tasks where logic and data patterns can drive decision-making. If your job doesn't require much in the way of creativity, problem-solving, or interpersonal skills, you should start thinking about how you can adapt.
- **Heavy on the Admin:** Jobs that are administrative in nature are some of the easiest to automate. Think about how often you're scheduling meetings, filing reports, or managing data. If that's the bulk of your work, it's time to upskill.

What Can You Do?

If your job falls into one of these categories, start by identifying tasks that rely on human creativity or judgment. Focus on shifting your role towards areas that require strategic thinking or interpersonal skills—areas where AI can't easily replace you. This will make you more adaptable and irreplaceable as the landscape changes.

But don't panic—just because your job has some of these characteristics doesn't mean it's getting axed tomorrow. The timeline of change depends on the industry, and some sectors are slower to adopt new technologies. That said, if your job fits the description, you should start preparing for the shift sooner rather than later.

Rising from the Ashes: Emerging Roles in the AI Era

Here's the good news: while some jobs are disappearing, new roles are rising from the ashes. The AI revolution is creating a whole new landscape of careers, and the people who get ahead will be those who understand where the opportunities lie.

So, what are these new roles? Let's talk about a few of the hottest job titles in the AI era:

- **AI Trainers:** Think of this role as a bridge between human workers and AI systems. AI trainers help teach machines how to interpret data more effectively by providing examples of how humans would solve specific problems. It's part human insight, part data science, and a crucial role in ensuring AI systems perform accurately.
  Action Step: To prepare for roles like this, consider upskilling in data literacy or taking an introductory AI course.

- **Data Scientists:** Data has always been valuable, but now it's the fuel that drives AI. Data scientists are in high demand because they're the ones who understand how to collect, clean, and analyze the massive amounts of data that AI systems rely on. They turn raw data into actionable insights that can help businesses make smarter decisions.[1]
  Action Step: This is a more advanced role, but learning basic data analysis skills, such as Excel, Python, and SQL, will add value to any role. Look into free online resources to familiarize yourself with data science principles. **Pro Tip**: YouTube has many free tutorials about data analysis and Python.

- **AI Ethics Consultants:** As AI becomes more integrated into decision-making processes, ethical questions arise. Who's accountable when AI makes a mistake? How do we ensure that AI doesn't reinforce biases? AI ethics consultants help organizations navigate these tricky questions, ensuring that their AI use is re-

---

1. Hiport of Miami. (n.d.). *Why Should You Choose a Data Scientist?* Retrieved from http://www.hiportofmiami.com/education/why-should-you-choose-a-data-scientist.html

sponsible, fair, and transparent.
Action Step: Explore courses or literature on AI ethics and stay informed about how ethical standards are evolving in your industry. Become the go-to person at your organization for ethics and AI by knowing more than others.

- **Automation Specialists:** These are the folks who help companies integrate AI and automation into their processes. They don't necessarily need to be coders, but they need to understand how AI tools work and how to apply them to make operations more efficient.
Action Step: Research automation tools relevant to your field and start experimenting with simple automation tasks in your current role. You won't automate yourself out of work; instead, you'll create efficiencies that can't be ignored. And let's be honest—how good would "Automated processes resulting in a 17% increase in efficiency" look on your resume?

- **Human-AI Collaboration Managers:** This is a new role emerging in companies that recognize the need to strike a balance between human workers and AI systems. These managers focus on optimizing the interaction between people and AI, ensuring that both work together smoothly to achieve the best results.
Action Step: Start building your leadership and project management skills and get familiar with the AI tools being used in your industry. Mastering the balance between human and AI collaboration could set you up to lead teams that emerge as the workplace evolves.

- **Prompt Engineers:** As large language models (like ChatGPT and Claude) and other AI tools become more prevalent, there's a growing need for experts who know how to communicate with these systems effectively. Prompt engineers specialize in crafting precise inputs, or "prompts," that guide AI systems to deliver the best possible output. Whether it's generating creative content, answering complex queries, or solving specific problems, prompt engineers know how to speak the language of AI to get results. This role combines technical understanding with creativity and is rapidly becoming one of the most sought-after skills in the AI-driven job market.
Action Step: Begin experimenting with AI tools like ChatGPT to understand how prompts influence output and explore resources on optimizing prompts for better results. Focus on learning frameworks (like the PREPARED frame-

work) and iteration to stand out as a skilled prompter (more on this later). It may not be a flashy addition to your resume, but crushing prompts will make *everything* you do easier.

These emerging roles aren't just for tech gurus, and the skills behind them can be used in nearly any role. Many emerging career paths will require some of the same skills you already have—problem-solving, communication, and project management—just applied in new ways.

Future-Proofing Your Career Path: Navigating the New Normal

The disruption caused by AI isn't something that will pass you by; it's here to stay. While some roles are evolving or disappearing, the key to future-proofing your career is not just about reacting to changes—it's about leading the charge by carving out your unique value in this new world.

To stay ahead, you need a mindset shift, moving from survival mode to growth mode. This is about safeguarding your current job and adapting to new opportunities, positioning yourself as indispensable where you are, and being ready when opportunities emerge in an AI-enhanced future. Let's dive deeper into how you can ensure long-term career security and growth.

Think Like a Problem-Solver, Not Just a Doer

AI will handle the routine, but it's your human creativity that brings innovation. The future of work will rely on people who not only see problems but can also frame them in unique ways and generate innovative solutions. **Don't just ask, "What needs to be done?" but instead ask, "What hasn't been thought of yet?"** Shift your approach from task completion to problem identification, process improvement, and innovative solutions.

Embrace the Synergy of Human-AI Collaboration

The most successful professionals won't fear AI—they'll collaborate with it. Beyond using AI for routine tasks, think about how you can bring creativity, empathy, and human intuition into the equation. The next frontier in the workforce is mastering **collaborative intelligence**: understanding what AI can do and knowing how to complement it with your unique human judgment (more on this later).

Capitalize on Adaptability and Emotional Intelligence

AI will never lead with empathy, intuition, or emotional insight. Being adaptable and able to handle constant change will become one of the most valuable traits in the future workforce. Your ability to build meaningful relationships, lead with compassion, and navigate uncertainty will set you apart. As much as technology advances, human connection remains critical—AI doesn't understand personal growth, conflict resolution, or cultural nuances, but you do.

Anticipate and Respond to Shifting Roles

The roles that AI disrupts today are not necessarily going away—they're evolving. It's up to you to anticipate where those roles are going and how you can be part of their transformation. Future-proofing means actively shaping your own career, rather than waiting for others to decide its course. Think of your role as fluid, not fixed, and stay on top of industry trends and emerging skills. This is how you secure your relevance in a rapidly changing market.

By shifting from a survival mentality to one of continuous growth and adaptability, you won't just navigate the disruptions AI brings—you'll actively seize the opportunities it creates. Embracing change with an open mindset ensures that your career evolves alongside technology, positioning you to lead and innovate in the AI-driven future.

AI-Proof Action Plan

Securing Your Place in the AI-Driven Workplace

Now that you've got a clearer picture of where AI is making moves and where your job stands, it's time to get proactive. This isn't about guessing which way the wind blows—it's about taking control of your career before AI forces the change. The steps below will help you identify areas where AI might replace certain tasks and, more importantly, how you can strengthen the skills that make you irreplaceable. Let's make sure you're ahead of the curve, not scrambling to keep up.

1. Audit Your Job for Vulnerabilities: Spend 30 minutes evaluating your current role and identify which tasks are repetitive, data-driven, or administrative. Write down three tasks that could be automated by AI. The goal is to identify where your job may be at risk.

2. Strengthen One Non-Automatable Skill: Choose one skill that AI can't easily replicate (e.g., creative problem-solving, emotional intelligence, managing relationships) and commit to improving it. Set a well-defined goal to significantly improve your skills in this area within the next six months. Create a development plan, including books, courses, or mentoring opportunities to ensure you're growing in areas where AI can't compete.

3. Have a Conversation About AI with Your Manager: Schedule a 15-minute conversation with your boss or team leader. Ask how AI is being used in the company and where it might be introduced. Use this opportunity to showcase your forward-thinking mindset and adaptability. Ask for chances to be involved in projects or initiatives that explore AI solutions, positioning yourself as a proactive contributor to the company's growth.

4. Shadow a Colleague in a Different Department: Find a colleague in a department that's more technical or involved in implementing AI. Ask to spend a few hours observing or assisting them. This helps you understand how AI is being used across the company and positions you as a learner. If shadowing isn't an option, explore online forums or communities where AI applications in your industry are discussed. This will give you similar insights into how AI is being implemented in other roles without the need for direct observation.

That's it—four direct, simple steps you can start today. By now, you've done more than just recognize the changes AI is bringing—you've started mapping out a strategy to secure your place in this new landscape. The key to staying relevant isn't about fearing AI or hoping it passes you by—it's about adapting, learning, and focusing on what you do best as a human. Keep building those skills that AI can't touch, stay curious, and position yourself as someone who isn't just surviving the changes, but thriving in them.

Skilling Up for the AI Age

So, YOU'VE MADE IT this far. And yes, I know, you've heard it a thousand times already—AI isn't some distant force hovering in the future, it's here, blah blah blah. We all get it. But here's what really matters: this shift doesn't have to leave you behind. Even better? If you're willing to learn and adapt, the AI age could be one of the greatest opportunities of your career.

But here's the catch: just because you're aware of the changes AI is bringing doesn't mean you're fully prepared. It's not just about having the right mindset—it's about having the right skills. And no, you don't need to learn computer programming (unless you want to), but you do need to understand which skills are going to matter most in the AI era. We've touched on the human-centered skills already, but now it's time to dig deeper. This chapter will help you pinpoint the skills you need to develop now—and how to do it efficiently.

Let's dive in.

The New Career Currency: Skills That Pay the Bills

In the AI age, skills are the new currency. Forget about job titles and fancy degrees—what will truly determine your career's future is your ability to bring relevant, in-demand skills to the table. So, what are those skills? Let's break them down into two categories: human skills and technical skills.

Essential Human Skills That AI Can't Replicate (Yet)

You've probably heard this before, but let me hammer it home: the most valuable skills in the AI era aren't technical. They're human. AI may be great at crunching numbers, recognizing patterns, and making data-driven decisions, but what it can't do (yet) are things like building relationships, thinking creatively, or leading teams. Those are the skills that will keep you valuable. I know what you might be thinking—*"I'm not a people person."* Well, guess what? You are now. In a world where AI handles the technical stuff, mastering these human skills is non-negotiable and will be the reason you keep your job, and Steve starts packing his desk. Now, let's break down the essentials.

Emotional Intelligence (EQ): While AI excels at analyzing data and making logical decisions, it falls short when it comes to understanding human emotions or navigating the complexities of interpersonal relationships. This is where EQ comes in. EQ enables you to connect with others on a personal level, lead effectively, and manage conflicts in ways that machines never can. For instance, high EQ can help you better read social cues, build stronger relationships, and create a positive team culture. Whether you're dealing with office politics, leading a diverse team, or handling tough conversations, your emotional intelligence is your competitive edge in a world increasingly driven by AI. It's not just about being liked—it's about influencing outcomes and fostering collaboration in ways that AI simply can't replicate. Improving your EQ can make you indispensable in your workplace, no matter how much automation takes over. And don't worry, we'll be diving even deeper into EQ in the next chapter, so you'll get plenty of guidance on how to sharpen this critical skill.

Creative Problem-Solving: AI can find solutions to problems, but it can't think outside the box. AI can't innovate or generate entirely new ideas because it relies on patterns and pre-existing information. That's where your creative problem-solving skills come into play. This skill involves more than just finding a solution—it's about tackling challenges from fresh perspectives, generating innovative ideas, and developing strategies that aren't solely driven by data or past trends. For example, creative problem-solving might involve thinking of ways to disrupt the status quo, blending unrelated concepts into something new, or identifying opportunities others overlook. It's about taking calculated risks, exploring unconventional solutions, and adapting quickly when things don't go as planned. In an AI-dominated world, your ability to innovate and craft solutions that machines can't is one of the most valuable assets you can bring to the table.

Adaptability and Resilience: In a rapidly evolving workplace where AI and new technologies are constantly emerging, the ability to adapt is crucial. Adaptability means being open to learning new tools, processes, and even taking on unfamiliar roles. It's about thriving in change, not just tolerating it. But adaptability alone isn't enough—you also need resilience. Resilience is the ability to recover from setbacks, whether it's a project failure, a technological hiccup, or unexpected shifts in the market. It's about learning from mistakes and continuing to push forward with confidence. In practice, being adaptable and resilient allows you to face challenges head-on, embrace uncertainty, and stay productive even when things don't go according to plan. Together, these qualities ensure that no matter how fast technology moves or how frequently the workplace changes, you remain an essential and forward-thinking part of your team.

Leadership and Collaboration: AI might be able to automate tasks and optimize operations, but it can't replace the human touch when it comes to leading teams and fostering collaboration. Strong leadership will always be essential, particularly in guiding teams through change, inspiring creativity, and managing diverse groups of people with different strengths and ideas. As AI takes over routine tasks, the demand for leaders who can motivate, build trust, and drive innovation will only increase. Collaboration, on the other hand, is more important than ever. AI tools might assist in productivity, but it's the human ability to communicate, share ideas, and work together to solve complex problems that ensures success in any organization. The future workplace will need leaders who not only understand how to leverage AI but also excel at bringing people together, facilitating open dialogue, and encouraging innovation.

Technical Skills Worth Investing In (and Ones to Skip)

You know that soft skills are important, and increasingly so as AI advances in the workplace. That being said, technical skills still matter. But you don't need to become a coding wizard or an AI engineer to stay relevant. Instead, focus on understanding the skills that complement AI and make you more effective in your role. Investing a little time now to get familiar with a few key technical skills will go a long way. These are just the basics, and you can explore them further if you want, but having this foundation will help set you apart.

Data Literacy: AI is driven by data. Being able to understand, interpret, and work with data is becoming an essential skill across industries. You don't need to become a data scientist, but you should be comfortable reading reports, analyzing trends, and making data-driven decisions.

AI Tool Proficiency: You don't need to build AI systems from scratch, but you do need to know how to use the tools that are relevant to your industry. Whether it's a CRM system with AI capabilities, a project management tool that uses machine learning, or AI-powered marketing platforms, being familiar with these tools is key.

Automation Software: Learning how to leverage automation platforms like Zapier or Microsoft Power Automate can make your job easier and more efficient. Automation is a big part of how AI is changing work, and knowing how to set up workflows that eliminate repetitive tasks can save you time and increase your productivity.

AI Literacy: This doesn't mean you need to understand every algorithm or the technical nitty-gritty behind machine learning. AI literacy is about understanding what AI can and can't do, knowing where it applies in your industry, and being able to talk about it with colleagues, clients, or leaders.

There are plenty of **resources to build your technical skills** without breaking the bank—or even spending a penny. Depending on the software your company uses, there are often many opportunities to explore free training. Microsoft and Google, for example, offer extensive training modules for their products, covering everything from automation tools like Power Automate to AI-powered platforms. Microsoft's free training includes everything you need to get more out of their Office 365 suite, making it easier to integrate automation and AI into your workflow. Additionally, platforms like Coursera, edX, LinkedIn Learning, and Google's own training modules provide accessible options to grow your AI literacy and data skills. The key is to explore these resources and build your skill set at your own pace, without feeling the need to spend a fortune.

And as for the **skills you can skip**? Unless you're interested in a tech career shift, deep coding knowledge or machine learning engineering probably isn't necessary for you. Focus on understanding the basics of data and how to use AI tools rather than building them. There you go—short and sweet. You can scratch the surface on technical tools or you can dig a well. The key to staying employed (and hopefully promoted) is knowing more than what's expected, so always look for ways to go one step past your job description—or maybe take enough steps to rewrite it.

The Unexpected Talents That Will Matter Most in an AI World

Sometimes, the skills that set you apart aren't the obvious ones. In the AI era, having "soft skills" like communication and creativity is essential—but so are talents like storytelling and design thinking, which you might not immediately think of. These are the skills that bridge the gap between raw data and human understanding, ensuring that technology works for people, not just alongside them.

Storytelling: While AI can process and present data, it doesn't know how to create an emotional connection or a narrative that resonates with people. That's where storytelling comes in. Whether you're in marketing, product development, or customer service, your ability to craft a compelling narrative around AI-generated insights or data can make all the difference. Storytelling is how you take cold, hard facts and turn them into something that inspires action, from influencing decision-makers to engaging clients or motivating teams.

Design Thinking: AI can suggest optimizations based on patterns, but it can't empathize with a user's needs. Design thinking focuses on human-centered solutions by keeping the user experience at the core of problem-solving. In roles like product development or service innovation, design thinking allows you to take AI insights and turn them into real-world applications that not only work but also feel intuitive and user-friendly. It's this creative approach to designing solutions that AI can't replicate.

Curiosity: I have already mentioned that curiosity is important as AI technology advances, but I will continue to remind you because it ***is*** important. It's more than just learning how to use these new tools—it's about continuously exploring ways to make those tools work better for you. While AI handles repetitive tasks, your curiosity can lead to finding new applications for AI in your work, discovering overlooked opportunities, or testing out experimental ideas that could set your organization apart. AI can't ask "what if?"—that's your job.

These talents might not fit neatly into a job description, but they're the kind of unexpected skills that will set you apart. AI might handle the technical heavy lifting, but it's your ability to connect the dots, think creatively, and shape AI's output into something meaningful that will keep you ahead in this rapidly evolving world.

Learning to Learn: Staying Ahead of the AI Curve

We've covered the skills you need, but here's the next challenge: how do you actually learn them? We're in a world where new skills are constantly in demand, and keeping up can feel overwhelming. The key is to master the art of *learning* itself—knowing how to pick up new skills quickly and effectively.

Strategies for Rapid Skill Acquisition

Let's face it—you're busy. You don't have the luxury of spending years acquiring new skills. The good news is, you don't need to. Here's how to learn smarter, not harder:

Focus on One Skill at a Time: Multitasking is a myth. If you're trying to learn multiple new skills at once, you're not going to get far with any of them. Pick the one skill that will have the biggest impact on your career right now, and focus on that.

Use the 80/20 Rule: This rule states that 80% of your results come from 20% of your efforts. When learning a new skill, focus on the 20% of knowledge that will drive 80% of your outcomes. For example, if you're learning data literacy, focus on mastering the basics of interpreting data and making decisions based on it, rather than trying to become an expert data analyst. Start by identifying the 20% of knowledge in your current role that drives most of your performance. By focusing on these key areas, you'll quickly see improvements in efficiency, which can be crucial in a rapidly changing work environment.

Learn by Doing: The fastest way to cement new skills is to put them into practice. If you're learning AI tools, start using them at work right away. If you're learning creative problem-solving, look for real-world challenges to tackle. The more hands-on you are, the quicker you'll learn.

Navigating the Sea of Online Courses, Bootcamps, and Certifications

The internet is flooded with learning resources, and that's both a blessing and a curse. How do you choose the right one? Here's how to navigate the sea of options:

Go for Reputable Platforms: Stick to well-known platforms like Coursera, Udemy, or LinkedIn Learning. These platforms offer a range of courses that are vetted by professionals and often come with certifications. Consider courses like "AI for Everyone" on Coursera for an accessible introduction to AI, or "Data Analysis Fundamentals" on LinkedIn Learning to enhance your data literacy.

Balance Free and Paid Resources: You don't need to break the bank on upskilling, but sometimes investing in a paid course will get you higher-quality content and more personalized feedback. Start with free resources, and if you feel it's worth the investment, move on to paid options.

Look for Industry-Specific Certifications: If you're in a field where certifications are respected (like IT or finance), earning a certification can give you a real edge. Research what's recognized in your industry, and go after the credentials that will boost your credibility.

Building a Personal Learning Network in the AI Community

You don't have to learn in isolation. One of the best ways to stay on top of trends and accelerate your learning is by building a network of like-minded professionals. Here's how:

Join Online Communities: Platforms like Reddit, LinkedIn, and Twitter are full of groups focused on AI and emerging technologies. Engaging with these communities can expose you to new ideas and help you stay ahead of the curve. Look for groups such as "AI in Business" on LinkedIn or the "Artificial Intelligence" subreddit, where professionals discuss AI's practical applications in various industries.

Attend Webinars and Conferences: Virtual events are an excellent way to learn from industry leaders and network with peers.[1] Keep an eye out for AI conferences or webinars in your field—many are free or low-cost.

Find a Mentor: If you're serious about upskilling, having a mentor who's already navigated the AI landscape can be a game-changer. Don't be afraid to reach out to people in your industry—many are happy to share their knowledge and guide others.

---

1. Business Soulwork. (n.d.). *Where to Learn about Emerging Technologies?* Retrieved from https://business-soulwork.com/where-to-learn-about-emerging-technologies/

Your AI Upskilling Game Plan

Now that you have a sense of the skills you need and how to acquire them, it's time to put it all together. Here's how to create a concrete plan that works with your schedule and goals.

Assessing Your Skill Gaps and Setting Priorities

Start by taking stock of your current skills. Which ones are solid, and which areas need work? Consider using a self-assessment tool or an online evaluation to pinpoint your strengths and weaknesses. Before diving into AI tools, take a few minutes to reflect on your most recent projects, successes, and challenges. This reflection will give you valuable insights into where you're excelling and where you might need to improve. The AI-Powered Action Plan at the beginning of this book offers a more in-depth guide to creating a comprehensive roadmap for your career growth, but here's a simplified approach to get you started.

- What skills are most relevant to my industry right now?
  AI Insight: Head to an LLM (e.g., ChatGPT) and ask, "What skills are most relevant to my industry right now? Before responding, ask me any questions you need answered to provide a thorough yet concise analysis."

- Which skills will be in demand over the next five to ten years?
  AI Insight: Ask AI, "What skills will likely be in high demand over the next five to ten years in my industry? Before answering, ask me any relevant questions about my industry, current role, and the broader market trends to provide a more customized response."

- Where am I weakest, and where can I improve?
  AI Insight: Prompt a GPT model, "Ask me about the challenges I've faced in my recent projects or tasks, and then probe into areas where I may have lacked efficiency or struggled to meet goals. Based on my responses, help me identify three key areas for improvement."

Once you have these insights, prioritize. Don't try to tackle everything at once—focus on the skills that will have the most immediate impact on your career.[2] Concentrate on areas where quick improvements will yield the greatest results. With those priorities in place, think about how to fit learning and growth into your schedule without feeling overwhelmed.

Time-Efficient Learning Strategies for Busy Professionals

If you're like most professionals, you're strapped for time. But upskilling doesn't have to consume your entire schedule. Here's how to make the most of the time you have:

- **Microlearning:** Break your learning into small, digestible chunks. Spend 15-30 minutes a day focused on a specific skill rather than trying to dedicate hours at a time. Leverage tools like Duolingo for learning or Todoist for setting microlearning goals. This way, you can track progress without feeling overwhelmed.

- **Incorporate Learning Into Your Workday:** Look for opportunities to learn on the job. Can you incorporate new AI tools into your workflow? Could you ask to shadow a colleague with expertise in an area you want to develop? Even small actions—like experimenting with AI automation—can enhance your daily tasks and help you grow.

- **Accountability:** Whether it's a peer, mentor, or learning group, having someone hold you accountable can make a huge difference in staying on track. Set milestones and check in regularly with someone who can motivate you and provide feedback. Keeping a log of your progress can also help ensure you're meeting your goals.

AI-Proof Action Plan

Developing the Skills That Will Keep You Relevant

Now that we've covered the skills you need to stay ahead in the AI era, it's time to roll up your sleeves and get to work. This action plan will help you take what you've learned and put it into practice. The goal here is simple: blend your human strengths with AI tools in a way that makes you indispensable. These steps are designed to focus your learning and skill development, so you can stay relevant no matter how much technology changes.

1. Pick One Human Skill to Deepen: Select one human skill (e.g., empathy, leadership, creative thinking) that AI can't replicate. Set a timeline to significantly improve it in three months. Breaking it down into daily or weekly actions ensures you're making steady progress and seeing real-world benefits quickly. This could mean reading a book, joining a class, or practicing in real-world scenarios.

2. Identify One AI Skill to Pair with It: Once you've chosen a human skill, find a complementary AI skill that can help you in your current role (e.g., using data analytics tools if you're working on leadership). This ensures you're blending human strengths with AI in your role.

3. Complete a Course on AI Literacy or Data Analysis: Find a short, focused course on AI literacy, data analysis, or automation. Aim to finish it within a month. The goal is to understand how AI and data apply to your role, even if you don't need deep technical knowledge.

4. Set Up a Skill Development Routine: Set aside 30 minutes, three times a week, to work on developing your chosen human and AI skills. This can be learning through courses, practicing in your job, or reading relevant content. Keep a log of your progress and review it monthly.

Now that you've built your roadmap and identified the steps to keep yourself ahead, it's time to put that plan into action. Having a strategy is one thing, but it's the consistent effort that will shape your future. AI can't replace your creativity, leadership, or resilience—but these skills don't sharpen themselves. Keep pushing forward, honing both your human strengths and AI capabilities. The world isn't slowing down, and neither should you. Apply what you've learned here, adapt as needed, and keep evolving. Your career won't AI-proof itself—you've got to make it happen.

The Human Edge: Outsmarting AI in the Workplace

By now, you've seen how AI is reshaping industries, roles, and even entire career paths. But let's pivot for a moment—because while AI is capable of many things, there are critical areas where it still can't compete: human intuition, creativity, and emotional intelligence. This chapter isn't about dwelling on what AI can't do, but instead focusing on how to leverage the things it can't replicate. Your unique advantage—the "human edge"—is what will set you apart and make you indispensable, no matter how advanced AI becomes.

This chapter is all about sharpening that edge. We're going to explore the skills that AI simply cannot replace—skills like Emotional Intelligence (EQ), creative thinking, and the art of collaboration. It's not just about being good at what AI can't do, but about using those strengths to work alongside AI in a way that amplifies your impact. In a world where AI handles the repetitive and technical tasks, mastering your human strengths will be your superpower.

Emotional Intelligence: Your Secret Weapon

In a workplace dominated by AI, the true differentiator isn't technical skill—it's your ability to navigate the complexities of human interaction. As AI takes over repetitive tasks, EQ becomes even more crucial because it equips you to handle the unpredictable, human side of work. We all know this side—the moments when John is in a bad mood and tensions rise, or when Peggy's not playing fair and team dynamics shift. Navigating these situations is what will set you apart. Knowing how a team excels and capturing the best of that human element will be the differentiator that keeps you on top. While entire books focus on EQ, we'll distill it down to what matters most in today's AI-driven landscape: self-awareness and social skills. Mastering these two components will help you thrive in the human dynamics of the workplace and position you to work alongside AI as a more effective, adaptable professional.

Self-Awareness: The Foundation for Success in an AI-Driven World

In the fast-paced, AI-driven workplace, where tasks are automated and data is processed at lightning speed, self-awareness emerges as one of the most important traits for success. AI might be excellent at handling repetitive tasks and providing data-driven insights, but it doesn't have the ability to reflect on its actions or adapt based on emotional intelligence. That's where self-awareness comes in. It's not just about understanding how you feel at any given moment; it's about recognizing your emotional triggers, understanding your strengths and weaknesses, and knowing how your behavior impacts others. In this rapidly changing world, self-awareness isn't just a personal trait—it's a professional asset that will keep you adaptable, effective, and AI-proof.

Why Self-Awareness Matters

Self-awareness is, in essence, the ability to look inward and understand how your thoughts, emotions, and behaviors align with the world around you. In a workplace increasingly dominated by AI, self-awareness allows you to recognize how you're contributing to the team and where you might need to adjust. Think of it as your personal feedback loop—one that AI cannot replicate.

In high-pressure situations, especially where quick thinking and complex decisions are required, being self-aware means you can regulate your emotions and make thoughtful decisions without letting stress cloud your judgment. While AI might offer solutions based on data, only a self-aware individual can balance that data with emotional and contextual nuances that machines simply can't process.

Self-awareness also plays a key role in collaboration. Being in tune with your own emotions helps you understand how your behavior affects others. Whether you're managing a team or working on a project with peers, self-awareness enables you to read the room, adjust your approach, and navigate conflict before it escalates. It's the foundation for strong leadership—helping you remain composed, understanding, and adaptable, all of which are traits that inspire trust and cooperation from others.

Moreover, self-awareness is what allows you to identify areas for growth. In a world where AI is constantly changing the way we work, being open to personal growth and professional development is key. Knowing your strengths enables you to capitalize on them, while acknowledging your weaknesses gives you the opportunity to improve. The self-aware employee is always looking for ways to adapt and grow, which makes them indispensable in a workforce that is evolving alongside technology.

How Self-Awareness Helps You Stay AI-Proof

AI might handle the technical, repetitive tasks, but it can't replace the human ability to reflect and grow. In fact, self-awareness is what will make you resilient in the face of AI advancements. As roles evolve, those who lack self-awareness may find themselves struggling to adapt to the changes. On the other hand, self-aware individuals are able to recognize when their skill set needs to shift or when they need to embrace new responsibilities.

For example, as AI takes over data-driven tasks, employees may need to focus more on creative thinking, leadership, or project management. A self-aware employee will not only recognize these shifts but will also proactively seek ways to develop the necessary skills to stay ahead. This adaptability is what makes self-aware individuals AI-proof—no matter how advanced AI becomes, the human capacity for reflection, growth, and emotional intelligence will always set them apart.

Self-awareness also helps you regulate your reactions to the growing presence of AI. For some, the rise of AI might feel threatening, sparking anxiety or resistance. A self-aware person, however, can acknowledge these emotions and respond with curiosity and adaptability rather than fear. They understand that while AI can enhance efficiency, it's their unique human qualities—like emotional intelligence and adaptability—that make them irreplaceable.

Practical Steps to Improve Self-Awareness

1. Reflect regularly: One of the best ways to cultivate self-awareness is by taking time to reflect on your thoughts, behaviors, and emotional responses. Whether through journaling or quiet contemplation, these moments of reflection help you identify patterns in your behavior—both good and bad. By reflecting on your day-to-day interactions, you'll gain insights into how you react under pressure, what triggers stress or frustration, and where you might need to adjust your approach.

2. Seek feedback: While self-reflection is important, it's equally crucial to get an outside perspective. Ask for feedback from peers, mentors, or supervisors to gain insight into how you're perceived by others.[1] Sometimes, we're not fully aware of how our actions affect those around us, and feedback can help us identify blind spots. Learning from others' perceptions allows you to refine your behavior and improve your relationships at work.

3. Leverage AI tools: Interestingly, AI can also be a helpful tool for improving self-awareness. Productivity trackers, time-management apps, and behavioral analytics tools can offer insights into your work habits and patterns. By using these tools to monitor your own performance, you can identify areas where you're most productive and where you tend to lose focus. This data can serve as a foundation for personal growth, helping you become more efficient and intentional in your work.

4. Practice mindfulness: Mindfulness is another powerful tool for developing self-awareness. By staying present and fully engaged in the moment, you can better understand your emotions and reactions as they happen.[2] Mindfulness exercises, such as deep breathing or meditation, can help you stay grounded and regulate your emotional responses in stressful situations, improving your overall emotional intelligence.

Social Skills: Navigating Relationships and Driving Collaboration

In an AI-driven workplace, it's easy to assume that technical skills are what will keep you competitive. But there's a critical component that AI can't replicate: social skills. These interpersonal abilities—like communication, empathy, and collaboration—are what enable you to work effectively with others, navigate complex relationships, and lead teams through the challenges that no algorithm can predict. As AI takes over repetitive tasks, the demand for strong social skills is only going to grow. After all, AI can crunch numbers

---

1. IT Education Centre. (n.d.). *The Power of Soft Skills*. Retrieved from https://www.iteducationcentre.com/the-power-of-soft-skills/

2. Smart Therapy PC. (n.d.). *How to Build Resilience and Bounce Back from Adversity*. Retrieved from https://www.smartherapypc.com/post/how-to-build-resilience-and-bounce-back-from-adversity

and provide data-driven insights, but it cannot build trust, resolve conflicts, or negotiate outcomes in the nuanced ways humans can.

Empathy: The Cornerstone of Social Skills

At the heart of strong social skills is empathy. Empathy is the ability to understand and share the feelings of others.[3] It's what allows you to see beyond the data and recognize the human emotions and motivations driving decisions, actions, and behaviors. In an AI-powered world, empathy is more important than ever because it's the one skill that can't be automated. It's essential for collaboration, conflict resolution, and leadership—areas where humans will always outshine machines.

Consider a situation where a project hits a roadblock. While AI might suggest data-driven solutions to solve the problem, empathy is what allows a team leader to understand the frustrations and concerns of the team, ensuring that emotions are addressed and that morale stays high. Without empathy, team dynamics can crumble, and communication can break down, leading to a less productive and more tense work environment.

Empathy also helps you navigate difficult conversations. Whether you're managing a team, negotiating a deal, or resolving a conflict, the ability to truly understand and respond to others' emotions is what keeps relationships intact and strengthens collaboration. This skill doesn't just make you likable—it makes you effective. Empathy enables you to anticipate problems before they arise, foster trust within your team, and create an environment where people feel valued and heard.

Key Social Skills for an AI-Proof Career

While empathy is the foundation, there are other social skills that are essential for thriving in an AI-powered workplace. These skills help you manage the complexities of human interaction, ensuring that you can communicate clearly, collaborate effectively, and influence outcomes in a way that AI simply can't.

1. Communication: Clear and effective communication is essential for sharing ideas, building consensus, and ensuring that everyone is on the same page. AI might assist with communication tools—such as automated email responses or chatbots—but the ability

---

3. School Education Solutions. (n.d.). *Tips for Developing Empathy Skills*. Retrieved from https://www.rajeevelt.com/tag/tips-for-developing-empathy-skills/

to navigate human conversations is still a uniquely human strength. Whether you're giving feedback, leading a meeting, or discussing a project with clients, strong communication skills ensure that your message is understood and that misunderstandings are minimized.

2. Collaboration: As teams become more diverse and distributed across locations, effective collaboration is crucial. AI may streamline processes, but it's your ability to work well with others that will keep projects on track. Successful collaboration requires understanding different perspectives, managing conflicts, and finding common ground. In an increasingly globalized and AI-driven workplace, your ability to collaborate across departments, cultures, and time zones is a competitive edge that AI can't replicate.

3. Negotiation and Persuasion: AI can provide data-driven insights to support arguments, but it can't negotiate deals or persuade others to see your point of view. Negotiation requires understanding the motivations, concerns, and emotions of the other party—something that only human interaction can achieve. Whether you're negotiating a contract, advocating for a new project, or persuading a team to adopt a new strategy, your ability to influence others will always set you apart from the machines.

How Social Skills Give You a Competitive Edge

In a workplace where AI handles much of the technical work, it's easy to feel like humans are becoming less relevant. But the truth is, strong social skills will always be in demand. These skills—empathy, communication, collaboration, and negotiation—are what keep teams motivated, projects on track, and relationships intact. AI can handle tasks, but it can't manage people, ideas, or emotions. That's where your social skills come in. They allow you to bridge the gap between technology and human needs, ensuring that the work gets done while maintaining a positive, productive environment.

By honing your social skills, you position yourself as someone who can not only manage the work but also the people and relationships that drive success. Whether you're leading a team, working with clients, or managing stakeholders, your ability to navigate the human side of work is what will keep you indispensable, no matter how advanced AI becomes.

Practical Steps to Develop Social Skills

Improving your social skills takes practice, but it's a worthwhile investment. Here are some practical steps you can take to strengthen your interpersonal abilities:

1. Practice Active Listening and Empathy: In your daily interactions, focus on really listening to others—what they're saying, how they're feeling, and what they need. By practicing active listening, you'll improve your empathy and strengthen your relationships with colleagues, clients, and team members.

2. Engage in Role-Playing or Scenario-Based Exercises: To improve your negotiation, persuasion, and conflict resolution skills, try role-playing or scenario-based exercises with colleagues or mentors. These exercises can help you practice handling difficult conversations and situations, allowing you to refine your approach in a low-stakes environment.

3. Gather Input: Ask for input from mentors, peers, or colleagues on how you communicate and interact with others. Constructive feedback can provide valuable insights into areas where you can improve, helping you refine your social skills over time.[4]

In an AI-driven world, your social skills are your competitive edge. They allow you to connect with others, lead teams, and navigate the complexities of human interaction—areas where AI simply can't compete. By continuously developing your empathy, communication, collaboration, and negotiation abilities, you ensure that you remain indispensable, no matter how much technology advances.

The Art of Working with AI: Sharpening Your Human Edge

Now that we've covered what sets us apart from AI, let's shift focus to how we can make AI a valuable part of our team—like a skilled assistant, not a leader. AI can drive results when used strategically, but it's not a replacement for the critical, nuanced thinking only humans bring to the table. The key to success lies in blending the strengths of both worlds, and this is where you'll have the opportunity to truly shine.

Working with AI isn't about competing with it; it's about using it to amplify your unique abilities. When done right, AI can make you more productive, creative, and indispensable

---

4. Richards Mooney, H. (n.d.). *4 Action Steps to Take on in the next three weeks to close out the year*. *Medium*. Retrieved from https://heidirichardsmooney.medium.com/4-action-steps-to-take-on-in-the-next-three-weeks-to-close-out-the-year-7965a09163b8

in the workplace. The real art of working with AI is in mastering how to guide it, and that begins with understanding the power of well-crafted prompts. Providing AI with clear, targeted instructions can elevate the quality of its output, allowing you to leverage its processing power while maintaining your distinct human touch. Learning to prompt AI effectively will unlock its full potential as a tool for innovation, problem-solving, and idea generation.

Mastering the Human-AI Partnership

The best outcomes come when humans drive the collaboration. Taking the back seat to a machine is not why you picked up this book. Heck, if you're content taking the back seat to a machine, you might as well ask an AI where the breadline is. But enough chit-chat. Let's dive into the best practices to maintain control and enhance your role through strategic prompting and human insight.

Become a Master of Prompts: The real power of AI is unlocked through effective prompting. The better your prompts, the better the output. For example, instead of simply asking an AI to "analyze data," provide specific context and goals: "Analyze sales data for the past quarter and identify three areas where customer retention could be improved, focusing on product usage patterns." This ensures the AI's responses are focused, actionable, and relevant to your needs. There are whole books about mastering prompts, but I will give you just a couple more things I have found particularly useful throughout my journey.

- **Prompt AI to Ask Questions:** This works wonders. Adding "ask me any relevant questions to provide a comprehensive response" improves most prompts.
- **Learn Frameworks:** Prompt frameworks, like the PREPARED framework, help structure and refine your prompts for better results. While there are many out there, they all serve the same purpose—ensuring your prompts are clear, focused, and drive actionable responses.
- **Iterate and Iterate and...:** You get the point. Iteration is the process of refining your prompts based on AI's responses, tweaking until the result is satisfactory. It's a loop: ask, review, adjust, repeat. Adjusting prompts and giving feedback allows you to tailor results to your specific needs, unlock creative possibilities, and streamline the process for better efficiency.

Leverage AI for Tactical Tasks, Retain Strategic Oversight: Use AI to handle tasks that don't require human judgment—like automating data entry, scheduling, or pulling reports. This frees you up to focus on the strategic, high-level thinking AI can't do. For instance, instead of spending hours sifting through data, prompt the AI to analyze key metrics and provide a summary, then use that insight to guide your decision-making or focus for deeper analysis.

Drive Innovation with Human Creativity: While AI can generate ideas, it lacks the ability to innovate in the way humans can. Combine your creative thinking with AI's analytical power by using prompts to explore new approaches. Ask questions like, "What are three unconventional solutions to this problem, based on industry trends?" and then use your human judgment to assess the feasibility and potential impact of those ideas. Exploring these suggestions can sometimes get answers quicker than racking your brain until it hits you.

Keep a Human at the Helm: AI works best when it supports human decision-making, not when it takes over. For any AI-driven task, maintain oversight and add your own critical thinking to ensure the output aligns with your goals. AI can offer suggestions, but only you can determine the best course of action based on your unique understanding of the situation.

Managing AI Tools for Maximum Impact

Don't get overwhelmed by AI's capabilities. Instead, focus on how it can streamline your tasks, allowing you to hone the skills that truly set you apart.

Focus on High-Impact Tasks: Use AI to take over the smaller, time-consuming tasks, so you can dedicate more energy to the complex work that demands human intuition. Tools like Grammarly or automation features in Trello can handle mundane tasks, giving you more bandwidth for strategic initiatives.

Evolving with AI: As AI tools continue to develop, the real differentiator will be those who stay curious and continuously adapt. The more familiar you are with prompting AI for advanced outputs, the more you can leverage it to stay ahead in your field. Stay open to learning and exploring new AI features that can enhance your workflow without detracting from your unique human strengths.

Case Studies: Humans and AI Collaborating on Breakthrough Innovations

There are countless examples of humans and AI successfully collaborating to improve our quality of life, simplify processes, and enhance product design. Let's explore a few real-world examples where this partnership is driving creativity and innovation.

AI-Assisted Personalized Learning: Platforms like **DreamBox Learning** and **Carnegie Learning** use AI to adapt lesson plans based on how well students are grasping the material. While AI helps deliver personalized content at scale, it's the human teachers who interpret the data, understand students' emotional and developmental needs, and adjust their teaching strategies accordingly. AI can analyze learning patterns, but teachers use their expertise to motivate and engage students, tailoring lessons that AI alone couldn't perfect.

AI-Powered Inventory Management: At **Zara**, AI is used to monitor sales patterns and predict demand for clothing items, ensuring the right amount of stock is on hand. However, it's the human teams that decide on trends, seasonal collections, and fashion aesthetics. AI suggests what's selling based on data, but humans bring creativity and intuition into deciding which designs will connect with customers emotionally and drive future trends.

Fraud Detection with Human Oversight: Banks like **JPMorgan Chase** use AI to detect suspicious financial activities, flagging potential fraud in real time. But human analysts still play a crucial role in reviewing flagged transactions, making nuanced decisions, and determining whether an action truly indicates fraud. AI provides a first line of defense by analyzing patterns, but humans provide judgment and context that algorithms alone cannot.

AI and Human Hybrid Models: Companies like **Zendesk** and **H&M** use AI chatbots to handle basic customer inquiries, such as order tracking or FAQs. However, when it comes to more complex queries, AI hands off the conversation to human customer service agents. The AI streamlines routine requests, allowing human agents to focus on empathetic communication and problem-solving for more intricate issues, which leads to better customer satisfaction.

AI-Assisted Music Composition: Musicians like **Taryn Southern** have used AI tools like **Amper Music** to co-compose songs. The AI generates various musical components, but it's the human artist who selects, refines, and arranges these elements, adding emotional depth and creativity. AI can assist with the structure, but human creativity drives the final product, ensuring the music resonates on a deeper level.

These case studies emphasize how AI and human skills complement each other—AI handles the data, while humans bring creativity, judgment, and emotional intelligence to the table. It's the combination of AI and human insight that drives real innovation and success. Hopefully, these examples make one thing clear: AI is here for us... not here for us (as in, it's not coming to take your job or plot your demise!).

AI-Proof Action Plan

Strengthening Your Unique Human Value

Now that we've covered the significance of human resources, it's time to put this into practice. The following steps are designed to help you flex your human strengths while integrating AI into your workflow. Think of this as a way to sharpen the skills that make you irreplaceable, while learning how to let AI handle the tasks it's best at. These small but powerful actions will help you reinforce your value in the workplace.

1. Develop a Creative Problem-Solving Routine: Set aside time each week (15-30 minutes) for creative brainstorming on problems you face at work. Whether it's improving a process, solving a customer issue, or thinking of a new approach, practice flexing your creative muscles regularly.

2. Run an AI-Human Collaboration Experiment: Pick one small project or task at work that involves using AI (e.g., using a tool for analysis or automation). Work on this project while actively deciding when and where your human input is crucial. Reflect on what the AI does well and where your creativity or judgment is needed most.

3. Build Emotional Intelligence at Work: Each week, focus on a specific EQ skill in real-life situations. In your next team meeting, practice active listening by summarizing a colleague's point before responding. During one-on-one conversations, work on managing conflict by staying calm and solution-focused. In customer interactions, adjust your communication to recognize and respond to their emotions. After each interaction, reflect on how applying EQ improved the outcome.

4. Create a Personal Development Plan: Outline a six-month plan to consistently work on the human skills that differentiate you from AI (e.g., leadership, communication, innovation). Set clear goals for each skill, and track your progress at the end of each month. Review industry trends quarterly to make adjustments.

As we close this first part on AI's impact on careers, remember, AI can handle a lot, but the secret to thriving in this new landscape is mastering what it can't. The things that make you human can only be topped by another human, so keep them in sight and stay one step ahead in the race to master these skills. You will never be faster than the machine but you can damn sure outpace Rob in accounting, so beat him to the punch, develop your human edge, and grab a seat in that corner office.

Embracing the AI-Driven Workforce

Rivanna Heights Media

Navigating the Ethical Minefield of AI at Work

As we begin part two, where we explore the new era of work in the age of AI, it is critical to note that AI is powerful but not without its risks. We've talked about how AI can boost productivity, optimize workflows, and help you excel in your career, but there's a darker side that we need to address. I'm not talking about science fiction scenarios where AI takes over the world—I'm talking about the very real ethical challenges we face as AI becomes more integrated into the workplace.

In this chapter, we'll explore the ethical minefield that comes with AI and how you, as a professional, can navigate it. From issues of bias and privacy to the role of regulation and responsibility, it's critical to understand the potential pitfalls and how to advocate for ethical AI in your organization. Because the last thing you want is to be caught off guard by AI decisions that don't just affect the bottom line but also people's lives. Becoming well-versed in AI ethics is another core component of the AI-proof career, preparing you to navigate a workplace where the human aspect of HR is increasingly mediated by machines.

The Dark Side of AI: What Could Go Wrong?

AI is like any other powerful tool—it can do incredible things when used responsibly, but it can also cause harm if mismanaged. The ethical issues surrounding AI are often complex, but they boil down to a few core areas: bias, privacy, and the unintended consequences of automated decision-making.

Bias, Privacy, and Other AI Ethical Hot Potatoes

Bias in AI is one of the most talked-about problems. You see, AI systems learn from data, and that data comes from us—humans. And believe it or not, humans aren't perfect, and our biases can sneak into the data we create. This means AI can reinforce or even amplify biases based on gender, race, or socioeconomic background. For example, an AI system designed to screen job applicants might favor certain candidates over others based on biased historical hiring data.

The important thing to understand is that bias isn't always intentional. Sometimes, biases in data reflect past demographics or trends that haven't yet caught up with today's shifts. As a knowledgeable professional, you can recognize where this might happen and adjust the input accordingly. For instance, if you're using AI to screen candidates and notice that more men are passing the screen than women, you could recommend incorporating a dataset that better reflects recent hiring trends. This small adjustment could yield results that are more in line with your current workplace landscape.

Next, there's **privacy**, and this is another big one. AI systems are data-hungry, and they thrive on the vast amounts of personal information we produce every day. From your browsing history to your voice assistant's search logs, AI can use this data to make predictions about your behavior. But here's where it gets tricky—how much of your personal information should companies have access to? And what happens when that data falls into the wrong hands or is used in ways you didn't consent to?

Privacy issues go beyond *what* data is used and *how* it's applied. Some of the concern centers on whether data can be tied directly to a person. For instance, we may all agree that leveraging health data to find a cure for a deadly disease is valuable. However, opinions diverge on how this data is gathered and the measures taken to disguise it, ensuring individual privacy. As a standout employee, you can add value by advocating for data to be ciphered or de-identified, allowing meaningful analysis without compromising privacy. Even simply raising questions like, "Are we de-identifying this data?" can set you apart at the conference table, showing your commitment to responsible AI practices.

These are just a couple of the ethical landmines AI can step on, but there are many others. **Transparency** is another big one—how do we ensure that AI's decision-making processes are clear and understandable? And let's not forget **accountability**—who's responsible when AI makes a mistake? Is it the programmer, the company, or the AI system itself?

This leads to an entire industry and, in the case of your career, new roles and new departments—introducing AI-compliance. It may not sound like fun to write policies and procedures, but if you are already in the compliance department, add skills in AI oversight and compliance to your repertoire now. And, if you aren't in the compliance department, understanding these new responsibilities could be *exactly* what keeps you relevant—and valuable—in this new age.

Real-World Consequences of AI Gone Ethically Awry

We don't have to look far to see how these ethical concerns play out in the real—and why understanding them matters to you. Take facial recognition technology, for example. Many police departments and governments globally have adopted AI-driven facial recognition systems to catch criminals. Sounds great, right? But studies reveal that these systems are significantly less accurate when identifying people of color and women, leading to wrongful arrests and accusations. When AI missteps, real people bear the consequences.

Another example is the use of AI in hiring. As I mentioned earlier, several companies have tried to use AI to streamline their recruitment processes, but some have had to scrap these systems after realizing they were biased against women or minority candidates. In one case, a major tech company found that its AI-powered hiring tool favored male applicants because it was trained on resumes submitted over the past decade—a period when most candidates were men.

These examples underscore a critical point: AI's mistakes aren't just theoretical. They have real-world consequences that can hurt people and damage the reputations of the companies using these technologies.

The Blurry Line Between Innovation and Invasion

Now, let's talk about the fine line between innovation and invasion. AI is incredibly powerful when it comes to collecting and analyzing data, but that power can be a double-edged sword. While AI can help businesses innovate and deliver better products and services, it can also lead to invasive practices that erode trust and privacy.

Consider companies that use AI to monitor employees' productivity. Some organizations have started tracking keystrokes, email patterns, and even facial expressions to assess how "engaged" their employees are. Sure, this might lead to higher efficiency, but at what cost? Where's the line between improving productivity and violating someone's right to privacy?

The challenge here is balancing the need for innovation with ethical considerations. Just because AI can do something doesn't mean it should. As a professional, part of your responsibility is to question whether the AI tools you're using respect the boundaries of privacy, fairness, and transparency.

Ethical AI: From Buzzword to Business Practice

So, what can we do about these ethical concerns? The good news is that many companies are starting to take AI ethics seriously. But turning "ethical AI" from a buzzword into a meaningful business practice requires more than just good intentions—it requires action.

Key Principles of Responsible AI Development and Use

Companies should follow a few key principles to ensure AI is used responsibly. This is not an exhaustive list but basic guidelines for development and use.[1] For an AI-proof career, making these principles core to your knowledge base strengthens your understanding of responsible AI and gives you a valuable edge as AI advances.

1. Fairness: AI systems must be designed to treat all individuals fairly. This means addressing and mitigating bias in the data and algorithms. AI tools should be audited regularly to ensure they're not reinforcing discriminatory practices.

2. Transparency: Users and stakeholders need to understand how AI systems make decisions. This involves making AI's decision-making processes as transparent as possible. Companies should be upfront about how AI systems work, what data they use, and how decisions are made.

---

1. BrisTechTonic. (n.d.). *Understanding Google Algorithm Updates and Minimising Their Impact*. Retrieved from https://www.bristechtonic.co.uk/blog/understanding-google-algorithm-updates-and-minimising-their-impact

3. Privacy: AI must respect individuals' privacy. Companies should have clear policies in place to protect personal data and ensure that AI tools are only using data with proper consent.

4. Accountability: When AI systems make decisions, there needs to be a clear line of accountability. This means establishing who is responsible for the actions of AI systems—whether it's the developers, the company, or even the users.

5. Security: AI systems must be secure. They should be protected from tampering, hacking, or misuse that could compromise their ethical integrity.

Companies Leading the Way in Ethical AI (and Those Falling Behind)

Some companies are already leading the charge when it comes to ethical AI. For example, Google has set up an AI ethics board and has committed to not using AI in applications that cause harm, such as autonomous weapons. Microsoft has been vocal about responsible AI use, releasing guidelines and developing tools to identify and address bias in AI systems.

On the flip side, there are companies that are falling behind. Take Clearview AI, a facial recognition company that scraped billions of images from social media without users' consent. The company's actions raised serious privacy concerns and sparked legal challenges. It's a reminder that without proper oversight, AI can quickly cross ethical boundaries.

The Role of Regulation and Self-Governance in AI Ethics

While some companies are taking proactive steps, there's also a growing movement toward regulating AI. The European Union has proposed legislation aimed at creating a legal framework for AI, and other countries are following suit. These regulations aim to ensure that AI is used in ways that protect individuals' rights and prevent harm.[2]

But regulation isn't enough on its own. Companies also need to engage in **self-governance** by establishing internal guidelines for responsible AI use. This includes setting up ethics boards, conducting regular audits of AI systems, and fostering a culture of

---

2. TechTuv. (n.d.). *Artificial Intelligence Enters 2024: Six Trends Shaping the GenAI Landscape*. Retrieved from https://techtuv.com/artificial-intelligence-enters-2024/

accountability. The bottom line is that ethical AI requires both external oversight and internal commitment—opening a wealth of opportunity for those keeping up with these evolving standards and understanding the frameworks that guide responsible AI.

Becoming an AI Ethics Advocate

Now that you have a better understanding of the ethical issues surrounding AI, it's time to take action. You don't need to be a CEO or an AI developer to advocate for ethical AI in your organization. No matter your role, you can help ensure that the AI systems your company uses are fair, transparent, and accountable. By approaching AI thoughtfully and responsibly, you show that you're tuned into the bigger picture—an asset that makes you indispensable to the organization. Here's how.

How to Spot and Address Ethical Issues in AI Systems

Start by learning to spot potential ethical red flags in AI systems. If you notice that an AI tool is making decisions that seem biased or unfair, don't ignore it. Speak up and ask questions. Why is the system making these decisions? What data is it using? Are there safeguards in place to prevent bias?

If you identify an issue, bring it to the attention of your team or manager. Ethical AI is everyone's responsibility, and addressing these issues early can prevent larger problems down the road.

Strategies for Promoting Responsible AI Use in Your Organization

To promote responsible AI use, here are a few strategies you can implement:

1. **Raise Awareness**: Start by educating your colleagues about the ethical implications of AI. Host lunch-and-learn sessions, share articles, or invite experts to speak about AI ethics.

2. **Advocate for Transparency**: Push for more transparency in how your company's AI systems work. Make sure that stakeholders understand how decisions are being made and what data is being used.

3. **Encourage Ethical Reviews**: Suggest that your organization conduct regular ethical reviews of its AI systems. These reviews can help identify and address potential issues before they become problems.

4. **Support Regulation and Governance**: Advocate for policies and practices that ensure AI is used responsibly. This could involve supporting new regulations or helping establish internal guidelines for ethical AI use.

AI-Proof Action Plan

Building Ethical Awareness in the AI Era

Now that we've explored the ethical challenges posed by AI in the workplace, it's time to take action. Navigating the ethical landscape of AI is crucial for ensuring fairness, transparency, and accountability—and approaching AI with an ethical mindset is key to securing your place in an AI-driven future. The steps below will help you become a proactive advocate for ethical AI use in your workplace, setting you apart as someone who not only understands the technology but also the importance of responsible AI practices.

1. Create an AI Ethics Checklist for Your Role: Take 20 minutes to list out the ethical concerns specific to your role or industry. Include areas such as data privacy, bias in AI decision-making, and transparency in AI use. Use this checklist as a reference whenever you implement or interact with AI tools to ensure you're adhering to ethical standards in your daily work.

2. Review Your Company's AI Use Policy: If your company has an AI or data usage policy, read through it carefully. Identify areas where the policy addresses—or fails to address—ethical concerns such as bias, discrimination, and privacy. If your company doesn't have a formal AI policy, make a note of that and consider advocating for one in the future. Understanding the gaps will allow you to contribute meaningfully to ethical discussions in your workplace.

3. Participate in an AI Ethics Workshop or Webinar: Set aside time this month to attend a workshop, seminar, or webinar focused on AI ethics. There are numerous free resources available online, ranging from short courses to live sessions. This will help you deepen your understanding of ethical AI and keep you updated on the latest best practices in the field.

4. Have a Conversation with a Colleague About AI Ethics: Engage in a 15-minute conversation with a colleague in your department or a related field about the ethical use of AI. Ask how they approach ethical dilemmas and where they see potential risks in your workplace. This not only raises awareness but also opens the door to collaborative solutions and improved ethical practices within your organization.

5. Track One Ethical Concern in an AI System You Use: Over the next few weeks, keep an eye on one specific AI tool or system you regularly use at work. Document any ethical concerns or questionable outcomes you notice (e.g., biases in decision-making, lack of transparency). Share your observations with your team or manager and propose adjustments or reviews to ensure the AI system is functioning ethically.

By implementing these steps, you'll develop the awareness and skills needed to navigate the ethical minefield of AI in the workplace. Ethical AI use is a major differentiator in today's workforce, and by proactively addressing these concerns, you'll not only ensure fair practices but also position yourself as a thoughtful leader in this evolving field. While AI can do a lot, it's the human responsibility to guide its use with integrity, and you're now equipped to be that guide.

The Global AI Race: Opportunities in a Borderless Job Market

THE WORLD IS SHRINKING—AND AI is speeding up the process. We're no longer confined by borders when it comes to the job market, especially in the tech and AI industries. AI is a global game now, and if you want to stay competitive, it's essential to understand how this technology is shaping careers across the world. Whether you're looking to land a job in an emerging AI hotspot, collaborate with a team in another country, or simply get ahead in your current role, understanding the global AI landscape is a game-changer.

In this chapter, we're going to take a tour of the AI world—looking at how different countries are approaching AI, the impact it's having on global workforce dynamics, and how you can position yourself to tap into the vast opportunities that a borderless job market offers. If you've ever thought about expanding your career globally, now's the time to act.

AI Around the World: A Global Tour

Let's start by taking a look at how AI is being approached around the world. While AI is transforming industries everywhere, each country has its own unique take on how to integrate it into business and society. These differences can offer a lot of opportunities if you know where to look.

How Different Countries and Cultures Are Approaching AI

The United States has been at the forefront of AI development for years, with major tech companies like Google, Microsoft, and Amazon leading the charge. Silicon Valley is still a hub for AI innovation, and the U.S. is home to some of the best AI talent and research institutions in the world. But it's not the only player anymore.

China is quickly closing the gap and, in some ways, even outpacing the U.S. The Chinese government has made AI a national priority, investing heavily in AI research, infrastructure, and education. Cities like Beijing and Shenzhen are becoming major AI hubs, with companies like Baidu, Alibaba, and Tencent pushing boundaries in AI development. China's AI strategy is aggressive and focused on achieving dominance by 2030.

In Europe, the approach is a little different. The European Union has been focused on the ethical use of AI, ensuring that privacy, fairness, and human rights are built into AI systems from the start. Countries like Germany and France are investing in AI research, but with a strong emphasis on regulation and ethics. The EU's GDPR (General Data Protection Regulation) is a prime example of Europe's cautious but deliberate approach to AI.[1]

Meanwhile, India has positioned itself as a major player in AI development, particularly in AI services and outsourcing. India's vast pool of tech talent, combined with its booming IT sector, makes it a go-to destination for AI-driven business solutions. Cities like Bangalore and Hyderabad are quickly becoming known as the AI outsourcing capitals of the world.

In Canada, cities like Toronto and Montreal are thriving AI ecosystems. Canada has become a magnet for AI talent, particularly in machine learning and deep learning, thanks to its supportive immigration policies, top-tier universities, and a growing tech scene.

As you can see, AI is a global phenomenon, and the way different countries are approaching it opens up new opportunities for professionals like you to tap into this evolving market.

The Impact of AI on Outsourcing and Global Workforce Dynamics

AI is also having a profound impact on how companies approach outsourcing and man-

---

1. IT Governance Deutschland. (n.d.). *EU General Data Protection Regulation GDPR*. Retrieved from https://www.itgovernance.eu/de-de/eu-general-data-protection-regulation-gdpr-de

aging global workforces. Traditionally, outsourcing meant offshoring jobs to countries with cheaper labor costs. But AI is changing that. Companies are now using AI to automate tasks that were previously outsourced, such as customer service, data entry, and even parts of software development.

What does this mean for the global workforce? For one, it's creating a shift in the types of jobs that are being outsourced. AI is making routine, repetitive tasks easier to automate, which means the demand for certain types of low-skilled outsourcing is declining. On the flip side, there's growing demand for higher-skilled workers who can manage, implement, and improve AI systems.

At the same time, AI is enabling companies to build **truly global teams**. With remote work becoming more common, AI tools are helping companies collaborate across borders. AI-powered translation tools, project management systems, and communication platforms are making it easier for teams from different countries to work together seamlessly. As a result, the global talent pool is expanding, and companies are no longer confined to hiring locally or needing to bring talent onshore through visas or relocation.

Emerging Global Hotspots for AI Careers

While not everyone will be directly involved in AI or looking to pack their bags for a move across the globe, understanding where AI is taking off can open up new perspectives and opportunities. For those directly involved in AI and ready to take on new cultures in new places, here are a few emerging hotspots to keep an eye on.

- **Toronto, Canada**: With a booming AI scene, Toronto is home to many AI startups and research institutions. The city's tech-friendly policies and proximity to the U.S. make it a great option for AI professionals looking to work in North America.

- **Shenzhen, China**: Known as China's "Silicon Valley," Shenzhen is a major hub for tech and AI innovation. With government backing and access to cutting-edge resources, this is the place to be if you want to be at the forefront of AI development.

- **Bangalore, India**: As India's tech capital, Bangalore offers opportunities in AI-driven business solutions and outsourcing. If you're looking to work on AI services, this is a key destination.

- **Berlin, Germany**: Berlin's startup scene is thriving, and AI is playing a big part in that growth. Germany's focus on AI ethics and industrial automation makes Berlin a unique spot for AI talent.

- **Paris, France**: With a growing AI research community and government support, Paris is becoming a key player in Europe's AI strategy. The city's focus on AI ethics and human-centric AI makes it an attractive destination for professionals interested in the social impact of AI.

Navigating Cross-Cultural AI Challenges

Working in a global environment comes with its own set of challenges.[2] One of the biggest is navigating the cultural biases that can sometimes creep into AI systems and working across diverse teams where language, expectations, and work styles may vary. Understanding these sometimes subtle implications will be a valuable addition to your AI-proof career toolkit.

Cultural Biases in AI Development

One of the key challenges of AI development on a global scale is cultural bias. As I have said, AI systems are only as good as the data they're trained on. If that data reflects biases from one particular culture or is heavily weighted toward a particular culture, the AI may produce biased results when applied in a global context.

For example, an AI system trained on data from Western cultures may not perform as well when used in Asia or Africa. Similarly, AI-driven hiring tools trained on data from predominantly male industries may inadvertently favor men over women when applied in another industry. This can have real-world consequences, from reinforcing gender or racial biases to creating products that don't resonate with diverse global markets.

Strategies for Working in Global Teams

When working in global teams, it's essential to recognize and respect cultural differences.

---

2. Tech Edition. (n.d.). *How to secure a job in the global tech market with the rise of remote work?* Retrieved from https://www.techedt.com/how-to-secure-a-job-in-the-global-tech-market-with-the-rise-of-remote-work

This is important with or without the addition of AI to the workforce. As AI continues to create global opportunities, being proactive in cultural understanding becomes a critical job skill. Here are a few strategies to help you navigate cross-cultural collaboration and make yourself indispensable in the global landscape.

1. **Embrace Cultural Diversity**: Different perspectives can lead to more innovative solutions. Encourage your team to share their unique insights, and make sure everyone's voice is heard.[3]

2. **Foster Open Communication**: Clear communication is key in any global team. Be mindful of language barriers and different communication styles. Use AI-powered translation tools if needed, but always make sure that everyone understands the goals and expectations.

3. **Be Aware of Time Zones**: When working across borders, be considerate of time differences. Use scheduling tools to find times that work for everyone, and be flexible with deadlines when possible.

Case Studies: Successful International Collaborations

Let's check out some real-world examples of how companies across borders are joining forces to drive innovation and create impactful solutions in today's global landscape.

- **DeepMind (UK) and Google (USA)**: DeepMind, based in London, partnered with Google to pioneer systems that learn and adapt without human input. Their cross-continental collaboration resulted in breakthroughs like AlphaGo, which pushed the boundaries of machine learning in strategic thinking and problem-solving.

- **Alibaba (China) and AI Startups in Israel**: Alibaba has been investing in startups worldwide, including in Israel, a global leader in research and development. This partnership is advancing innovations in logistics, e-commerce, and cybersecurity, demonstrating the strength of global networks in shaping digital

---

3. Edworking. (n.d.). *Building an effective in-house creative team structure.* Retrieved from https://edworking.com/blog/remotework/building-an-effective-in-house-creative-team-structure

infrastructure.

- **BMW (Germany) and Nvidia (USA)**: BMW teamed up with Nvidia to bring advanced automation and efficiency to its production lines. This partnership between German manufacturing and U.S. technology exemplifies how international collaboration can enhance traditional industries with cutting-edge capabilities.

Going Global: Expanding Your Career Horizons

Now that we've explored the global landscape of today's workforce and the challenges of working across cultures, it's time to think about how you can take advantage of these opportunities and expand your career, globally or at home, with a global organization.

Tapping into International Job Markets

If you're serious about taking your career international, start by looking at jobs in the global market. Many companies are open to hiring remote talent, especially as more businesses embrace global collaboration.[4] Keep an eye on job boards, particularly LinkedIn, and company career pages for opportunities in different countries.

You might also consider **relocating** to an emerging AI hotspot if you're interested in working in a more hands-on environment. Cities like Toronto, Shenzhen, and Berlin are home to growing AI ecosystems where you can learn from top talent and work on cutting-edge projects. Remember, not all jobs for companies are focused on AI development or engineering jobs. These hot spots offer opportunities at companies in accounting, HR, marketing, and any other function you would expect top talent to flock to.

Building a Global Professional Network

Networking is essential for any career, but it's especially important if you're looking to expand globally. Start by building connections with professionals from other countries. There are many ways to do this in today's internet-based world, but here are a few to get you started.

---

4. AllRemote. (n.d.). *How to get a remote job with no experience in 2023?* Retrieved from https://allremote.jobs/blog/How-to-get-a-remote-job-with-no-experience-in-2023

- **Online Communities**: Join AI-focused LinkedIn groups, forums, or Slack and Discord channels that have an international presence.

- **Conferences and Webinars**: Attend international conferences (virtually or in person) to connect with professionals from different countries. These events are great for learning about global trends and building your network.

- **Collaborating on Open-Source Projects**: Many AI projects are open-source, meaning you can contribute to them from anywhere in the world. This is a great way to gain experience, meet other professionals, and showcase your skills to potential employers.

AI-Proof Action Plan

Exploring Global Career Opportunities
If you're ready to explore how AI is opening doors for remote work possibilities and doors to jobs in your home country, this action plan will guide you through key steps to begin your journey. These actions are designed to help you assess your interest in international opportunities and gather the resources needed to position yourself for global success.

1. Assess Your Interest: Take 15 minutes to reflect on whether working for a foreign company or taking a remote position is something that excites you. Consider factors like time zone differences, cultural diversity, flexibility, and work-life balance. Write down your pros and cons to help clarify your thoughts on whether you'd be comfortable with international or remote work.

2. Research: Spend 30 minutes researching which countries and companies hire people with your skillset, not just AI experts. Use platforms like LinkedIn or Glassdoor to search for roles that align with your current profession but are focused on how you can use AI to improve productivity, data analysis, or efficiency. Start with the AI hotspots mentioned in this chapter—Canada, Germany, China, and India.

3. Explore Cross-Cultural Dynamics: Take a free online course or watch videos on cross-cultural communication and working with international teams. Platforms like Udemy or Coursera offer short, introductory courses on these topics. Understanding how to work with people from different countries will help you succeed if you decide to pursue global or remote opportunities.

4. Identify Resources for Learning: Subscribe to industry newsletters, job boards, and online communities where professionals in your field discuss AI-enhanced global work opportunities. Look for AI-focused LinkedIn groups or websites like Remote.co, which offer resources for remote work. Stay updated on global trends that intersect with your career field and AI technology.

5. Test the Waters: Consider joining a project or freelance platform where you can start using AI in collaboration with international teams. Websites like Upwork or Freelancer can offer short-term projects that let you explore working across borders. This will give you practical experience using AI in a global context, without the need to commit to a long-term role.

By following this plan, you'll gain a better understanding of whether remote or international work aligns with your career goals and how to prepare for opportunities in the global job market. This isn't about becoming an AI expert—it's about using the skills you're developing to explore new paths, navigate cross-cultural work environments, and access roles that may not have been on your radar before. As AI reshapes industries worldwide, your chance to expand beyond borders is closer than ever—so reach out and grab it if you're ready.

The Entrepreneur's AI Playbook

If you've ever dreamed about starting your own business, there's never been a better time to dive into AI. We're in the midst of an AI gold rush, and the opportunities for innovators are endless. Maybe you're looking to develop a brand-new AI tool, integrate AI into an existing product, consult businesses needing AI help, or build a business that leverages AI to solve real-world problems. And it doesn't stop with AI products. Maybe you've been sitting on a traditional idea, one that AI can help get out there more quickly and efficiently—whether for market research, customer engagement, or financing strategies. The point is, whatever your entrepreneurial mind is thinking, the time to act is now.

But as with any gold rush, you've got to know where to dig. The AI space is filled with hype, but not every shiny idea is worth pursuing. That's why this chapter is your playbook for understanding how to tap into AI-driven opportunities as an entrepreneur. We'll look at the AI market landscape, walk you through the steps of launching an AI-driven business, and help you assess whether you're ready to take the leap into AI entrepreneurship.

The AI Gold Rush: Opportunities for Innovators

AI is transforming industries left and right. From healthcare and finance to retail and logistics, AI is at the heart of some of the most innovative business models today. But to take advantage of this AI boom, you need to know where the opportunities lie.

Identifying Gaps and Needs in the AI Market

The key to successful entrepreneurship is finding a gap in the market—a problem that no one else is solving effectively. In the AI world, those gaps are everywhere. Businesses are struggling to harness the full potential of AI, often because they don't have the right tools, expertise, or strategies. This opens the door for you to create solutions that fill those needs.

Start by asking yourself: What are businesses struggling with when it comes to AI? Here are a few areas where opportunities are emerging:

- **AI Integration**: Many companies are collecting massive amounts of data but don't know how to use it effectively. If you can build AI solutions that help companies make sense of their data, you've got a winning idea.
- **Automation**: AI-driven automation is reshaping industries, but many businesses still rely on manual processes that could be automated. Think about industries where repetitive tasks are still the norm—whether it's manufacturing, customer service, or supply chain management—and how AI could streamline operations.
- **AI Tools for Small Businesses**: Big companies often have the resources to invest in custom AI solutions, but small and medium-sized businesses (SMBs) are left behind. There's a huge gap in the market for affordable, easy-to-use AI tools designed specifically for SMBs.
- **Ethical AI Solutions**: With growing concerns around AI bias, privacy, and transparency, there's a demand for AI solutions that prioritize ethics. If you can build AI tools that are transparent, fair, and accountable, you'll be ahead of the curve.

AI-Driven Business Models That Are Reshaping Industries

The great thing about AI is that it doesn't just create new products—it creates entirely new business models. Let's take a look at a few examples of AI-driven business models that are changing the game:

- **Subscription-Based AI Services**: AI is perfect for subscription models because it offers continuous value. Companies like Netflix and Spotify use AI to personalize content recommendations, while B2B companies offer AI-driven analytics and automation services on a subscription basis.

- **AI as a Service (AIaaS)**: AIaaS is becoming a hot trend, where companies offer AI tools and platforms that businesses can use on-demand. This allows smaller companies to access advanced AI capabilities without needing to build them in-house. Companies like Google Cloud, Microsoft Azure, and Amazon Web Services (AWS) are leading the charge in this space.

- **AI-Driven Marketplaces**: AI can help match buyers and sellers in more intelligent ways. Whether it's using AI to recommend products on e-commerce platforms or matching freelancers with clients on gig economy platforms, AI is driving smarter, more efficient marketplace models.

The Startup Landscape: What's Hot and What's Not in AI Ventures

While AI presents massive opportunities, not every idea is going to take off. Let's talk about what's hot and what's not in the AI startup world:

- **Hot**: **AI in Healthcare**. AI is revolutionizing everything from medical imaging to drug discovery. Startups that focus on improving healthcare outcomes through AI are attracting significant investment. Think about how AI can make healthcare more personalized, efficient, or accessible.

- **Hot**: **AI in Fintech**. AI is transforming the financial services industry, from fraud detection to personalized banking experiences. Fintech startups that leverage AI to enhance customer service, reduce risk, or streamline financial operations are in demand.

- **Not**: **Over-Hyped AI Assistants**. While virtual assistants like Siri and Alexa have proven useful, the market is saturated with AI chatbots that don't deliver on their promises. Be cautious about launching a chatbot unless it truly adds value and solves a specific problem.

- **Not**: **AI Without a Clear Business Case**. Just slapping "AI" onto a product doesn't make it valuable. Investors and customers are becoming more skeptical of AI startups that don't have a clear business case. Make sure your AI solution solves a real problem and has a viable market.

From Idea to Implementation: Launching an AI-Driven Business

Having a great idea is only the first step. The real challenge is turning that idea into a successful business. Let's walk through some key considerations for launching an AI-driven startup, the pitfalls to avoid, and how to turn your idea into reality.

Key Considerations for AI Startups

When starting an AI-driven business, there are a few key things you need to consider:

1. **Data Access**: AI thrives on data, so having access to high-quality, relevant data is crucial. Whether you're using customer data, operational data, or third-party data sets, your AI system will only be as good as the data it's trained on. Make sure you have a plan for acquiring, storing, and analyzing data effectively.

2. **AI Expertise**: Do you have the technical skills to build the AI system yourself, or will you need to bring in experts? If you're not a developer, consider partnering with someone who has the technical expertise to bring your idea to life.

3. **Ethics and Privacy**: AI is under increased scrutiny for issues around bias, privacy, and accountability. From the start, think about how you'll build an AI system that is ethical and transparent. This isn't just a "nice to have"—it's becoming a business necessity.

4. **Customer Understanding**: AI solutions are only valuable if they solve real problems. Spend time talking to potential customers to understand their pain points, and make sure your AI solution addresses their needs.

Pitfalls to Avoid When Integrating AI into Your Business Model[1]

Building an AI-driven business comes with its own set of challenges. Here are a few common pitfalls to avoid:

- **Over-Promising and Under-Delivering**: It's easy to get caught up in AI hype

---

1. TofuHQ. (n.d.). *The Dos and Don'ts of Using AI in Your B2B Content Marketing Efforts*. Retrieved from https://www.tofuhq.com/post/the-dos-and-donts-of-using-ai-in-your-b2b-content-marketing-efforts

and over-promise what your system can do. Be realistic about what your AI solution can achieve and set clear expectations with customers.

- **Ignoring the User Experience**: AI is powerful, but it's also complex. Make sure your product is easy to use and integrates smoothly with your customers' existing workflows. A clunky or overly technical user experience will drive customers away.
- **Underestimating the Cost**: Building an AI system can be expensive. From data acquisition to hiring AI talent, costs can quickly add up. Make sure you have a solid financial plan in place and don't underestimate the resources you'll need.

Case Studies: AI Entrepreneurs Who Struck Gold and Who Struck Out

Let's look at a couple of real-world examples of AI entrepreneurs who struck gold—and a few who didn't.

Success Stories

UiPath, an AI-driven company focused on robotic process automation (RPA), is a perfect example of how AI can revolutionize a traditional industry. By automating repetitive tasks for businesses, UiPath created a massive market and became one of the fastest-growing AI companies in the world.

OpenAI began as a research lab with the ambitious mission to ensure AI benefits all of humanity. They struck gold with the development of GPT-3, a language model that revolutionized natural language processing. By making their models accessible via API, they created immense value for businesses across industries, leading to lucrative partnerships and widespread adoption.

C3.ai, founded by Tom Siebel, created a niche in enterprise AI by focusing on software solutions that help large organizations harness AI for predictive maintenance, energy management, and more. By targeting specific needs in heavy industry and energy, C3.ai carved out a profitable segment and became a leading name in enterprise AI.

Epic Fails

Jibo, a social robot designed to assist families with everyday tasks, was an AI startup that captured a lot of attention but ultimately failed. Why? Despite the impressive technology,

Jibo struggled to deliver real value to customers, and the novelty of a social robot wasn't enough to sustain long-term demand.

While not purely an AI company, **Theranos** leveraged data analytics and AI to promise faster, cheaper blood tests. The company gained massive attention but ultimately collapsed when it was revealed it couldn't deliver the promised technology. This case underscores the importance of transparency and realistic expectations, especially in industries like healthcare.

Anki, a company that created consumer robotics like Cozmo, an AI-driven toy robot, failed to keep its momentum. Despite early enthusiasm and clever technology, the company struggled with production costs and couldn't sustain profitability, leading to its shutdown in 2019.

Your AI Startup Launchpad

Now that you have a solid understanding of the AI market, let's focus on you. Are you ready to launch your AI-driven business? In this section, we'll assess your readiness, look at resources and support systems for AI startups, and create a game plan for turning your AI business idea into a reality.

Assessing Your Readiness for AI Entrepreneurship

Before you dive in, it's important to ask yourself: Am I ready to be an AI entrepreneur? Here are a few questions to consider:

- Do I have a clear business idea that solves a real problem?
- Do I have access to the data and resources needed to build my AI solution?
- Do I have the technical expertise (or a partner who does) to bring this idea to life?
- Am I prepared for the financial investment and time commitment required to launch an AI-driven business?

If you're confident in your answers, you're off to a great start.

Resources and Support Systems for AI Startups

The good news is that there are plenty of resources and support systems available for AI entrepreneurs. Here are a few you should tap into:

- **Incubators and Accelerators**: Programs like Y Combinator, Techstars, and AI-specific incubators can provide funding, mentorship, and resources to help you get your startup off the ground.
- **AI Communities**: Join AI communities like AI startups on LinkedIn, Reddit, or specialized forums where you can network with other entrepreneurs, developers, and potential investors.
- **Online Courses and Certifications**: If you need to brush up on your AI skills, there are plenty of online courses from platforms like Coursera, Udacity, and edX that can help you gain the technical knowledge you need.

AI-Proof Action Plan

Launching Your AI Venture: A Practical Guide for New Entrepreneurs

It might not be for everyone, but if you're serious about starting an AI-focused business, this plan will give you the steps to go from idea to execution. These aren't theoretical exercises—each step is designed to move you closer to a functioning AI product or service and guide you through the process of testing, refining, and securing your first clients or investors.

1. Define Your AI Business Idea with Market Validation in Mind

Spend a focused hour brainstorming and refining a clear problem that your AI solution will solve. Think about pain points within industries you know well and ask: *Can AI make a tangible difference here?* Use this to draft a simple business hypothesis. Then, validate the idea by talking to potential customers in that field. Gather direct feedback to see if your solution resonates—don't assume market need; confirm it.

2. Draft a Lean Business Model Canvas for Your AI Product

Take the time to build a one-page business model using the Lean Canvas framework. This includes defining key elements: the problem, customer segments, unique value proposition, solution, and revenue streams. This step forces you to articulate a scalable, sustainable business model. Identify any major assumptions, and make a plan to test them as you build.

3. Build a Minimum Viable Product (MVP) with Focused Functionality

Develop a simple version of your AI product focusing on one core feature that solves the primary customer problem. This could mean using open-source AI frameworks or low-code/no-code platforms to get an initial product out quickly. The goal here is to create something tangible you can show potential customers, even if it's basic. Spend 1-2 weeks assembling a demo or prototype, focusing on the core functionality rather than perfection.

4. Seek Out Early Adopters and Pilot Opportunities

Approach five to ten companies or individuals who could benefit from your AI solution and offer to run a pilot at a discounted rate or for free in exchange for feedback and testimonials. This will give you invaluable insights into how your product performs in real-world scenarios and build credibility as you refine it. Prioritize users in your target market to ensure feedback is relevant.

5. Secure Initial Funding or Partnerships

If you need capital to advance beyond the MVP, research funding options specific to AI startups, such as government grants for tech innovation, AI-focused venture funds, or angel investors interested in AI. You can also consider accelerator programs that provide seed funding and mentorship. Alternatively, explore partnerships with established tech companies looking to support AI startups through collaborative projects or investment.

6. Refine and Scale Based on Feedback

Use the feedback from your pilot phase to identify necessary improvements and adjustments. Address any usability issues, enhance features based on user needs, and ensure that your product can handle scaling as you grow. With a more polished product, you'll be ready to start actively marketing and onboarding new clients.

Success in entrepreneurship doesn't come from having a one-off breakthrough idea—it comes from building something that genuinely adds value. By following the steps outlined in this action plan, you're laying the foundation for a venture that's innovative, practical, and market-ready. If your entrepreneurial fire was sparked in this chapter but an AI venture isn't up your alley, look for traditional business ideas you can start and collaborate with AI using the skills you have learned throughout this book to validate this venture. Whatever path you choose in the start-up arena, AI can be the product you sell, the tool that streamlines your processes, or the service that sets you apart—and it will certainly be a powerful ally in launching any business.

Future-Proofing Your Career: The Long Game

WE'VE COVERED A LOT of ground so far, from understanding AI's role in the workplace to positioning yourself as a leader in this new era. But let's face it—AI is not a static technology. It's evolving rapidly, and so is the job market. The big question now is: How do you future-proof your career when the future is so unpredictable?

The answer lies in your ability to adapt. The key to staying relevant isn't just about learning today's skills but also preparing for tomorrow's challenges. In this chapter, we'll take a deep dive into what's coming next, how AI will continue to reshape the workplace, and how you can build a long-term strategy that keeps you ahead of the curve—no matter what the future holds.

Crystal Ball Gazing: The Next Wave of AI Disruption

If you think AI has already transformed the workplace, buckle up. We're just at the beginning. Emerging AI technologies are set to disrupt industries in ways we can barely imagine right now. But let's look at some of the trends and technologies on the horizon, so you can start preparing for what's next.

Emerging AI Technologies and Their Potential Impact on Careers

I know you have heard about machine learning, natural language processing, and AI automation. But what's coming next? Here are a few emerging AI technologies that could have a huge impact on careers in the not-too-distant future:

- **Generative AI**: This is AI that can create. From writing music and designing products to generating realistic images or even code, generative AI is taking creativity to the next level. Tools like OpenAI's GPT models are already showing how AI can produce human-like content. For you, this means continuing to develop collaboration skills with AI.

- **AI in Healthcare**: AI's impact on healthcare is about to explode, with technologies like predictive diagnostics, AI-assisted surgery, and personalized treatment plans. Careers in healthcare will shift as AI starts taking over routine diagnostic tasks, which means the human roles will become more focused on complex problem-solving and patient interaction.

- **Edge AI**: Unlike traditional AI that relies on cloud computing, edge AI operates locally on devices like smartphones, sensors, and IoT devices. This is going to change the way industries manage data and make real-time decisions, creating new roles for people who can build and manage these systems.

- **AI in Education**: We're going to see a surge in AI-driven personalized learning platforms that adapt to the way each student learns best. If you're in education, prepare for AI to augment teaching and tutoring, allowing professionals to focus more on the human aspects of learning, like mentorship and emotional support.

The long-term impact? Many tasks we handle today will be taken over by AI systems, which means the value we bring to the table will be increasingly **human**—creativity, critical thinking, and emotional intelligence. Yes, the staples of human ingenuity once again.

Long-Term Trends in AI and Employment

As AI advances, the way we work will continue to evolve. Here are some of the key long-term trends that we expect to see in the AI-driven job market:

1. **The Rise of Hybrid Roles**: The future belongs to professionals who can integrate AI into their daily tasks. These "AI-augmented" roles will combine human skills with AI tools. Think marketing professionals who use AI for customer analytics or product managers who rely on AI to predict market trends.

2. **Continuous Learning Will Be Essential**: Gone are the days when a degree or a certification would carry you through an entire career. As AI evolves, so will the skills you need. Lifelong learning will be the norm, and professionals will

need to continually update their skill sets to stay relevant.[1]

3. **New Industries and Jobs Will Emerge**: Just as the internet created jobs that didn't exist a few decades ago, AI will spawn entirely new industries and roles. From AI ethics consultants to robotic process automation managers, we'll see new professions emerge that we can't fully predict yet.

Preparing for the Unknown: Building Adaptability into Your Career

No one can predict the future with 100% accuracy, but you can prepare for uncertainty by building adaptability into your career strategy. The key is to develop **transferable skills**—skills that are valuable across different roles and industries. Human skills that will only grow in importance as machines handle the grunt work will remain to be creativity, critical thinking, and emotional intelligence. While we're beating this into your head, let's remember a few others that will never go out of style:

- **Problem-solving**: The ability to approach complex problems and find creative solutions will always be in demand.
- **Communication**: As AI takes over more technical tasks, your ability to communicate complex ideas clearly and persuasively will become a critical asset.[2]
- **Leadership**: Leading teams through change, managing emotions, and inspiring innovation are all human skills that AI can't replicate.

It may sound repetitive, but the more adaptable you are, the more prepared you'll be for whatever the future brings, and having a core of highly developed soft skills will make you

1. McLaughlin, S., Sherry, M., Doherty, E., Carcary, M., Thornley, C., Wang, Y., Kolding, M., Cattaneo, G., Korte, W. B., Birov, S., Heusing, T., Steinbach, M., Fanning, F., Valdelin, E., Stoerk, M., & Krmek, M. (2014). *E-Skills: The international dimension and the impact of globalisation - Final report 2014*. Retrieved from https://core.ac.uk/download/297017576.pdf

2. College Tutors Michigan. (n.d.). *The Surprising Benefits of Teaching Others to Enhance Your Learning*. Retrieved from https://collegetutorsmichigan.com/the-surprising-benefits-of-teaching-others-to-enhance-your-learning/

stand out in any job market. Let someone else focus on programming the machine that will eventually program itself while you focus on strategic planning and innovating team dynamics.

The Augmented Professional: Humans 2.0

One of the most exciting possibilities AI brings is the potential to enhance—not replace—human capabilities. As we move into the future, professionals won't just be working with AI; they'll be **augmented** by it. Let's explore what this human-AI symbiosis looks like and what it means for your career.

The Future of Human-AI Symbiosis in the Workplace

Imagine having an AI-powered assistant that can anticipate your needs, organize your day, and even help you brainstorm creative ideas. This isn't science fiction—it's happening now. Tools like Microsoft's AI-powered Copilot are designed to work alongside professionals, enhancing productivity by handling repetitive tasks and offering data-driven insights.

In the future, we'll likely see deeper integration between humans and AI, where the AI doesn't just assist but actually *enhances* human decision-making, creativity, and problem-solving abilities. This could extend from tools on your computer or wearable devices to even more integrated forms of AI interaction. While it may seem futuristic, innovations like these are much closer than we think.

Enhancing Human Capabilities: From Brain-Computer Interfaces to AI Assistants

One of the more futuristic trends on the horizon is the development of **brain-computer interfaces** (BCIs). [3] Companies like Neuralink are exploring ways to link the human brain directly to machines, allowing for seamless interaction between thought and technology. While this is still in its early stages, it's not hard to imagine a future where professionals can "think" their way through tasks with the help of AI.

---

3. Icy Destiny. (n.d.). *Everything About Brain-Computer Interfaces (BCI) - 13 Amazing Facts*. Retrieved from https://icydestiny.com/everything-about-brain-computer-interfaces-bci/

Even without BCIs, AI assistants are becoming incredibly sophisticated. These assistants will become more than just digital helpers—they'll become collaborators. AI will help you manage information overload, make data-driven decisions faster, and even suggest new strategies based on trends it identifies in real-time.

Ethical and Practical Considerations of Becoming a "Cyborg Professional"
With all this talk of AI enhancing human abilities, there are some ethical questions we need to consider. As we integrate AI more deeply into our work, where do we draw the line between human and machine? How do we ensure that human creativity and decision-making aren't overshadowed by AI systems?

As AI continues to augment human capabilities, it's essential to strike a balance between leveraging AI and maintaining the **human touch**. AI can help you be more efficient and informed, but the key to future-proofing your career is ensuring that the **human side**—you guessed it: emotional intelligence, creativity, leadership, and critical thinking—remains front and center. Remember, AI is *our* tool. It is nothing without us, and it can never be. We create the data that feeds it. Without us, it is a loop of nonsense, creating nothing of value.

Charting Your Course in the AI Future

With all the potential changes on the horizon, how do you chart your course? It's not about having a crystal ball—it's about being smart, strategic, and **resilient** in your approach to career planning.

Techniques for Long-Term Career Planning in a Rapidly Changing Landscape
Here are a few techniques to help you stay ahead of the game as AI reshapes the job market:

1. **Scenario Planning**: Instead of betting on one career path, prepare for multiple futures. Think about several different scenarios that could unfold in your industry and plan how you would respond to each one. This gives you flexibility in a world that's constantly changing.
2. **Skill Mapping**: Regularly assess your skills and how they align with emerging trends. Map out the skills you have, the ones you need to stay relevant, and create

a timeline for acquiring them. This keeps you proactive rather than reactive to changes in the market.

3. **Continuous Learning**: Build learning into your daily routine. Whether it's listening to AI podcasts, taking online courses, or attending industry webinars, make lifelong learning a habit. The faster you can learn new skills, the more agile you'll be in responding to change.

Building Resilience and Adaptability into Your Professional Identity

Your professional identity shouldn't be tied to a specific job or title—it should be tied to your ability to adapt. The most successful professionals are those who can pivot when necessary, learn new skills, and take on new roles as industries evolve.

Here's how to build resilience and adaptability into your career:

- **Embrace Change**: Instead of fearing change, embrace it as an opportunity.[4] Look for ways to turn challenges into growth opportunities.
- **Cultivate a Growth Mindset**: A growth mindset is the belief that you can improve and adapt through hard work, learning, and resilience. This mindset is critical for thriving in an AI-driven world where the only constant is change.
- **Stay Curious—sound familiar?**: The most adaptable people are those who stay curious about the world around them. Ask questions, explore new technologies, and never stop seeking out new ways to improve.

AI-Proof Action Plan

Creating Your 10-Year AI Career Roadmap

This is what it all comes down to. As AI reshapes industries and transforms the way we work, your success will hinge on your ability to adapt, grow, and stay ahead of the curve. This roadmap isn't just another career strategy—it's the key to thriving in an AI-driven world. By mapping out your path, seizing opportunities, and continuously refining your

---

4. Coach Yas. (n.d.). *What is a Paradigm Shift*. Retrieved from https://www.coachyas.com/blog/what-is-a-paradigm-shift

skills, you'll ensure that you're not just reacting to change, but actively shaping your own future. This is your blueprint for long-term success in a rapidly evolving landscape.

1. Set Your Long-Term Vision

Start by picturing where you want to be in ten years. What industries, roles, or technologies inspire you the most? Think about the AI-driven sectors that align with your passions or where you see the most potential for growth. Whether it's healthcare, finance, education, or something else entirely, identify what truly excites you. Consider the trends you've seen emerging and imagine how you could position yourself as an expert or innovator in that space. This vision will serve as your North Star, guiding every decision and step you take over the next decade. Be specific—do you want to lead a team that integrates AI into business processes, become an expert in AI ethics, or perhaps launch your own AI-driven startup? The clearer your vision, the easier it will be to craft a meaningful roadmap.

2. Identify Key Milestones

Once your long-term vision is clear, break it down into smaller, actionable goals that will guide you toward that destination. Think of these milestones as checkpoints along your 10-year journey. In the next year, what essential skills do you need to acquire to build a strong foundation? Perhaps this includes gaining a deeper understanding of AI tools, or acquiring certifications relevant to your industry. Over the next three to five years, consider what roles you should aim for to further your experience—whether it's shifting to a position where AI plays a central role or seeking leadership opportunities that allow you to influence AI integration. By setting these tangible milestones, you'll create a realistic path for development, ensuring you're not just following trends but leading them.

3. Adapt as You Go

AI is evolving rapidly, and so will your career. The most important aspect of your 10-year roadmap is the ability to remain flexible and open to change. As new technologies, tools, and opportunities emerge, don't be afraid to pivot. For example, you might start out focused on a particular application of AI, like automation, only to find that your industry shifts toward AI-enhanced customer experience or decision-making tools. Staying agile means continuously reassessing your goals and updating your milestones to reflect the latest advancements and industry demands. Don't view your roadmap as set in stone—it's a dynamic tool that evolves as the world of AI does. Keep your long-term vision intact, but be prepared to adjust your path when unexpected opportunities arise.

The future of work may be unpredictable, but you're now equipped with the tools and mindset to navigate it. The key to thriving in an AI-driven world isn't just mastering today's skills; it's about staying adaptable, continuously learning, and evolving as technology does. AI won't replace what makes us human, but it will amplify our ability to succeed when used wisely. By following this roadmap, you're not only future-proofing your career but positioning yourself to lead in an ever-changing landscape.

Moving to Part Three, we'll turn our attention to the other aspects that influence your long-term success and well-being. From branding yourself to stand out in a crowd to balancing your life and career—we will focus on what matters most: *you*, crushing it in an AI-dominated world.

Thriving in an AI World

Rivanna Heights Media

AI and Remote Work

REMOTE WORK ISN'T JUST a trend; it's the new reality. For some of you, this means freedom—no more commutes, the chance to build a workspace that actually works for you, and the flexibility to work in sweatpants if that's your thing. But with that freedom comes a new set of challenges. Without the structure of an office, it's all too easy to drift into a rhythm that's less productive, less collaborative, and ultimately, less fulfilling. You're expected to be just as engaged, just as connected, and just as sharp—all without physically being in the same space as your team. And in an AI-driven world, those expectations are only going to get more intense.

So, how do you make remote work work for *you*? Enter AI. This isn't about using AI to replace what you do; it's about using it to level up your game. From automating your workflow to keeping you organized, AI can be the ultimate tool in your remote work arsenal if you know how to wield it. In this chapter, we're diving into the ways you can use AI to sharpen your focus, strengthen team communication, and maximize productivity—ensuring that you're not just another remote worker but a remote *force* to be reckoned with.

Optimizing Workflow and Productivity

Remote work is all about finding your rhythm, hitting deadlines, and getting results without anyone looking over your shoulder. That freedom is golden—until distractions sneak in, or tasks start to pile up. Here's where AI can make a huge difference in how you organize, prioritize, and complete your work. This isn't about micromanaging yourself; it's about setting up a framework that keeps your focus sharp and your productivity at its peak. So let's dive into how you can tap into AI-driven tools to keep your workflow smooth and maximize productivity, leaving you more time to focus on delivering your best work.

Automating Repetitive Tasks with AI

When you're working remotely, every minute counts, and one of the quickest ways to increase your efficiency is by offloading repetitive, time-consuming tasks to AI. AI-powered automation tools can handle many administrative tasks you would otherwise have to manage yourself. For instance, tools like Zapier and If This Then That allow you to create "recipes" or "zaps" that connect different apps and automate actions between them. With a few simple steps, you can set up automations to handle everything from data entry to customer responses, freeing you up to focus on the tasks that require a human touch.

For example, if you're managing a project that involves regularly updating spreadsheets, you can use an AI-driven tool to automatically pull in data from emails or other sources directly into your spreadsheets. This keeps your data current without you having to break focus every time there's an update. Or, if you're in a role that requires client engagement, you can automate certain aspects of email communication, like setting up responses for common questions or scheduling follow-ups. These small automations might seem minor, but they can add up to hours saved each week—time you can redirect to high-impact tasks.

Streamlining Task and Project Management

Remote work requires a level of self-discipline and organization that's often backed by solid task and project management. Tools like Trello, Asana, and Monday.com offer AI-driven features that simplify task tracking and project management. For instance, Trello's automation bot, Butler, can help organize your workflow by setting up automatic actions based on the criteria you choose. This means you can set reminders for due dates, assign tasks based on priority, or even move tasks between lists as they're completed.

Then there's the AI-powered project management platform, ClickUp, which can help you keep everything in one place—your to-do lists, notes, project updates, and even your time-tracking. AI assists by suggesting the best way to organize tasks based on your previous workflows, and it can even predict when you'll likely complete a project based on your current pace. With these tools, you're not just managing your tasks—you're optimizing your workflow, so every step flows smoothly into the next.

These AI tools can also assist with team communication, which is vital when you're working remotely. By integrating with tools like Slack or Microsoft Teams, project management platforms can ensure you stay in the loop on project updates without having to sift through countless messages. Notifications can be personalized, so you only get alerts when something relevant to your work changes, helping you avoid the unnecessary distraction of constant pings and messages.

Time Management and Schedule Optimization

AI can also help remote workers manage their time more effectively. Time management is one of the trickiest aspects of remote work since it's easy to lose track of time or fall into unproductive patterns. Tools like Clockwise and RescueTime leverage AI to analyze how you spend your time and provide actionable insights. Clockwise, for instance, integrates with your calendar and helps you block out "focus time" based on your meetings and appointments, rearranging your schedule to maximize productivity and minimize context-switching.

Meanwhile, RescueTime goes a step further by tracking your activities throughout the day, providing reports on which tasks are eating up your time and where you might be able to reclaim lost minutes. The tool can suggest when to take breaks and when you're most productive, so you can align your workload with the times you're at your best. This kind of insight is invaluable in a remote setting, where maintaining a work-life balance can be a challenge.

If you're working across time zones, AI can also optimize scheduling with apps like x.ai, which helps coordinate meeting times by suggesting optimal slots based on participants' availability. It acts as a virtual assistant that manages the back-and-forth of scheduling, saving you from the hassle of endless emails. With AI managing the logistics, you're free to focus on more meaningful tasks.

Reducing Distractions and Staying Focused

Staying focused is one of the biggest hurdles in remote work, where your workspace might be a home office, a coffee shop, or even your kitchen table. AI tools can help minimize distractions and keep you on track. For instance, Freedom is an app that lets you block distracting websites or apps during designated focus periods. You can customize it to block specific sites based on your habits, so if social media tends to pull you away from work, Freedom can keep you on task.

Additionally, Serene is another AI-driven productivity tool that helps you create deep focus sessions by allowing you to set daily goals, block distractions, and track your progress throughout the day. The tool will guide you through focus and break cycles, nudging you back to work if you get off track and providing gentle reminders to stay on task. These AI-based focus tools don't just manage your time—they help you create a productive environment, no matter where you're working from.

Optimizing Workflows for Collaboration

Remote work often involves collaborating with team members who may not share the same physical space. AI tools like Otter.ai for transcription and Grammarly for real-time editing feedback can make it easier to work together effectively, even from a distance. Ot ter.ai can transcribe your meetings in real time, allowing you to focus on the conversation instead of taking notes. This not only saves time but also ensures that all team members have access to accurate meeting minutes, which can be essential for maintaining alignment on projects.

Grammarly, on the other hand, ensures your communication is clear and professional. It goes beyond simple grammar checking by analyzing tone and offering suggestions to make your writing more engaging or persuasive, which can be particularly helpful in remote communication. By using AI to streamline written communication, you can ensure that messages are clear, professional, and effectively convey your intent.

Enhancing Productivity through Routine Analysis

One of the most valuable aspects of using AI for productivity is its ability to help you analyze and adjust your routines. Apps like Todoist and Forest use AI insights to assess your productivity patterns, identifying when you're most and least productive. Todoist's productivity tracker offers insights into which tasks you're consistently completing and which tend to linger, allowing you to make adjustments that improve efficiency. Forest uses a unique approach by gamifying your focus sessions, encouraging you to "grow a tree" every time you complete a focus period without interruptions. This analysis can provide you with valuable feedback on your habits and routines, helping you refine your approach to remote work over time.

By leveraging these AI tools to automate repetitive tasks, manage your time, minimize distractions, and streamline collaboration, you can create a remote work setup that's as productive as any traditional office. With AI as your ally, you're not just working remotely—you're working smart, with tools that support you at every step.

Communication and Collaboration in Virtual Teams

In a traditional office setting, communication flows naturally—there's the impromptu chat at the water cooler, the quick exchange in the hallway, and the ease of reading body language in meetings. Remote work disrupts these informal interactions, often leaving team members feeling isolated or out of sync. The beauty of AI, however, is that it can help bridge the distance, facilitating not only communication but the kind of collaboration that goes beyond just getting tasks done. Let's dig into how AI tools can make remote communication as effective (if not more so) than the in-person experience, transforming you into a team player who thrives, no matter the physical distance.

AI for Clearer Communication: Breaking Down Language and Tone Barriers
One of the biggest challenges remote teams face is maintaining clear, consistent communication. Unlike face-to-face interactions, where you can read visual cues, virtual communication relies heavily on written and video mediums, which can easily be misinterpreted. AI-powered tools are stepping in to bridge this gap, enhancing the clarity and tone of our messages, so they land as intended.

Grammarly Premium and Hemingway App are excellent examples of AI tools that refine written communication. While Grammarly offers more than just grammar checking by assessing tone, clarity, and readability, Hemingway takes it a step further by simplifying language to ensure messages are concise and clear. These tools are particularly useful in remote teams where quick, clear communication is critical. In a remote setting, you don't have the luxury of verbally clarifying everything; every word counts. Imagine sending a message to a global team—Grammarly can help you avoid cultural missteps by suggesting alternative phrases if your message might sound too direct or unclear. This can reduce misunderstandings and ensure a consistent tone across the board.

Another AI tool making waves in global communication is DeepL Translate, which outperforms traditional translators in accuracy and nuance. In multicultural teams, language barriers are often an issue, but with AI-powered translation, team members from different regions can communicate seamlessly. DeepL Translate goes beyond literal translations, capturing the subtleties of language, so a message in English can maintain its intended tone when translated to German, Japanese, or any other language. This promotes inclusivity and enables remote teams to work together without language being a limiting factor.

AI-Powered Video Conferencing: Keeping Remote Meetings Engaging and Productive

Remote meetings can be a double-edged sword—necessary for collaboration but often prone to fatigue and miscommunication. That's where AI-driven video conferencing tools come in, transforming the typical online meeting from a static presentation to a more interactive, productive experience.

Take Zoom's AI features as an example. While many know Zoom for its standard video conferencing, its AI-driven features like automated transcription and real-time translation make it a powerful tool for remote teams. Automatic transcription isn't just about note-taking; it creates a permanent, searchable record of meetings, allowing team members to revisit discussions and avoid miscommunication. If you've ever found yourself multitasking during a meeting, this feature ensures you don't miss essential points, making you a more informed and engaged participant.

For teams that rely heavily on brainstorming and real-time feedback, Miro—an AI-enhanced virtual whiteboard—is a game-changer. Miro uses AI to recognize and structure hand-drawn ideas, translating rough sketches or mind maps into clean, shareable visuals. Its intelligent templates adapt based on your inputs, making collaborative planning or design sessions feel almost like you're in the same room, jotting down ideas together on a shared whiteboard. This visual collaboration keeps teams aligned and energized, making remote work feel as dynamic as in-person meetings.

Meanwhile, Otter.ai enhances the meeting experience by acting as an "AI notetaker." Otter not only transcribes meetings in real time but also identifies key topics and summaries. This can be immensely valuable when meeting with stakeholders across time zones—team members who can't attend live can still engage with the main points later, ensuring everyone remains on the same page. AI-driven tools like Otter eliminate the need for endless post-meeting debriefs and help remote teams operate with a shared understanding of priorities and decisions.

AI Tools for Better Project Tracking and Accountability

Accountability and transparency can be challenging in a remote work environment, where team members aren't visible, and it's easy for tasks to slip through the cracks. Here, AI-powered project tracking tools ensure that everyone remains accountable, connected, and informed on project progress, deadlines, and dependencies.

Consider Notion, which is much more than a note-taking app. With its AI-powered search and task management features, Notion allows teams to organize and access project details in a way that's intuitive and easy to navigate. For example, if you're in the middle of a project and need information on a previous decision, Notion's AI search can quickly find relevant notes, ensuring you don't waste time hunting through documents. Notion also integrates with tools like Slack and Trello, giving your team a centralized platform to track tasks, assign responsibilities, and monitor timelines, enhancing overall transparency.

Trello's Butler AI—a project manager's dream—further elevates accountability by automating task assignments based on rules you set. Say you're in a team managing multiple projects; Butler can automatically assign tasks based on who has the fewest responsibilities, ensuring a balanced workload. This intelligent assignment system prevents task bottlenecks and keeps the entire team moving in sync. Butler also offers automated notifications, reminding team members of upcoming deadlines and overdue tasks, helping remote workers stay accountable without a manager's constant oversight.

For more complex project tracking, Jira leverages AI to help remote teams in tech-heavy roles, like software development, manage their workflows. Jira's AI-driven features can predict the time required for tasks based on previous work patterns and can alert teams when projects are veering off-schedule. In a remote setting where it's easy to feel isolated, having visibility into your team's progress and potential bottlenecks can foster a sense of cohesion and accountability, making you feel like you're moving forward as a unit.

Enhancing Social Connections and Team Cohesion with AI

One of the greatest losses in remote work is the informal social bonding that naturally happens in a shared office. Casual chats, spontaneous team lunches, and celebratory moments foster a sense of belonging and strengthen team dynamics. AI can play an unexpected yet impactful role in recreating these social connections.

Donut is an AI-driven Slack integration designed to facilitate team bonding in virtual environments. It pairs team members for casual "water cooler" chats, encouraging organic conversations and strengthening relationships. This AI bot promotes team cohesion by ensuring that everyone, regardless of location, has an opportunity to connect with their peers. Building strong relationships, even digitally, can be vital for collaboration, as familiarity and trust improve communication and productivity.

Additionally, Know Your Team is an AI-powered tool designed to foster transparency and camaraderie within teams. It provides structured prompts and activities that encourage open communication, personal sharing, and regular check-ins, even in a remote setting. This tool can help managers assess team morale, allowing them to step in with support if needed. For employees, it provides a safe space to express concerns or celebrate achievements, ensuring everyone feels valued and heard, which is crucial for maintaining morale in a remote team.

Cultivating Emotional Intelligence in Communication with AI Insights

In virtual communication, where body language and tone are harder to gauge, emotional intelligence becomes even more important. AI tools are emerging to help remote workers read between the lines, ensuring interactions remain positive, constructive, and emotionally intelligent.

For example, Receptiviti analyzes text-based communication to provide insights into team sentiment. By monitoring language in team chats and emails, it can detect shifts in morale or tone, flagging when certain team members may be feeling overwhelmed or disengaged. This type of AI-driven emotional intelligence is invaluable for managers who can't physically observe their team's well-being. By identifying when morale dips or tensions rise, Receptiviti empowers leaders to respond proactively, making remote work feel more supportive and connected.

Similarly, Crystal uses AI to analyze personality traits and provide insights into how best to communicate with team members. If you're working with a team member who prefers direct, data-driven conversations, Crystal will suggest aligning your communication style accordingly. In a remote setting, where misinterpretation is a risk, this kind of personalized insight can make all the difference, allowing you to connect more effectively with colleagues and foster a culture of understanding.

In today's remote work environment, effective collaboration relies on more than just the right tools—it's about how we use these tools to stay connected, motivated, and focused as a team. AI isn't just a mediator; it's a facilitator, helping remote teams bridge gaps and build relationships in a virtual landscape. By leveraging AI to improve clarity, maintain team cohesion, and enhance emotional intelligence, you're setting yourself up to be a proactive, valuable team player—one who can navigate the nuances of remote work and excel in any collaborative environment.

Staying Engaged and Building Presence in a Remote Environment

In a remote work environment, staying engaged and building a strong presence can feel like an uphill climb. You're not surrounded by coworkers, managers, or clients in the same way, and the casual interactions that might naturally foster connection and visibility just aren't as organic in virtual spaces. But with AI tools, you can be proactive about keeping engagement high, building rapport, and showing up in ways that make a difference, all without the "branding" angle.

Staying Top of Mind with Colleagues and Managers

One of the challenges in remote work is keeping your contributions visible. Without face-to-face time, it's easy for your work to go unnoticed, especially when you're not in the habit of sending regular updates. AI can help bridge this gap by making it easier to stay present and visible without feeling like you're overcommunicating.

For example, using a tool like Notion AI to create weekly project logs or progress updates allows you to share your accomplishments and ongoing tasks with your team in a simple, streamlined format. These updates help colleagues and managers see what you're working on and the value you're adding without needing to ask. As a result, you keep your role and contributions in their minds, which is critical for staying engaged and acknowledged in a remote environment.

Another approach is using Microsoft Teams' MyAnalytics feature to analyze your engagement patterns within the team. MyAnalytics provides insight into your collaboration habits, showing how often you interact with key team members or participate in shared projects. By keeping an eye on these patterns, you can identify colleagues you may need to reach out to more often or key areas where you can contribute more actively. This data-driven insight can help you stay connected and engaged with your team, so you're not just showing up—you're showing up where it matters most.

Maximizing Participation in Virtual Meetings

Virtual meetings offer one of the few real-time opportunities for interaction, and making the most of them is crucial. Using AI-powered tools like Grain or Otter.ai for real-time transcription and summarizing can free you from note-taking, allowing you to focus more fully on the conversation. With these tools handling documentation, you can participate actively and bring thoughtful responses to the table, which strengthens your presence and engagement during meetings.

With Grain, for instance, you can also highlight important sections of the meeting to share later, so you're not only engaged but actively contributing to the team's understanding of key takeaways. After the meeting, sending these snippets can reinforce the points you raised and show that you're invested in the team's progress. When team members can count on you to bring both attention and follow-through to meetings, it builds a sense of trust and respect that stands out.

Otter.ai offers similar functionality, providing live transcripts that let you stay fully engaged in the discussion without the distraction of note-taking. Later, when you're compiling action items or making follow-up points, you can rely on the transcript to back up details, making sure nothing important slips through the cracks. By focusing on the conversation itself, you're able to contribute more thoughtfully and leave an impression beyond just "showing up" to meetings.

Creating Moments of Connection in Virtual Spaces

Building rapport with colleagues is different in a remote environment, but it's no less important. Using AI-driven tools, you can maintain—and even enhance—the connections that keep team cohesion strong. A tool like Slack's Donut integration helps foster those connections by scheduling informal "virtual coffee" chats with colleagues. By setting up these casual one-on-one sessions, you're actively creating opportunities for connection that can strengthen teamwork and rapport.

Microsoft Teams AI can also support engagement by flagging important updates from team members and suggesting responses. Maybe a colleague shares a project update or milestone—Teams can prompt you to congratulate them, showing that you're paying attention and engaged with the team's overall success. These small gestures go a long way in creating a positive team atmosphere and demonstrating that you're invested in others' achievements as well as your own.

Another effective tool is Crystal Knows, which uses AI to offer insights into communication styles and preferences. While Crystal isn't strictly a "remote work tool," it can help you navigate different personalities on your team, making it easier to engage with people in a way that resonates. If you know that a teammate prefers concise, bullet-pointed updates, you can tailor your messages accordingly. These small adjustments make your interactions more effective, so you're not just communicating but genuinely connecting in a way that strengthens the virtual team dynamic.

Keeping Engagement Strong Through AI-Driven Feedback and Reflection

One of the key challenges in remote work is maintaining engagement over the long term. Without regular in-person feedback or the energy of an office environment, it's easy to feel disconnected. Using AI tools to collect feedback and self-reflect can be a proactive way to stay engaged and continuously improve.

For example, Leapsome is an AI-driven platform that helps remote teams by providing real-time feedback and performance tracking. By regularly checking in with your own progress and seeking feedback from colleagues, you can gauge how well you're engaging and where you might need to improve. This habit of consistent self-reflection keeps you motivated, showing that you're not just working in isolation but actively growing and contributing to the team's goals.

Friday is another AI-enabled tool that allows you to set weekly goals, reflect on progress, and share updates with your team. This structured reflection helps you stay engaged with your work by setting intentional goals and reviewing them regularly. Sharing these reflections can also encourage other team members to do the same, fostering a culture of continuous improvement and collective engagement.

Leveraging AI for Balanced Engagement and Preventing Burnout

While staying engaged and visible is important, remote work can also lead to burnout if you're not careful. Balancing active participation with personal boundaries is crucial, and AI can help here too. For example, Microsoft Viva offers insights into your work habits, such as when you're most active and how often you work outside regular hours.

By tracking these patterns, Viva can alert you when you're at risk of burnout, so you can adjust and take the necessary breaks to stay refreshed and productive.

Another helpful tool is RescueTime, which tracks how you're spending your time and provides alerts if you're veering into overwork territory. By helping you understand your own work patterns, RescueTime enables you to set boundaries and manage your workload sustainably. In a remote setting where it's easy to blur the lines between work and personal time, this level of insight can be a game-changer for maintaining long-term engagement without sacrificing well-being.

Creating a Strong Presence While Staying True to Yourself

Ultimately, AI can enhance your engagement and presence in remote work, but it's not about creating a forced or artificial persona. The goal is to use AI to amplify the strengths you already bring to the table—your insights, your dedication, and your collaborative spirit. Tools that help streamline communication, improve your responsiveness, and keep you connected are just aids; your unique contributions and authenticity are what truly stand out.

In the end, the key to building a meaningful presence in a virtual setting is being consistently engaged, showing up for your team, and being proactive about the ways you add value. AI can help you stay organized, connected, and effective, but your commitment to the work and your team is what makes you irreplaceable.

AI-Proof Action Plan

Thriving in Remote Work

As remote work continues to shape the modern workplace, using AI effectively can help you stay engaged, efficient, and connected. This action plan will guide you through steps to optimize your workflow, enhance communication, and maintain a strong presence—all powered by AI tools.

1. **Streamline Your Workflow with AI Task Management**
   Select an AI-driven task management tool like Notion, ClickUp, or Trello, and commit to using it consistently for one week. Track how it helps you organize tasks, prioritize effectively, and save time on routine work. Additionally, automate at least two repetitive tasks using AI tools like Zapier or IFTTT, such

as scheduling or data entry. At the end of the week, assess the impact on your workflow to ensure these tools support higher productivity.

2. **Enhance Communication with AI-Powered Transcriptions and Feedback**
   Try using real-time transcription tools like Otter.ai in your next virtual meeting to capture key points. This will allow you to focus on the conversation while ensuring accurate records. Afterward, share the transcription with your team to reinforce takeaways. You can also experiment with AI feedback tools like TINYpulse to gather insights on team engagement and collaboration. These tools will help you communicate more effectively and stay in sync with your virtual team.

3. **Stay Engaged and Visible with AI-Driven Reminders**
   Use AI-driven scheduling tools like Microsoft MyAnalytics or Google Calendar to set reminders for critical engagement opportunities, like checking in with teammates or acknowledging their achievements. Set weekly goals for staying visible and connected, and review them each week to identify areas for improvement. By consistently using these reminders, you'll ensure that your presence remains strong and supportive, even in a remote setting.

4. **Long-Term Engagement Tracking and Toolkit Refresh**
   Every month, review your communication and engagement patterns using MyAnalytics or similar AI tools to monitor consistency and visibility. Additionally, set a quarterly reminder to evaluate your toolkit and integrate at least one new AI feature or tool if it aligns with your goals. Staying up-to-date with AI innovations ensures that your remote work approach remains effective and relevant.

By following this action plan, you're setting yourself up to excel in the evolving landscape of remote work. With AI handling the routine, you'll have the time and focus to make impactful contributions and stay truly connected with your team—no matter where you are.

AI and Personal Branding

In the age of AI, standing out in the job market requires more than just technical skills—it requires a powerful personal brand. With AI automating many tasks and reshaping industries, professionals must position themselves uniquely and clearly in the workforce. How do you differentiate yourself in a world where machines can handle so much? By emphasizing the human element, showcasing your unique value, and becoming an expert in leveraging AI to solve real-world problems.

In this chapter, we'll dive deep into how you can craft and enhance your personal brand in the age of AI. From using AI tools to boost your visibility to positioning yourself as an AI thought leader, this chapter will equip you with actionable strategies for standing out in an AI-saturated job market.

Defining Your Unique Brand

Let's cut through the noise and focus on the real deal: in the age of AI, you're not just another cog in the machine. If you want to stand out, you've got to know what makes you humanly irreplaceable. AI might be able to sift through data, spit out patterns, and make complex predictions, but it lacks something fundamental—*your unique perspective and personality.* That's where your edge comes in.

Think of it this way: while AI runs on code and algorithms, you run on creativity, intuition, and experiences that have shaped how you see the world. Your unique edge is the culmination of what makes you different. It's that blend of skills, perspectives, and quirks that AI can't replicate. But to truly wield this edge, you need to pinpoint it and amplify it. This isn't about padding your resume or dropping buzzwords. It's about digging into the core of what makes you valuable and finding a way to articulate it so powerfully that it becomes the reason people seek you out.

Start with Self-Reflection: Define Your Core Value

First, let's address the foundational step: defining your core value. You might think you already know your strengths, but personal branding in the AI era requires a deeper look. It's not just about what you're good at but what you can offer that is irreplaceable. To get a handle on this, try a self-reflective exercise that looks at three critical aspects: your strengths, your passions, and the problems you love to solve.

Start by listing out your top strengths—not just the technical stuff, but the deeper skills. Are you a natural problem-solver who thrives under pressure? Do people rely on you for innovative ideas when others hit a wall? These are the kinds of skills that make you valuable in ways AI can't match. Think about what you bring to the table when everything else falls apart, and don't hold back. You might even find it helpful to think about situations where you've gone above and beyond or stood out. What did you do that others couldn't or wouldn't?

Now, layer in your passions. What kind of work makes you lose track of time? It's easy to overlook passion in professional branding, but in an era where everyone's vying to be the next data whiz, passion can set you apart. It's the spark that drives you to bring your best, even when it's challenging. And trust me, people notice when you're doing work you actually care about. AI can't feel passion, and in a world where it's automating more jobs every day, people are increasingly drawn to those who are genuinely invested in what they do.

Lastly, think about the problems you love to solve. AI can churn out answers, but problem-solving often requires that human touch—a combination of empathy, creativity, and nuance. Where do you shine when there's a challenge? Maybe you're the person who brings order to chaos, or perhaps you have a knack for breaking down complex issues in a way that makes sense to everyone. Pinpointing the kinds of problems you love to tackle gives you a lens through which you can approach branding that's authentic and impactful.

Seek Outside Perspectives: Ask for Feedback

Even with introspection, it can be tough to get a fully rounded picture of yourself. This is where feedback comes into play. If you want to know what your unique edge is, ask the people who've worked with you. Approach trusted colleagues, mentors, or friends who've seen you at your best. Ask them directly: *What do you see as my superpower? What makes me stand out from others you've worked with?*

You might feel a bit vulnerable asking these questions, but the responses can be eye-opening. You may discover qualities you weren't fully aware of or downplayed. Sometimes, others see strengths in us that we take for granted. Maybe you're the one who keeps a team calm under pressure, or you have an intuitive knack for understanding client needs. AI can't offer that level of human connection or inspire trust in the same way you do. Understanding what others value in you helps you refine your brand with a sense of clarity and confidence.

If you want an even deeper dive, consider using feedback tools like 360-degree reviews or surveys. Some people shy away from structured feedback, but in the AI era, real-time insights into your strengths and weaknesses are invaluable. Getting this feedback allows you to make adjustments to how you present yourself, aligning more closely with the impact others see in you. Remember, your edge isn't something that should stay static; it should evolve as you gather more insight and adapt to the changing landscape.

Craft Your Core Message: Sharpen Your Unique Value Proposition

Once you've identified your strengths, passions, and the problems you're driven to solve, it's time to pull it all together into a unique value proposition. This is the message you want people to remember when they think of you—the answer to why they should choose you over anyone else. But remember, this isn't an elevator pitch; it's a brand statement. It should be concise, memorable, and encapsulate the heart of what you bring that AI can't.

Here's an example: "I help teams turn complex data into clear strategies by connecting the dots that others miss, blending deep technical insight with a creative approach that brings a human touch to decision-making." This statement is specific, it emphasizes your human edge, and it's memorable. Your value proposition should be simple enough to be easily remembered but layered enough to convey depth. Avoid bland generalizations like "hard-working" or "dedicated"; those don't distinguish you. Instead, think of what you bring that's uniquely yours.

Build Authenticity into Your Brand

Personal branding isn't about showing a polished version of yourself—it's about showing the real, unfiltered version of you that adds value. Authenticity is more than a buzzword; it's the foundation of any effective brand, especially in the AI age, where people crave real connections. Don't try to hide your quirks or pretend to be something you're not. Embrace your unique style, whether that's a direct approach, a sense of humor, or an unconventional way of thinking. AI can simulate a lot, but it can't replicate authenticity.

Consider creating content or engaging in discussions that highlight your personal views and insights. Share the lessons you've learned, the challenges you've overcome, or even your failures. These human experiences are what make your brand relatable and memorable. People are more likely to trust and connect with someone who owns their story, warts and all, than someone who only highlights their successes. AI doesn't have a backstory; you do. Make it count.

Be Consistent and Intentional

Your edge isn't something you discover once and forget. It's a living, breathing part of your professional identity that should show up consistently in everything you do. From the way you handle meetings to how you interact on LinkedIn, your brand should communicate the same message over and over. Consistency is key because, in a world where AI tools are being widely adopted, people crave reliability and authenticity. If you're scattered in your messaging, it can dilute your brand and leave people uncertain about what you stand for.

Being intentional doesn't mean over-curating your image; it means staying true to the strengths and values you've identified. When new opportunities arise, consider how they align with your core value proposition. Staying true to your edge may mean saying "no" to projects or roles that don't align with your brand. It might feel counterintuitive in the short term, but in the long run, it reinforces your identity and strengthens your value in the eyes of others.

Bringing It All Together: Your Edge as a Foundation

Finding your unique edge isn't just about defining who you are—it's about setting the foundation for every professional move you make in an AI-dominated world. It's your answer to why someone would choose you over a machine. Once you've identified it, own it with confidence and let it guide how you present yourself. Remember, AI may automate the basics, but it can't replace the human nuances you bring. Define your edge, hone it, and make it your unbreakable foundation. That's how you stay relevant—and indispensable.

Amplifying Your Brand

Here's the thing: it doesn't matter if you're the best strategist, the sharpest problem-solver, or the most empathetic leader—if no one knows it, your brand is invisible. In a world where AI is reshaping how we communicate and gather information, you've got an opportunity to use these tools to boost your visibility, not replace your voice. Think of AI as your sidekick in this mission, enhancing your reach, expanding your influence, and helping you stay on top of the trends. In this section, we'll dive into how to use AI to get your personal brand in front of the right people, ensuring your unique value doesn't get lost in the noise.

Automate Your Outreach: Make Connections While You Sleep

First, let's talk about one of AI's best tricks: automation. Building a brand used to mean hours spent on repetitive tasks—sending emails, responding to messages, following up with contacts, and staying active on social media. Now, AI tools can handle a lot of these tasks for you, freeing up your time while keeping you connected. Use AI-powered automation to manage email sequences, social media scheduling, and even some personalized outreach. Tools like LinkedIn automation bots (when used smartly) can help you reach out to new contacts, introduce yourself to potential mentors or clients, and build connections—all while you focus on the work only you can do.

But here's the golden rule: automate without losing the personal touch. Set up templated responses, but tweak them. AI can help you scale, but it's your personality that will keep people engaged. For instance, you might use AI to schedule posts and messages at optimal times or automate follow-up emails to people you've met at networking events. Just remember, people connect with people, not bots, so make sure your personality comes through in every interaction.

Analyze Your Impact: Get Real-Time Feedback on Your Brand

Your personal brand isn't just what you put out there; it's also how people perceive it. And AI can give you a real-time look at how your brand is landing. With sentiment analysis tools, you can gather insights on how your messages, content, and interactions are resonating with your audience. These tools analyze words and tone in comments, reviews, and feedback to show whether the response to your brand is positive, neutral, or negative. This isn't about obsessing over every comment or like, but rather about understanding trends in how your brand is perceived.

For example, if you're posting industry insights on LinkedIn, a sentiment analysis tool can give you a feel for how these posts impact your reputation. Maybe people are finding your tone overly technical, or perhaps they're responding positively to posts where you add a bit of humor. This feedback is gold. It allows you to adjust your brand in real time, steering your content and interactions in a way that resonates more deeply. It's almost like getting an instant focus group for your brand—insightful and immediate.

Curate a Strong Online Presence: Be Seen Where It Counts

Having a great personal brand won't do you any good if it's hidden in a corner of the internet no one visits. AI can help you position your brand in the spaces where it's most likely to get noticed by the right people. With AI tools for social listening, you can monitor keywords, track trends, and understand what topics are gaining traction in your industry. Armed with this insight, you can tailor your content to stay relevant, and show up in places where your target audience is already looking.

Use AI to identify when your network is most active and what content resonates best. If your industry is buzzing about a new technology or regulation, join the conversation. Tools like BuzzSumo or Google Trends can help you pinpoint what's hot in your field so you can engage thoughtfully, showing that you're tuned in and offering unique perspectives on timely topics. Posting at the right time and engaging on relevant content shows that you're not just visible—you're *strategically* visible, appearing in discussions that add weight to your brand.

Stay Updated on Trends: Position Yourself as a Thought Leader

AI moves fast, and if you want to maintain a personal brand that stays relevant, you need to stay ahead of the curve. Fortunately, AI tools can make it easier to keep up with trends, new technologies, and emerging topics in your industry. Set up AI alerts for news and updates on your key topics, using tools like Feedly, Pocket, or even Google Alerts. By keeping tabs on the latest trends, you can incorporate timely insights into your posts, content, and conversations, positioning yourself as someone who's not only up-to-date but also has a unique perspective on where things are heading.

Think about it: if you're regularly sharing insights that others are only beginning to notice, you're no longer just another professional in the field—you're a thought leader. Thought leaders aren't just tuned in to what's happening now; they're looking ahead, helping others see the bigger picture. Using AI tools to stay informed means that you're always one step ahead, ready to contribute something meaningful instead of merely reacting. It's a subtle shift, but it can elevate your brand immensely.

Expand Your Influence: Use AI to Connect with Like-Minded Professionals

Building a network isn't just about the number of people you know; it's about who those people are and how they align with your brand. AI can help you find and connect with like-minded professionals, mentors, or potential collaborators by identifying people with shared interests, skills, or industry focus. LinkedIn, for instance, uses AI to suggest connections based on mutual connections, shared interests, and work history. Tools like Shapr or Meetup can help you find professional events, groups, and communities where you can connect with others who share your interests.

AI's suggestions aren't perfect, of course, but they can be a powerful starting point. Once you're connected, bring the human element into play. Set up one-on-one conversations, and build genuine relationships rather than just collecting contacts. These connections are valuable because they help you expand your reach and influence in circles that matter to your brand. And remember, AI can help you get in the door, but it's your authenticity and insight that keep you there.

Bottom Line: Amplify, Don't Replace

Using AI to amplify your personal brand is about finding ways to extend your reach without diluting your message. It's a powerful sidekick for handling the repetitive tasks, monitoring trends, and making connections, but it's not the star of the show—you are. Let AI do the heavy lifting in the background, gathering insights, automating tasks, and analyzing impact, while you stay focused on what truly matters: the human connections, insights, and creativity that AI simply can't replicate.

Remember, this isn't about creating a robotic brand that checks every algorithmic box. It's about using AI to help you maximize the impact of your unique edge, ensuring that what makes you irreplaceable doesn't go unnoticed. By strategically amplifying your brand with AI, you're not just keeping up—you're setting yourself apart in a way that even the smartest algorithms can't touch.

AI-Proof Action Plan

Building Your Unique Brand in the Age of AI

With AI automating various tasks and reshaping industries, establishing a powerful personal brand is essential for standing out in today's job market. This action plan will guide you through defining, amplifying, and maintaining your brand—all with the support of AI tools that enhance, not replace, your unique impact.

1. Define Your Unique Value Through Self-Reflection

Identify your core strengths, passions, and the types of problems you enjoy solving. Spend a week reflecting on your experiences, skills, and personal qualities that set you apart. Focus on attributes that highlight your unique perspective, empathy, and creativity—qualities that make you irreplaceable.

2. Share Your Brand Consistently Using AI-Driven Content Tools

Use tools like Buffer or Hootsuite to schedule weekly posts that align with your brand's message. Share insights, experiences, and perspectives that illustrate your human qualities and expertise. This consistency helps reinforce your brand and ensures it stays visible to your network.

3. Refine Your Brand Based on Audience Feedback and Perception

Track how your content is received using sentiment analysis tools like Brandwatch. Monthly, review audience reactions and feedback to fine-tune your messaging, ensuring it aligns with how you want to be perceived. Adjust as needed to keep your personal brand relevant and impactful.

With your brand now defined and amplified, you've established a powerful foundation that sets you apart in an AI-driven world. This approach ensures that your unique qualities, insights, and strengths are seen and valued. By bringing clarity and reach to your brand, you're positioning yourself as indispensable and ready to thrive in a rapidly evolving landscape.

LOVING THE AI-PROOF STRATEGIES?

"Success isn't just about what you accomplish, it's about what you inspire others to do." – Lewis Howes

You've made it this far, and I hope you're enjoying the book and finding valuable insights to help advance your career. If you have found even one piece of information helpful, your fellow readers would love to hear about it. Or, maybe this guide has helped you rethink your career in the age of AI, take a moment to share your experience!

Why Your Review Matters:

- Helps other professionals find proven strategies for navigating the AI revolution
- Guides the development of future books and resources
- Contributes to a community of forward-thinking professionals

Leave Your Review in 60 Seconds: Simply click or scan the QR code below to leave your review on Amazon. It only takes a minute, but your influence could last a lifetime.

Quick Prompt: Which strategy sparked your biggest "aha moment"? What surprised you most about AI's impact on your industry?

AI and Work-Life Balance

AI HAS REVOLUTIONIZED THE workplace, driving productivity to levels we couldn't have imagined a decade ago. But with this increased efficiency comes a challenge we're all familiar with: how do you balance the constant demand for performance in an AI-powered, always-on world with the need for downtime, self-care, and maintaining relationships?

In this chapter, we'll explore the double-edged sword of AI when it comes to work-life balance. We'll look at how AI can help streamline tasks, but also how it can blur the lines between work and personal life. We'll also tackle how AI impacts mental health in the workplace and provide strategies to build resilience. Finally, you'll learn how to create a plan for achieving harmony between your career in AI and your personal life, so you can thrive without burning out.

The Double-Edged Sword of AI Productivity

AI tools have transformed the way we work. They automate repetitive tasks, analyze data faster than we can, and even predict outcomes that help us make better decisions. With AI, it feels like there's no limit to what we can accomplish. But here's the catch: just because we *can* be more productive doesn't mean we *should* always be pushing ourselves to the limit.

How AI Can Both Improve and Complicate Work-Life Balance

Let's start with the positives. AI has the potential to give you back some of your time by taking over the mundane, repetitive tasks that usually bog down your day. Imagine an AI tool that handles all your scheduling, reminds you of important deadlines, or even automates certain reports you once had to manually put together. AI tools like these allow you to focus on high-impact tasks that really matter and, ideally, free up more time for your personal life.

But—and it's a big but—AI also has the downside of making work feel ever-present. AI-powered apps are so good at keeping us connected that it's easy to feel like you're never truly off the clock. Emails, Slack messages, and notifications don't stop when you leave the office (or close your laptop if you work from home). AI-driven productivity tools may encourage an "always-on" mentality, where boundaries between work and life blur, creating pressure to be constantly available.

Strategies for Setting Boundaries in an Always-On AI World

So how do you make sure AI works *for* you and not the other way around? The key is setting boundaries—and sticking to them. Here are a few strategies that will help you keep your work and personal life in balance, even in the face of AI-enabled productivity tools:

1. **Turn Off Notifications**: AI might help keep you productive, but you're not a machine. Set clear boundaries by turning off non-essential notifications after work hours. Many apps and tools now offer "do not disturb" modes or scheduled times where notifications are paused. Use these features to protect your personal time.

2. **Automate with Intention**: Just because AI can automate something doesn't mean you should let it take over every aspect of your work. Be intentional about which tasks you delegate to AI. For example, automate the repetitive parts of your job, but make sure the work that requires creativity or personal interaction stays on your plate. This keeps you engaged without overwhelming you.

3. **Set AI-Free Zones**: Create spaces in your day where AI doesn't intrude. For instance, you might decide that dinner with your family is a no-tech, AI-free time, or that you won't check work-related AI tools after 7 p.m. Giving yourself some AI-free time helps reset your mind and maintain the boundaries between work and life.

The Importance of Digital Detox in Maintaining Human Skills

We live in a digital world, but that doesn't mean we should be tethered to our devices 24/7. One of the most important things you can do for your mental health and long-term career success is to take a regular "digital detox." This doesn't mean abandoning technology entirely, but rather creating intentional breaks where you step away from screens and focus on offline activities that nurture your creativity and well-being.

The irony is that the more you rely on AI and tech tools, the more important it becomes to give your mind time to disengage. A digital detox helps recharge your brain, reduces stress, and keeps you sharp, allowing you to bring your best self back to work when it's time to plug in again.

Mental Health and Wellbeing in the AI Workplace

As AI continues to reshape the workplace, we're seeing both incredible opportunities and new challenges when it comes to mental health and well-being. While AI can enhance productivity, it can also create stress, anxiety, and a feeling of being left behind in an ever-changing job market.

Addressing Stress and Anxiety in Rapidly Changing AI Environments

Let's be real—navigating the AI revolution can be stressful. The rapid pace of change, the constant demand to learn new tools, and the fear of becoming obsolete are all common sources of anxiety for professionals today.[1] But here's the good news: you're not alone, and there are ways to manage this stress while staying adaptable.

1. **Embrace Lifelong Learning**: One of the best ways to reduce anxiety about AI is to embrace the idea of continuous learning. Instead of fearing the next AI update, see it as an opportunity to expand your skill set. When you're always learning, you won't feel blindsided by new technology.

---

1. Aquarius AI. (n.d.). *Understanding Education Technology: A Comprehensive Guide.* Retrieved from https://aquariusai.ca/blog/education-technology-revolutionizing-the-way-we-learn-and-teaching-students-for-success-in-the-digital-age

2. **Practice Mindfulness and Resilience**: Mindfulness can be an effective tool for managing stress in a fast-paced AI environment. Take short breaks during the day to practice mindfulness, whether it's a few minutes of deep breathing or a walk outside.[2] These moments help calm your mind, making it easier to handle the pressures of a rapidly changing workplace.

3. **Seek Support**: Don't be afraid to reach out for support if you're feeling overwhelmed. Whether it's talking to a mentor, seeking professional counseling, or simply connecting with coworkers who are facing similar challenges, building a support network is key to maintaining your mental health in an AI-driven workplace.

Building Resilience and Adaptability for Long-Term Career Success

Resilience is a muscle that gets stronger the more you use it. In an AI-driven world, where change is constant, building resilience will be one of your greatest assets. But how do you develop this trait?

1. **Focus on What You Can Control**: You can't stop AI from advancing, but you can control how you respond to it. Focus on the skills you can develop, the projects you can contribute to, and the relationships you can build. When you take proactive steps, you'll feel more empowered in your career.

2. **Celebrate Small Wins**: AI advancements can make it feel like you're always trying to catch up, which can be demoralizing. Combat this by celebrating your small wins. Every new AI tool you learn or project you complete is a step forward—acknowledge those victories to keep yourself motivated.

3. **Stay Connected to Your Purpose**: One of the most effective ways to build resilience is to stay connected to your "why." Why are you in this career? How does AI help you fulfill your purpose? When you focus on the bigger picture, it becomes easier to adapt to the smaller changes AI introduces.

---

2. Half The Sky. (2023, December). *Office SOS: Ways to Beat Stress at Work*. Retrieved from https://www.halftheskyasia.com/blog/2023/12/office-sos-ways-to-beat-stress-at-work

The Role of Human Connection in an AI-Dominated Workplace
We know that AI might be great at handling tasks and, more importantly, that it can't replace the value of human connection. As more work becomes automated, the relationships you build with your colleagues, clients, and network will become even more critical.

Human skills like empathy, collaboration, and leadership are irreplaceable—and they're becoming increasingly important as AI takes over more technical tasks. Make it a priority to foster genuine connections at work. Whether that's through virtual coffee chats, team-building activities, or simply making time to listen to a coworker, these relationships are what will keep you grounded in a high-tech world.

Your Work-Life Harmony Plan

Achieving work-life balance in the AI era isn't about creating a perfect 50-50 split between work and personal time—it's about finding harmony. It's about integrating AI tools into your work in a way that maximizes efficiency without sacrificing your well-being or personal fulfillment. Here's how to create a work-life harmony plan that works for you.

Techniques for Integrating AI Tools Without Sacrificing Personal Time
1. Use AI to Automate, Not Overload: Use AI tools to take things off your plate, not pile more on. For example, if an AI tool can handle routine tasks, don't fill that newfound time with more work—use it to take a break, reflect, or focus on personal growth.

2. Set Tech-Free Times: Establish clear times in your day when you disconnect from AI tools. Whether it's during meals, family time, or weekends, having tech-free moments is essential for maintaining your mental and emotional health.

3. Work in Sprints: AI can help you maximize productivity by working in focused "sprints" where you tackle specific tasks for a set period, followed by a break. This technique helps you stay productive without feeling burned out by constant work.

Creating a Sustainable Career Path in the High-Paced AI Industry
Sustainability isn't just about preserving the environment—it's about creating a career path that's sustainable for your life. In a fast-paced AI industry, this means pacing yourself, prioritizing self-care, and not falling into the trap of thinking you need to work 24/7 to keep up with the machines.

- **Set Realistic Goals**: Understand that you don't need to be an AI expert overnight. Set achievable goals for learning AI tools, and allow yourself time to grow into new responsibilities.
- **Prioritize Downtime**: Building a successful AI career is a marathon, not a sprint. Make time for hobbies, exercise, and relationships—these are what sustain you in the long run.

AI-Proof Action Plan

Achieving Balance and Fulfillment in Your AI Career Journey

In an AI-driven workplace, maintaining a balance between productivity and personal well-being is essential. This final action plan outlines three steps to help you use AI tools effectively without sacrificing mental health or relationships.

1. Set Boundaries for AI Use to Protect Personal Time

Create clear boundaries to prevent AI tools from overwhelming your personal time. Turn off non-essential notifications after work hours, using "do not disturb" settings on your devices. Establish AI-free times, such as family meals or weekends, to ensure genuine downtime. Limit automation to repetitive tasks, leaving creative or high-engagement activities for yourself.

2. Prioritize Mental Health with Digital Detoxes and Mindfulness

Schedule regular digital detoxes to unplug and recharge. Aim for at least one day per week where you step away from screens and engage in offline activities that nurture mental well-being. Incorporate mindfulness practices into your routine, such as short breathing exercises or walks, to manage stress. Build a support network by connecting with colleagues or groups that focus on maintaining work-life balance in an AI-driven environment.

3. Develop a Sustainable Career Growth Plan

Set achievable goals for learning new AI tools, focusing on mastering one feature or tool each month to avoid overwhelm. Use AI to support productivity sprints—work in focused 45-50 minute intervals followed by short breaks to maximize efficiency while preventing burnout. Celebrate small wins weekly to build resilience and stay motivated for long-term success in the AI industry.

In the new era of work, achieving balance might seem like an elusive goal, but it's entirely within your reach if you're intentional about it. AI can be a powerful ally in helping you get more done in less time, but only if you maintain clear boundaries and prioritize your mental health. By integrating AI thoughtfully into your work and setting limits, you can create a sustainable, fulfilling career that doesn't come at the expense of your personal well-being.

Conclusion: Your Next Chapter

As you turn the last pages of *AI-Proof Your Career*, you might feel a mix of excitement, curiosity, and perhaps even a sense of relief. If so, you're not alone. Embracing AI in your career can feel like stepping into uncharted territory—but it's also an unprecedented opportunity. This isn't the end of a journey; it's the beginning of a transformative new chapter.

Reflect on the stories we discussed at the beginning: a junior copywriter who outpaced her team, a radiologist who doubled his impact, and a small business owner who transformed his business model. None of these individuals succeeded simply because of a flashy new AI tool. They succeeded because they saw beyond the hype, understanding that AI wasn't a threat to their career—it was a force multiplier. They saw AI not as a replacement, but as a partnership, enhancing their unique human skills and allowing them to reach new heights.

Throughout this book, you've gained insights into the principles, strategies, and mindsets that empower people to navigate and excel in this rapidly changing landscape. You've examined the fundamental shifts that AI is bringing to the workplace and learned how to leverage those shifts—from tackling ethical considerations to building a distinctive personal brand. By understanding AI's impact on careers, embracing the AI-driven workforce, and mastering the skills needed to succeed in an AI-enhanced world, you've equipped yourself with the tools to stay ahead.

The Power of Adaptability

One theme has run through every page: adaptability. In an era where technology evolves faster than ever, the most crucial skill you can cultivate is your ability to adapt. But remember, adaptability isn't just about learning new software or keeping up with industry trends. It's about being open-minded, resilient, and constantly willing to redefine what success looks like for you. Embracing AI in your career requires flexibility, curiosity, and an eagerness to reinvent yourself as often as needed.

You're not just adapting to the AI age; you're helping to shape it. Whether you're an entry-level employee or a seasoned executive, your decisions, actions, and attitude toward AI contribute to how it's integrated into your industry. By staying proactive, continuously learning, and seeking out ways to contribute uniquely, you're defining your path and ensuring that AI enhances, rather than dictates, your professional journey.

Building Your Unique Edge

AI may be powerful, but it's not infallible. It lacks creativity, intuition, empathy, and the ability to make ethical decisions with true understanding—qualities that only humans possess. As you move forward, remember that your human strengths are your most valuable assets. Use AI to complement those strengths, not overshadow them. Cultivate a strong personal brand, stay attuned to ethical implications, and prioritize your personal growth as much as your technical skills.

You've learned in this book how critical it is to identify your unique human edge and leverage AI to amplify it. Instead of focusing on what AI can replace, focus on what it can empower you to do better, faster, and on a larger scale. As AI automates the routine, you're free to invest your energy into creative problem-solving, strategic thinking, and relationship-building—the irreplaceable pillars of career success.

A Future Full of Possibilities

The AI-driven world presents endless opportunities. You can reshape your role, lead innovation in your field, and even break into new career paths that didn't exist before. Imagine the possibilities: starting your own AI-enabled business, becoming a sought-after leader in ethical AI practices, or pioneering remote work strategies that prioritize human connection. The future is what you make of it.

Think of this book as a launchpad—a foundation of insights and strategies to help you soar in the AI era. As AI continues to evolve, so too will the skills and strategies needed to succeed. Keep learning, stay curious, and don't hesitate to question the status quo. The professionals who thrive will be those who constantly ask, "What's next?" and are willing to push boundaries.

Your Role in the AI Narrative

In this journey, you have a choice: you can be a passive participant, waiting to see how AI will impact you, or you can take an active role, steering your career in the direction you want it to go. By choosing the latter, you're securing your own future and contributing to a broader narrative. You're helping shape the ethical, innovative, and inclusive integration of AI in our society.

Remember, AI is a tool, but the vision and values that guide it are human. Every step you take in your career reflects on how AI is applied in the workforce. Lead with integrity, remain mindful of the ethical implications, and use AI to advance not just your career, but also the welfare of those around you. This isn't just about AI-proofing your career; it's about setting a standard for what responsible, impactful AI integration looks like in your industry.

Moving Forward with Confidence

The journey may not always be straightforward, and there will be moments of doubt and setbacks. But know this: you have the tools, the insights, and the resilience to navigate the challenges ahead. You've equipped yourself to handle the AI era and thrive within it. The AI world is vast and complex, but it's also full of potential—potential that's now within your reach.

As you close this book, keep the momentum going. Start by implementing one or two strategies you found most impactful. Revisit this book when you need guidance, fresh insights, or a reminder of why you embarked on this journey. And most importantly, stay engaged, keep learning, and share your journey with others. Whether you're inspiring your colleagues, mentoring younger professionals, or advocating for responsible AI practices, your actions can create a ripple effect, helping others find their way in the AI world.

So here's to the future—the future you're not just part of, but one you're actively shaping. Embrace the challenges, seize the opportunities, and remember: in this AI-driven world, the power lies not in the technology itself, but in how you choose to use it.

The AI age is here. Make it yours.

Appendix: Tools Featured in This Book

Grammarly: AI-powered writing assistant that improves grammar, spelling, clarity, and style.
Career Boost: Enhances written communication skills for emails, reports, and presentations, allowing professionals to convey ideas clearly and professionally.
Experience Level: Beginner-friendly; intuitive interface with instant, easy-to-understand feedback.

Trello's Butler: Automates tasks within the Trello project management tool.
Career Boost: Improves productivity in project management by automating repetitive board tasks.
Experience Level: Beginner-friendly; uses simple, rule-based automation.

Google Analytics: Tracks and analyzes website traffic and user behavior.
Career Boost: Enables data-driven marketing and content strategy, essential for roles involving web analysis.
Experience Level: Moderate; some familiarity with data analysis is helpful, but tutorials are widely available.

Zapier:
Purpose: Connects applications to automate repetitive tasks across platforms.
Career Boost: Streamlines workflows by linking multiple tools, reducing manual work.
Experience Level: Highly beginner-friendly with an intuitive drag-and-drop interface.

ChatGPT (and similar tools like Claude and Gemini): Generates text, assists with prompts, and supports creative and analytical tasks.

Career Boost: Enhances content creation, idea generation, and problem-solving, useful in many career fields.
Experience Level: Extremely intuitive; chat-based interface for easy use.

Google Assistant: Virtual assistant for scheduling and reminders.
Career Boost: Increases productivity with quick access to scheduling and task reminders.
Experience Level: Very beginner-friendly; accessible with voice or text commands.

IFTTT (If This Then That): Connects apps and devices to automate workflows.
Career Boost: Saves time by automating repetitive digital actions through simple "If-Then" rules.
Experience Level: Highly accessible for beginners.

Microsoft Power Automate: Automates workflows within the Microsoft suite and beyond.
Career Boost: Improves efficiency by integrating and automating tasks across Microsoft applications.
Experience Level: Moderate; templates assist with setup, but some familiarity with automation helps.

Todoist: Task management tool with goal-setting and tracking features.
Career Boost: Enhances organizational skills, helps set and meet productivity goals.
Experience Level: Very easy to use with a straightforward interface.

Google Cloud, Microsoft Azure, AWS: Provide scalable AI-as-a-Service (AIaaS) platforms and tools.
Career Boost: Offers advanced AI tools, useful for developing technical skills in tech-driven roles.
Experience Level: Moderate to advanced; technical knowledge is beneficial, but tutorials are provided.

UiPath: Focuses on robotic process automation (RPA) to automate repetitive business tasks.
Career Boost: Reduces manual workload, freeing up time for high-value activities in operations.

Experience Level: Moderate; basic understanding of RPA is helpful, but training resources are available.

OpenAI: Advanced language models (e.g., GPT-3) accessible via API for varied applications.
Career Boost: Supports business functions like customer service, content creation, and data analysis.
Experience Level: Moderate; API use may require some technical setup.

C3.ai: Enterprise-level AI solutions for predictive analytics and other applications.
Career Boost: Valuable for managing enterprise functions like predictive maintenance and energy management.
Experience Level: Less beginner-friendly; designed for industry professionals.

Copilot: AI-powered assistant in Microsoft tools that handles repetitive tasks and offers insights.
Career Boost: Boosts productivity by summarizing data, generating reports, and assisting with content.
Experience Level: Very accessible, especially for Microsoft Office users.

Clockwise: AI scheduling tool that optimizes calendar for focus time.
Career Boost: Helps professionals manage their time effectively by blocking out dedicated focus periods.
Experience Level: Beginner-friendly with automated scheduling features.

RescueTime: Tracks time spent on activities and provides productivity insights.
Career Boost: Helps identify time-wasters and improve personal productivity habits.
Experience Level: Very user-friendly with a simple dashboard.

x.ai: AI scheduling assistant that coordinates meeting times.
Career Boost: Streamlines scheduling, reducing back-and-forth communication for meetings.
Experience Level: Very easy to use, accessible via calendar integrations.

Freedom: Distraction-blocking app that limits access to time-wasting websites.
Career Boost: Supports focus and productivity by blocking distracting sites.
Experience Level: Very easy to set up and manage.

Serene: Creates deep focus sessions and minimizes distractions for enhanced productivity.
Career Boost: Helps users work in concentrated sprints, improving focus and task completion.
Experience Level: Beginner-friendly with pre-set focus session options.

Otter.ai: Transcribes meetings and conversations in real-time.
Career Boost: Useful for documentation and reviewing meeting minutes, ideal for collaborative roles.
Experience Level: Simple setup with intuitive transcription features.

Forest: Gamifies focus sessions by letting users "grow a tree" for each focused work period.
Career Boost: Encourages concentration and productivity through gamified focus sessions.
Experience Level: Easy to use with an engaging, gamified design.

ClickUp: AI-enhanced project management platform that organizes tasks and workflows.
Career Boost: Streamlines task management, improves team collaboration, and increases productivity.
Experience Level: Beginner-friendly with templates and workflows.

MyAnalytics: Provides insights into work habits and collaboration patterns.
Career Boost: Allows professionals to optimize productivity and collaboration within the Microsoft ecosystem.
Experience Level: Accessible for Microsoft Teams users with helpful insights.

Miro: Collaborative virtual whiteboard with AI enhancements for brainstorming.
Career Boost: Supports remote team brainstorming and project collaboration with interactive tools.
Experience Level: Very user-friendly with intuitive tools.

Donut: Slack integration that pairs team members for casual, virtual chats.
Career Boost: Strengthens team relationships and fosters workplace culture remotely.
Experience Level: Easy to set up and use within Slack.

Notion AI: Assists with note-taking, task management, and intelligent search.
Career Boost: Organizes information effectively, supporting project management and personal productivity.
Experience Level: Beginner-friendly; works seamlessly within the Notion platform.

Grain: Offers real-time transcription and meeting highlights.
Career Boost: Facilitates documentation and helps with engagement in virtual meetings.
Experience Level: Simple to use in virtual meeting settings.

Know Your Team: Builds team transparency and communication through structured activities.
Career Boost: Enhances team bonding and openness in remote or distributed teams.
Experience Level: Beginner-friendly with guided team activities.

Crystal Knows: Analyzes communication styles to improve interpersonal skills.
Career Boost: Supports personalized communication strategies for improved team interactions.
Experience Level: Moderate; setup required, but insights are valuable.

Receptiviti: Analyzes team sentiment and morale from communication patterns.
Career Boost: Helps managers understand team morale, fostering a positive workplace.
Experience Level: Moderate; useful for team leads and HR professionals.

Leapsome: Facilitates performance tracking and real-time feedback.
Career Boost: Boosts team engagement and alignment on goals, enhancing performance.
Experience Level: Beginner-friendly with team collaboration in mind.

Friday: Weekly goal-setting, reflection, and team updates.
Career Boost: Encourages accountability and alignment within teams.
Experience Level: Intuitive with simple prompts for goal setting.

Microsoft Viva: Tracks work-life balance and wellness insights.
Career Boost: Helps monitor and maintain work-life balance, promoting employee well-being.
Experience Level: Simple integration with other Microsoft tools.

Brandwatch: Sentiment analysis for brand perception.
Career Boost: Aids in managing professional reputation and understanding audience engagement.
Experience Level: Moderate; ideal for social analysis or marketing roles.

Buffer: Schedules social media posts, aiding in consistent personal branding.
Career Boost: Streamlines social media management to enhance visibility and personal brand.
Experience Level: Very easy to use with clear setup instructions.

Hootsuite: Social media management tool for scheduling and audience engagement.
Career Boost: Supports brand presence and consistency across platforms.
Experience Level: Simple to use with beginner-friendly tutorials.

BuzzSumo: Content analysis tool that tracks trending topics.
Career Boost: Identifies popular topics, assisting in content creation and industry engagement.
Experience Level: Very accessible; straightforward search functions.

Feedly: Aggregates news and industry updates.
Career Boost: Keeps users informed on industry trends and developments.
Experience Level: Beginner-friendly with customizable feeds.

Pocket: Saves and organizes articles for later reading.
Career Boost: Supports continuous learning by creating a personal knowledge library.
Experience Level: Extremely easy to use with browser extensions.

Shapr: Networking app that connects professionals based on shared interests.
Career Boost: Facilitates professional networking and relationship building.
Experience Level: Very beginner-friendly with matchmaking features.

Meetup: Platform to find professional events and networking groups.
Career Boost: Connects users with events for career growth and networking.
Experience Level: Beginner-friendly with event recommendations.

TINYpulse: Collects real-time feedback on team engagement and morale.
Career Boost: Improves workplace culture by gathering insights on team sentiment.
Experience Level: Simple to use with clear feedback prompts.

Google Alerts: Monitors specified keywords to track industry news.
Career Boost: Keeps users updated on industry developments and relevant news.
Experience Level: Extremely easy to set up and customize.

Power BI: Business analytics tool for data visualization and insights.
Career Boost: Assists in data-driven decision-making for business analysis.
Experience Level: Moderate; requires basic data skills but has accessible tutorials.

Evernote: Note-taking tool for organizing information and tasks.
Career Boost: Enhances productivity and research management through organized notes.
Experience Level: Very beginner-friendly with tags and organizational features.

Acknowledgments

This book is built from a mix of sources—books, podcasts, documentaries, blogs, and straight-up experience. Alongside the footnoted references, I've pulled from real conversations with people who know their stuff, life lessons learned the hard way, and plenty of late-night deep dives into AI-driven media. It's not just theory; it's the collective wisdom of folks who've been there, done that.

And yes, AI played its part too. I used it to double-check facts and keep things tight, making sure the insights in these pages were as sharp and accurate as possible. The real credit goes to the creators, mentors, and thinkers who contributed directly and indirectly to this book's foundation. To each of them, thank you.

To everyone who shared a piece of their knowledge—whether in print, a podcast, or just a late-night conversation—thank you. This book is a team effort, built from the ideas and experience of many. My hope? That it helps you bring your A-game, stay sharp, and dominate whatever field you're in.

www.ingramcontent.com/pod-product-compliance
Lightning Source LLC
LaVergne TN
LVHW090322210926
848480LV00001B/332